COBOL FOR STUDENTS

D1439646

COBOL FOR STUDENTS

Fourth Edition

Andrew Parkin
Managing Director, Ethitec
Previously Professor of Systems Analysis
De Montfort University

Richard Yorke
Computer Consultant

A member of the Hodder Headline Group
LONDON • SYDNEY • AUCKLAND

First published in Great Britain 1975
Reprinted 1978, 1979, 1980
Second edition 1982
Reprinted 1983, 1984, 1985
Third edition 1990
Reprinted 1991, 1991 (with corrections), 1993
Fourth edition 1996 by
Arnold, a member of the Hodder Headline Group
338 Euston Road, London NW1 3BH
Second impression 1998

British Library Cataloguing in Publication Data
A catalogue record for this book is available from the British Library

ISBN 0 340 64552 0 (pb)

Typeset in 10/12pt Times by Wearset, Boldon, Tyne and Wear
Printed and bound in Great Britain by J W Arrowsmith Ltd, Bristol

Contents

Preface

Notes for teachers

We think the major questions the COBOL teacher has to ask are these:

1 Do I teach the Divisions in the order they are coded or in the order of their importance to the task of programming? The first method is straightforward, but the details of the Environment and Data Divisions at best can be meaningless to the learner until he has learned something of the Procedure Division, and at worst are boring. The alternative method can leave the student puzzled about the whole picture right until the end.

2 Do I cross all the t's and dot all the i's as I go along in lectures, or do I concentrate on broad essentials, to get the students writing a simple program quickly? The first can be tedious or can lead to the student losing the important concepts in the mass of detail. The second is attractive but means that either the student ends the course without knowing the complications, or the teacher must go back and cover the same territory in finer detail.

3 Do I teach the COBOL dialect that applies to the computer I am using, or do I try to distinguish the particular from the general? The first is clearly a more practical approach in the short term, but the second may prove of more value to the student in the long term.

4 How do I keep the threads developing with a mixed ability group? If the teacher goes too quickly, he will lose the slower or less-experienced students, or he will be building on misconceived foundations. If the teacher goes slowly, spending a lot of time anticipating misconceptions. he risks turning the quicker student off the subject altogether.

5 Should I organise the course so that program structure is introduced first, showing how these designs can be implemented in COBOL, or should I give a grounding in elementary COBOL and introduce structured programming on this foundation?

Each of these problems is a dilemma, and there is room for discussion of the answer. We give below our reasons for adopting the solutions as developed here, but we hope you will find sufficient flexibility in this text to put into effect the method you personally prefer (e.g. by covering the material in a different order).

The method of this book

The book is in three parts. Part 1 concentrates on the fundamentals of the language and takes the student to the point where he can write a modestly sized COBOL program using sequential files. Part 2 assumes a competence in elementary COBOL and explains program design and other programming techniques that should be part of the professional programmer's repertoire. Part 3 extends the student's knowledge of the language by explaining some of the more advanced features of COBOL and includes the newer COBOL 89 functions.

Each Part has sections that can accompany a course of lectures. The teacher explains the material in the section (which takes about one hour), concentrating on concepts and skipping as much detail as desired to this end. He then invites the students to study the text for that section.

The text consists of a few frames of fast-moving narrative followed by questions designed to be a real test of the student's understanding of both concept and detail. Quick-learning or experienced students will be able to complete the section in approximately one hour. Many students will be able to complete the text without assistance. The teacher can concentrate his attention on those students who are unable to complete the text on their own.

To return to the five questions, this book answers them as follows:

1 After the introductory Section A (which can be omitted for experienced students) a brief look is taken at all four Divisions. Thereafter, Procedure Division and Data Division entries are introduced in the order that we think to be natural for a good understanding. The student is reminded of the relationships of the Divisions at several points. For the practical exercise at the end of Section F, the teacher gives the student Identification Division and Environment Division entries to copy down. These latter Divisions are treated in the last section, J, in Part 1, together with a substantial exercise based on a data validation program.

2 The teacher can concentrate on concepts in his talk. The student learns the detail through the text.

3 The text is machine-independent and follows the 1985 American National Standard COBOL. Where the standard allows for interpretation by the compiler implementor, common variations are treated. Where we have found a contradiction between an implementation and the standard, we have mentioned the variation. Only the common entries in the Environment Division have been dealt with. Similarly, to go into all the ins and outs of USAGE COMPUTATIONAL and its

variations would be a major task in itself. The teacher will use his judgement at points such as these, knowing the machine the students will use.

4 Because all students will have worked the text for the previous section, they are at a more equal level of development at the outset of the lecture than may be the case with other methods. Many common misconceptions are dealt with in the text. Furthermore, while the text is being worked, the teacher can concentrate on helping those most in need of assistance.

5 On the whole a more precise and useful explanation of structured programming can be given if the student is assumed to have an existing knowledge of programming and has experienced the difficulties of problem solving with the control structures available in the language. Thus program design is deferred until Part 2. If the student is learning COBOL as a second language, though, there is a very good case to be made for starting with some of the topics in Part 2.

Keller plan teaching

If it is the teacher's aim that every student should master the skills of programming in COBOL, and he or she is prepared to deal with very different rates of progress towards such mastery, the system of 'personalised instruction' promoted by Professor F. S. Keller should be considered. Although this text is not intended to be fully self-instructional, a student who uses it for self-instruction can make good progress if tutorial help is available when needed.

A novice student can master Part 1 of the book in about 15 weeks with about three hours' study and practical work per week. A Keller plan of 10 or 11 units, plus two to four programming assignments, can be mastered in this time by virtually 100% of undergraduate students if they have two opportunities for tutorial advice and unit tests per week. The number of assignments expected is sensitive to the computer service. We usually set two assignments for a 'pass' and use additional assignments for grading, if this is required.

Notes for students

Have you got the right book?

This is not a teach-yourself text. It is intended to accompany a course of lectures. On the other hand, if you already have an appreciation of computer programming, you may find this book a very fast way of becoming proficient in COBOL. If you already know a little COBOL, Parts 2 and 3 of the book may extend your horizons.

How to learn COBOL

When you learn a foreign language – French, for example – you can understand its concepts and structure by listening to a teacher or by reading an educational book about it. This will not help you much when you step off the plane at Orly. The only way you can become fluent in the language is by speaking it. The reinforcement of saying the words, making up your own phrases and sentences, is an essential ingredient of learning and remembering.

Learning COBOL is similar, except that COBOL exists only as a written language. Proficiency in COBOL is acquired by writing it.

The book contains many exercises which call for written answers; it is essential that you do write down the answers. Eager students are sometimes tempted to answer the questions 'mentally' in their impatience to make progress with the subject. Resist this temptation, or you may end up arriving at Orly having only read a book about French.

How to use this book

Each section of the book (Section A, Section B, etc.) contains a number of **frames** (frame A1, A2, etc.). At the end of each frame there are some questions. Read the frame and write down your answers to the questions.

If you are unable to answer a question, read the relevant parts of the frame again. If you get stuck, or if there is a point that is not clear, ask the tutor.

Preface to the Fourth Edition

This edition has been updated to include the 'Intrinsic Function Module for COBOL'. This is the ANSI Standard X3.23a-1989 (COBOL 89) which has also been adopted as ISO International Standard 1989 Addendum 1. This is an Addendum to the ANSI Standard X3.23-1985 (COBOL 85) and consists mainly of 42 predefined functions related to many different application areas. As many lecture courses have been based upon earlier editions of this book, the basic style and structure of this fourth edition is unchanged, the COBOL 89 features being added as a separate Section W. However, minor improvements have been made throughout the text.

Acknowledgements

Acknowledgement is due to those organisations who have contributed to the development of the COBOL language. We reproduce here a statement at their request:

'COBOL is an industry language and is not the property of any one company or group of companies, or of any organisation or group of organisations.

No warranty, expressed or implied, is made by any contributor or by the COBOL Committee as to the accuracy and functioning of the programming system and language. Moreover, no responsibility is assumed by any contributor, or by the committee, in connection therewith.

Procedures have been established for the maintenance of COBOL. Inquiries concerning the procedures for proposing changes should be directed to the Executive Committee of the Conference on Data Systems Languages.

The authors and copyright holders of the copyrighted material used herein: FLOWMATIC (Trademark of Sperry Rand Corporation), Programming for the UNIVAC I and II, Data Automation Systems copyrighted 1958, 1959, by Sperry Rand Corporation; IBM Commercial Translator Form No. F 28-8013, copyrighted 1959 by IBM; FACT, DSI 27A5260-2760, copyrighted 1960 by Minneapolis-Honeywell have specifically authorised the use of this material in whole or in part, in the COBOL specifications. Such authorisation extends to the reproduction and use of COBOL specifications in programming manuals or similar publications.'

Particular thanks are due to Mary Spence and Brian Watts of De Montfort University, Leicester who have supplied many clarifications and new ideas for this fourth edition.

Publisher's Note

Shortly before work began on this new edition Roger Barnes, a co-author of the previous edition, died. All involved wish to record their appreciation of the time and effort Roger spent working on the book. He is missed.

Part 1
Fundamentals

Part I
Fundamentals

A Background Concepts – A Review

A1 The computer

There are many different types of digital computer available ranging from small personal computers through to very large and very expensive mainframe computers. However, they do all have a similar basic structure consisting of a **central processing unit** (CPU) to which are attached certain **peripheral devices**. The CPU has three main parts:

- a **control unit** which controls all the operations of the machine and executes the instructions contained in a program
- an **arithmetic and logic unit** (ALU) which undertakes basic arithmetic operations, e.g. addition, multiplication, and various logic functions, e.g. testing for the equality of two items
- a **memory** which holds the program while it is being executed together with the data on which the program is currently working.

A **program** is a series of instructions. Typically, the control unit will fetch a program instruction from memory, execute it, using the ALU if necessary, fetch the next instruction, execute it, and so on.

Programs start with some raw data (the **input**) and process it in some way to produce some new data (the **output**). The computer slavishly executes the instructions given to it and it is very unusual for the hardware to execute an instruction incorrectly. Therefore, if the output is wrong, there is almost certainly an error in the input data or a logic error in the instructions of the program.

The peripheral devices are completely separate even though they are sometimes within the same physical box, e.g. in a microcomputer, a floppy disk drive is often held in the same box as the CPU but is still separate from it. There are **input devices**, e.g. a keyboard, for getting data and programs into memory, **output devices**, e.g. a printer, for outputting from memory the results of programs and **backing storage devices**, e.g. disk drives, which are mainly used to store output data that will need to be re-input at a later stage for further processing.

Exercises

Now write down the answers to the following questions, from memory if possible. If you are unable to answer a question, try to get the answer from the frame. If there is any point that is not clear, ask your tutor. This procedure applies to all the frames that follow.

When you are satisfied with your answers, check them with the solutions at the end of the section and continue to frame A2.

1 What is the purpose of an input device?
2 What is the purpose of a backing storage device?
3 What are the two main causes of error in computer output?
4 Where is a computer program held while it is being executed?
5 Can data which has been output also be used as input?

A2   Keyboard and screen

The most common input device is a **keyboard** and the most common output device is a **screen** (or **monitor**). Together, they are the basic means of communication between a user and a computer, the keyboard for entering data and the screen for displaying data. They are used with the smallest portable PCs (Personal Computers) through to acting as terminals for larger computers. When used in this latter context, the keyboard and screen together are sometimes referred to as a VDU (Visual Display Unit).

Monitors can display different types of data, e.g. letters for word processing, graphics in a variety of colours, different windows. Typically, for programming, a monitor might use 24 **rows** or lines with 80 characters in each row. The position of a character in a row is often referred to by its **column** number. Thus, the first character in a row is in column 1; the twentieth in a row would be column 20.

Each successive character input via the keyboard is usually displayed on the screen. The characters keyed are often held in a **buffer** until the RETURN key is depressed. When this happens, all the characters in the line concerned are transmitted to the CPU. Thus the basic unit being dealt with by the keyboard operator is a line of characters. The operator prepares a line then depresses the RETURN key to release the line to the CPU.

As well as a screen being used to **echo** any data input via the keyboard, it is also used as an output device in its own right, e.g. a message prepared in the memory of the computer can be output to the screen. Usually, only one line is sent at a time but, on a 24-line screen, the other 23 lines remain visible unless a command is given to clear the screen.

When a program requires data to be keyed in, it is up to the programmer to decide where on a screen each particular item of data is to be keyed. The columns allocated for a particular group of characters on one line are called a **field**. Thus, each line is usually divided into fields and each field contains one or more characters. Sometimes it is desirable to imagine that a field is divided into two or more smaller fields, e.g. a 'date' field could consist of a 'day', 'month' and 'year' field. In this case, the larger field is called a **group** field. Fields that are not subdivided are called **elementary** fields.

There are variations to the standard keyboard and screen facilities, e.g.

- **light pens** used to select input from information already displayed on the screen,
- **graphics and colour screens** for high-quality line drawings, draughtsman's drawings, design work, etc.,
- a **mouse** to allow visual selection of data on a screen as an alternative to, or in conjunction with, a keyboard.

Exercises

1 (a) When a monitor is used for programming, how many columns would typically be used?
  (b) How many characters can be entered on one line?

2 Is a mouse an input or an output device?
3 If a line contained a name (13 characters), an address (40 characters) and an account number (6 digits),

  (a) How many columns would be used?
  (b) How many elementary fields are there in one line?

4 The account number field in a line contains a one-digit area code field, a one-digit customer type field and a four-digit serial number field. How large is the group field?

A3   Printers

The most common means of generating output that people can read is via a printer. This is sometimes called producing **hard copy** because the output is permanent on a piece of paper, in contrast to screen output. We shall consider a few example printers.

A **dot matrix printer** is a low-speed, low-cost device where each character printed is made up from a series of dots. The greater the density of dots in the print head, the better the image. A typical page width is 80 characters, although they can go up to 160 characters.

An **inkjet printer** sprays ink on to the paper via a number of tiny jets and, therefore, is a non-impact printer, i.e. there is no mechanical striking to produce a character. It is usually faster than a dot matrix printer and produces a higher-quality print.

A **line printer** is medium to high speed, more expensive than either of the above and usually associated with larger volumes of output. As the name suggests, whole lines of output are set up in memory then released to the printer. An example is the **drum** (or **barrel**) printer which has a revolving drum containing all the possible characters for every column position on the printer. One revolution of the drum is required to print one line. Typically, a line printer has a line width of 120 or 132 characters.

A **laser printer** is another non-impact printer. It is high speed, expensive and prints whole pages at a time. The quality of output is much better than other printers and a whole range of different types of character may be mixed on the same page. Each character is formed by an electronically controlled laser beam marking out an image on the rotating surface of a special drum, then ink toner is electrostatically attracted to the image before the paper comes into contact with the drum.

Exercises

1 You are running your own small company and have a limited amount of money to spend. You require a printer for intermittent use, e.g. production of invoices or sales orders. What type of printer would you choose?
2 Impact printers are generally noisier than non-impact printers. Why is this?
3 You require a printer which is to be used in an open-plan office so that it should not disturb people working. Which type would you choose?
4 Line printers use continuous stationery with a perforation at the end of each page. If the various pages are destined for different people, the pages have to be 'burst' either by hand or by special machinery. Do laser printers have this problem?

A4   Backing storage devices

Not all the information held within a computer needs to be output in a form suitable for people to read. You may be halfway through keying a program into a computer and then want to stop for a while – perhaps somebody else wants to use the computer so you cannot just leave the half-completed program in memory. You need to be able to store your program on media that can later be used as input when you want to complete the keying in. On a personal computer, an appropriate medium could be a floppy disk and a floppy disk drive is one example of a backing or secondary storage device.

To use a business example, suppose a sales clerk is handling a customer

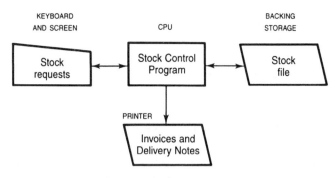

Fig. A.1 Updating a file on backing storage

order by phone. The computer the clerk is using needs the current stock levels to be available in some readable form so that it can check that there is enough of each stock item to satisfy the order and then reduce the figure representing the amount of stock held. This information is held in a stock file on a backing storage device. Any stock issues made can be printed on a Delivery Note and Invoice for the customer, but the updated stock levels are written back to the stock file on the backing storage device. This is illustrated in Fig. A.1.

These examples illustrate that backing storage media are used for both input and output. We shall now consider some of the more common backing storage media and relate these to general concepts about files.

Information is recorded on reels of **magnetic tape** by a **tape deck**. This may be thought of as working in the same way as a home cassette tape recorder except that with business computers they work much faster and use longer reels of tape. Since data can be recorded on the tape at a high density, several million characters can be recorded on a single reel of tape. This may be much more data than can be held in the memory of the CPU, so programs are written to process one **record** of data at a time. There are usually many records in one file on a tape and the processing mechanism involves reading the first record, processing it, writing it out to a second tape, reading the next record, processing it, writing it out to the second tape, and so on.

'Record' is the name given to any convenient group of related fields. Thus, the data in one line of a screen could make a record. Other examples of records that could be on a magnetic tape are:

Stock file: each record in the file could contain

1 a stock item number
2 a description of the type of stock
3 the current amount of stock in hand,
   etc.

Payroll file: each record in the file could contain

1 an employee number

2 an employee name
3 a rate of pay
4 the pay to date this year
5 the tax paid to date this year,
  etc.

In practice, the records in such files would have more fields than the ones listed but the nature of those extra fields would depend upon the exact use to which the files were put.

Information is recorded on magnetic tape in **blocks** of data, usually each block containing a number of records. Recording can only take place when the tape is moving at the designed tape speed. Since the tape must stop after each block is written out, a gap is left after each block to allow for deceleration (see Fig. A.2).

This gap is in practice about half an inch long. It will be seen that if blocks are short, say 80 characters, a reel of tape will contain a large quantity of inter-block gaps and very little data between them. For this reason, and to reduce the frequency of stopping at inter-block gaps, it is usual to write tape blocks as large as practicable – the limiting factor may be the amount of spare space available in memory for forming the block prior to writing it out.

In COBOL, facilities exist to specify the number of records per block (the **blocking factor**) required for a particular file. However, PCs have a standard block size so this blocking factor specification is only relevant to larger machines. In general, to specify a file completely for a COBOL program, it is necessary to define three levels:

FILE   its name and the medium on which it is recorded
RECORD   the fields that make up the record
FIELD   the characters that make up the field.

The first record on a reel of tape is a special one, the **header** label, which identifies the information held in the file. There is also a **trailer** label marking the end of the file.

In terms of speed, a modern commercial tape drive could read characters equivalent to the total number of characters in this book in about 4 seconds. The speed would depend, of course, upon the blocking factor used but this would be about the fastest.

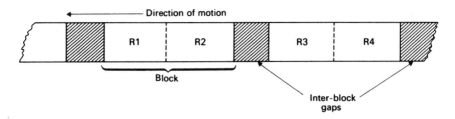

Fig. A.2 Format of blocks and records on magnetic tape

Magnetic disks are another form of backing storage and they are available in many different shapes and sizes. On large computers, it is common to have **fixed disks** which are permanently linked to the CPU and have fast access speeds. The fixed disks consist of a series of separate magnetic disks stacked together and data can usually be stored on both surfaces of the disk. Storage capacities vary but the larger ones can go up to at least 500 million characters.

Exchangeable **diskpacks** are similar in concept to fixed disks but they can be loaded and unloaded like magnetic tapes. For smaller systems, **hard disks** are a variation of fixed disks, though generally with a smaller capacity. Finally, **floppy disks** or **diskettes** are the most common form of exchangeable backing storage device for personal computers, but capacities do not generally go beyond one and a half million characters.

For all these types of disk, there are similar concepts of file, block, record and field as for magnetic tapes. The main difference between the two types of device is that tapes are **serial access devices** where you have to start at the beginning and physically pass over all the data on the tape to reach the end. Disks can also be processed in this serial way but they also have the capability of accessing individual blocks of data directly. They are, therefore, examples of **direct access devices**. More details of how direct access devices work are given in Section T.

Exercises

1 Name four types of peripheral device. Classify them as input, output or backing storage.
2 What is the purpose of a header label?
3 How are data blocks separated on magnetic tape?
4 What are the three levels of file definition required by a COBOL program?
5 Will a payroll program contain the name of each employee in the organisation? If not, where will the names be held?
6 Do floppy disks generally have a greater capacity than fixed disks?
7 What distinguishes direct access devices from serial access devices?

A5 The program specification

Before a COBOL program is written, a detailed specification must be drawn up showing exactly what is to be done by the program. This may have already been done for you by another more senior programmer or a systems analyst. However, you may be in a working situation where you have to do this yourself from a less-precise description of what the program is required to do. An important point is that you should not start trying to write COBOL before a clear specification has been created. Usually, such a specification is in three main parts:

1 Input   – a description of the file and record layouts for the input data.
2 Output   – a description of the file and record layouts for the output data.
3 Processing – a description of the processes the program must follow to get the output from the input.

The input and output descriptions can be defined on special forms which detail the various points to consider, e.g. the size and type of each field in a record.

The processing section of the specification may often be written in **Structured English**, also known as **pseudo-code** or **PDL** (**Program Definition Language**). This is a series of short phrases, called statements, defining precisely and concisely what processing is required. For example, here is a processing specification for a program to read serially through an input magnetic tape and copy each record read on to a line printer.

DO UNTIL end of tape file
    read next record
    IF record is not the trailer label
        print the record
    ENDIF
ENDDO

This is saying that until the end of the input tape file is reached, records should be read and then printed as long as the record read is not the special trailer label at the end of the tape file.

The general structure of a *DO UNTIL* statement is:

DO UNTIL condition
    statement
    statement
        |
        |
        |
ENDDO

It specifies that the inner list of statements should be repeatedly obeyed until the *condition* with the *UNTIL* becomes true. The *ENDDO* indicates the end of the statements to be repeatedly executed. The inner statements are indented to highlight that they are under the control of the *DO UNTIL* statement. A *DO WHILE* can also be used, where the *condition* relates to the continuing execution of the *DO* loop rather than its termination.

The general structure of an *IF* statement is:

IF condition
> *statement*
> *statement*
> |
> |

ELSE
> *statement*
> *statement*
> |
> |

ENDIF

It specifies that the first inner list of statements is only to be obeyed if the condition is true and the second inner list of statements, after the *ELSE*, is only to be obeyed if the condition is false. As illustrated in the example above related to the reading of a tape, the *ELSE* part is optional. The *ENDIF* is always required and indicates the end of the statements dependent upon either the true or false value for the condition and, again, all such statements are indented. An extension to the *IF* is the *CASE* statement. This is discussed later when problems requiring such a statement are met.

The uppercase words have fixed meanings and are called **keywords**. The lowercase words can be any short description related to the problem.

Exercises

1 Name the three parts of a program specification.
2 What are alternative names for 'Structured English'?
3 What is the purpose of the Structured English *IF* statement?
4 What is the purpose of the Structured English *DO UNTIL* statement?
5 Give a Structured English specification for the above tape-reading example, but this time to count the number of records printed and, when the end of the tape is reached, to print out the total number of records printed.

A6 The COBOL compiler

COBOL (COmmon Business Oriented Language) is a computer language developed in the United States of America in 1959. The body responsible for maintaining and further developing the language is CODASYL (the Conference on Data Systems Languages), a voluntary organisation that includes representatives of users and manufacturers of computers. In 1966, the USA Standards Institute proposed a standard version of the language based on the CODASYL recommendations as they stood in 1965. This standard version was ratified in 1968 and came to be called American National Standard COBOL (ANS COBOL) or, sometimes COBOL 68. In 1974, an extended and revised version of the language was standardised and this is known as COBOL 74. More recently, a further version, COBOL 85, was produced, followed by an addendum, COBOL 89. This book is based on COBOL 85 with the additional COBOL 89.

As it is a language resembling English and it is not limited to the facilities of a particular computer, COBOL is called a **high-level** language. A **low-level** language resembles the language used internally by the particular machine it is associated with. High-level languages are sometimes called **problem-oriented**, whereas low-level languages are **machine-oriented**.

Even though COBOL is high level, it is still a **procedural language** in that you as the programmer have to specify **how** a problem can be solved using COBOL program statements. **Fourth-generation languages** (4GLs) are a more recent development and tend towards being non-procedural, i.e. it is sufficient for the programmer to state *what* the problem is rather than *how* it can be solved. In this context, COBOL is sometimes referred to as an example of a third-generation language but it is suggested that the way COBOL will develop in the future is to incorporate some of the ideas of non-procedural languages.

After having received or created a program specification, a programmer produces the COBOL program usually by creating it on a computer with the help of special software, e.g. an editor or word processor. The resultant raw COBOL program is called a **source program**.

The source program needs to be translated into the language used internally by the computer. This language is called **machine code** and the program, after it has been translated into machine code, is called the **object program**. The translation process itself is done by a special computer program called the COBOL **compiler**.

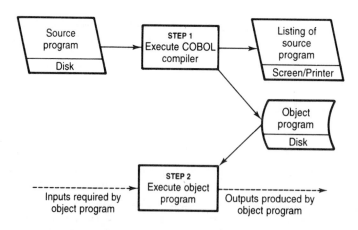

Fig. A.3 The compilation process

Thus, the COBOL compiler reads the source program into the computer, usually from a disk file or other backing storage, and translates this into a machine code object program. If the source program is not valid COBOL, the translation process will not take place and the compiler will inform you of any errors. You will then need to correct the source program using, say, an editor, but eventually, a completely valid COBOL program should be produced. The object program created from such a valid COBOL source program is usually written to a separate backing storage file and can then be loaded into the machine and executed. This process is illustrated in Fig. A.3.

As a programmer, you may think that this is the end of your task but, in fact, it is only the beginning because even though your program is valid COBOL, it may fail to do what the program specification said it ought to

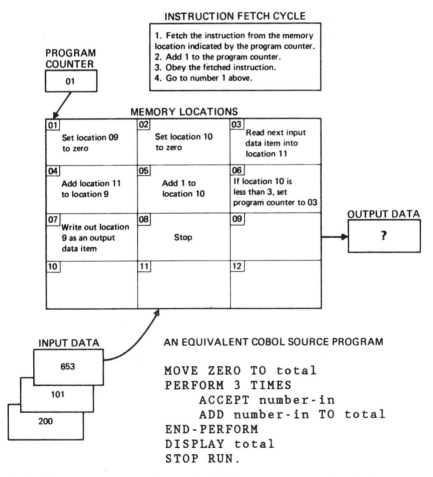

INSTRUCTION FETCH CYCLE

1. Fetch the instruction from the memory location indicated by the program counter.
2. Add 1 to the program counter.
3. Obey the fetched instruction.
4. Go to number 1 above.

PROGRAM COUNTER

01

MEMORY LOCATIONS

01 Set location 09 to zero	02 Set location 10 to zero	03 Read next input data item into location 11
04 Add location 11 to location 9	05 Add 1 to location 10	06 If location 10 is less than 3, set program counter to 03
07 Write out location 9 as an output data item	08 Stop	09
10	11	12

OUTPUT DATA

?

INPUT DATA

653

101

200

AN EQUIVALENT COBOL SOURCE PROGRAM

```
MOVE ZERO TO total
PERFORM 3 TIMES
     ACCEPT number-in
     ADD number-in TO total
END-PERFORM
DISPLAY total
STOP RUN.
```

Fig. A.4 How a computer works in more detail. The source program, written by the programmer, is translated by the compiler into a machine code object program. The object program is stored in the memory locations of the central processing unit. The control unit in the CPU has built-in logic which slavishly executes the instruction fetch cycle.

do. The next stage of program testing is considered in more detail in Part Two.

Exercises

1 What is a compiler?
2 What in general is the name given to the program that a programmer writes?
3 What is the name given to the version of the program that has been converted into machine code?
4 What does COBOL stand for?
5 When a compilation of a COBOL program has been successful for the first time, is the resultant program produced by the compiler ready for general use?
6 In Fig. A.4, pretend you are the control unit following the instruction fetch cycle for a machine code program. What data is output when instruction 7 is executed?

Answers – Section A

Frame A1

1 To read data and programs into the memory of the computer.
2 To store intermediate results that will be read back into the computer at a later time.
3 An error in the data. An error in the program.
4 In memory.
5 Yes. The results output to a backing storage device may be input at a later time.

Frame A2

1 (a) 80
  (b) 80
2 Input
3 (a) 59
  (b) 3 – note that this answer assumes there are no spaces between the fields.
4 The account number group field has 6 characters.

Frame A3

1 A difficult question, to which there is no one answer. The cheapest printer is probably a dot matrix but if speed and print quality are important, an inkjet or laser may have to be considered.

2 Because of the mechanical striking against an inked ribbon or paper.

3 An inkjet or laser, depending upon the money available.

4 No. Separate A4 sheets that you would use with a photocopier are the normal paper used with laser printers.

Frame A4

1 Keyboard (input) and Screen (output).
  Laser Printer – output.
  Magnetic Tape – backing storage.
  Floppy Disk – backing storage.

2 To identify the information held in a file.

3 By an inter-block gap.

4 File, record, field.

5 No. The employees' names, along with other data such as their rate of pay and tax paid, would be held in a file, possibly on magnetic disk, one record per employee.

6 No. Floppy disks have a relatively small capacity.

7 Direct access to blocks of data rather than having to wade through the whole file.

Frame A5

1 A description of the input, output and processing.

2 Pseudo-code and PDL (Program Definition Language).

3 To specify that the statements under the *IF*'s control should only be executed if the condition is true and, optionally, that the statements with the *ELSE* part should only be executed if the condition is false.

4 To specify that the statements under the *DO UNTIL*'s control should repeatedly be executed as long as the condition associated with the *DO UNTIL* remains false.

5 *set a counter to zero*
  DO UNTIL end of tape file
      read next record
      IF record is not the trailer label
          print the record
          add 1 to the counter
      ENDIF
  ENDDO
  print out the contents of the counter

Frame A6

1 A machine code computer program that translates instructions given in a high-level language into the machine's internal instructions.

2 Source program.
3 Object program.
4 COmmon Business Oriented Language.
5 No. It has to be tested to make sure it does what it is supposed to do.
6 954.

B COBOL Essentials

B1 COBOL syntax

A COBOL reserved word is a word within the COBOL language that has a special fixed meaning. For example, SUBTRACT is a COBOL reserved word that allows you to do subtraction. A COBOL **statement** is a series of words that starts with a COBOL reserved word. Thus,

```
SUBTRACT tax FROM pay
```

is a COBOL statement starting with the reserved word SUBTRACT, which, when translated by the compiler, subtracts the contents of a memory location you have called 'tax' from the contents of a memory location you have called 'pay' – we'll see later how these programmer-supplied names are associated with memory locations and how data is read into memory.

Statements may be grouped together into **sentences**. Thus

```
SUBTRACT tax FROM pay
ADD bonus TO pay.
```

is a sentence with two statements – notice the full stop, which indicates the end of the sentence. One or more sentences can be grouped together to form a **paragraph**. In a similar way, paragraphs can be grouped together to form a **section** and sections can be grouped together to form a **division**. You may be wondering how far this hierarchy can go on! Fortunately, not much further because a COBOL program consists of no more than four different types of division. They are:

```
IDENTIFICATION DIVISION.
ENVIRONMENT DIVISION.
DATA DIVISION.
PROCEDURE DIVISION.
```

Also, all of these divisions are optional. For example, it is possible with a very small program to have a PROCEDURE DIVISION only. If the divisions do appear, however, they must be in the above order. The complete hierarchy within a COBOL program, therefore, is:

program
division
section
paragraph
sentence
statement

although it is possible to skip some of the intermediate levels. For example, a division may contain paragraphs only, without the intermediate section level.

At some points within a program, the COBOL compiler expects certain sections and paragraphs to appear, i.e. ones with special reserved words, but in other parts the programmer can make up complete sections and paragraphs. Let us pursue more details of each of the four divisions.

IDENTIFICATION DIVISION. This shows the name of the programmer, the name and purpose of the program, where and when it was written. These are largely **comments** – special lines in the program which do appear on an output listing of the program, but once recognised in the program are ignored by the compiler.

ENVIRONMENT DIVISION. This shows the particular computer that will be used to compile and execute the program and identifies the kinds of peripherals that will be used for input and output of data.

DATA DIVISION. This describes all the data and files used by the program. The nature of each file is described in detail, as well as the structure of the records contained in the file. The compiler uses this information to assign memory locations for data when it is read in or before being written out. Data which is not directly part of input/output is assigned to a separate area called **Working-Storage**.

PROCEDURE DIVISION. This is the 'doing' part of the program, where the programmer provides statements telling the compiler what procedures should be performed on the data. The earlier SUBTRACT and ADD statements are PROCEDURE DIVISION entries.

In Fig. B.1, there is an example complete COBOL program which contains all four divisions. It does not achieve very much but if you supplied your name, the date and the computer's name in the appropriate places, it would compile and execute successfully.

Exercises

1 How does the compiler know when one sentence ends and another begins?

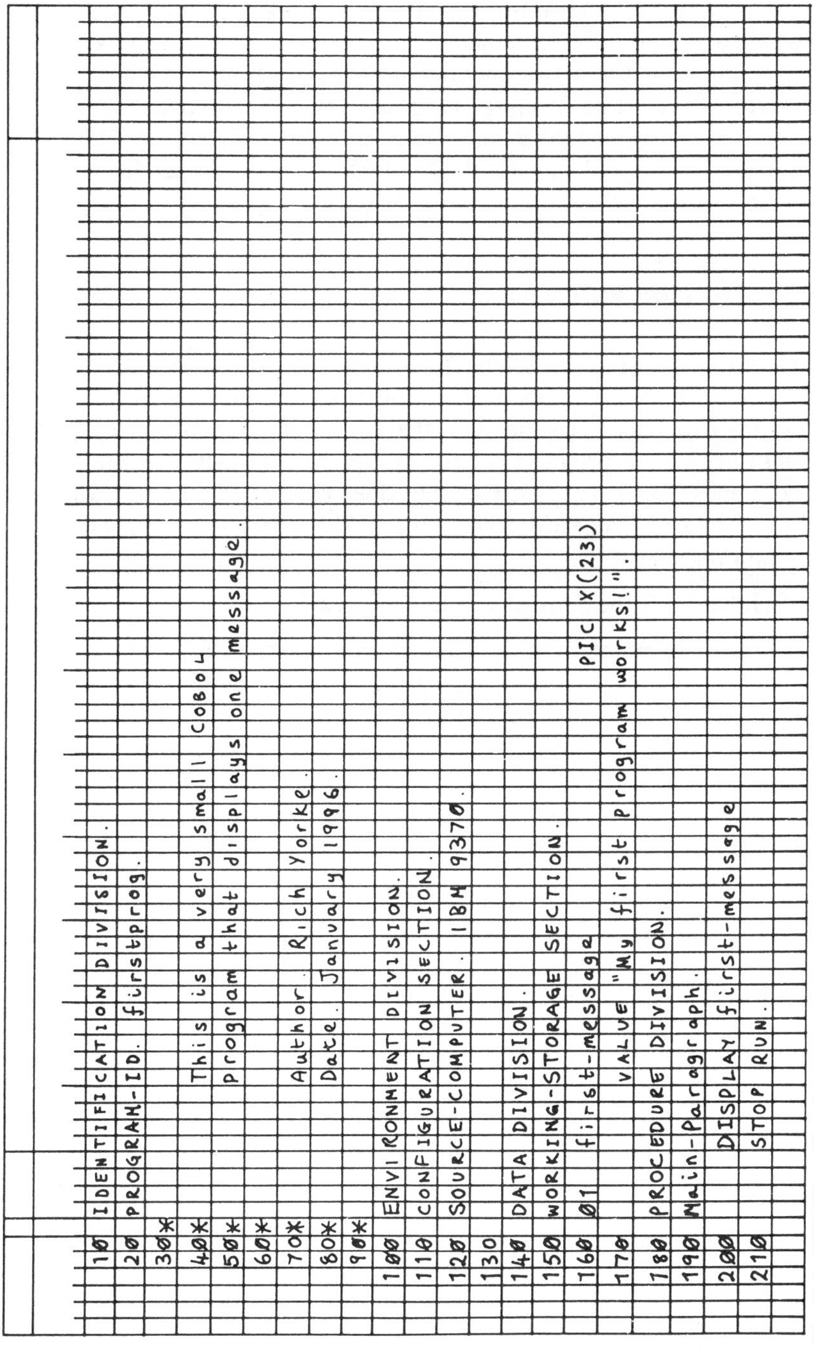

```
10   IDENTIFICATION DIVISION.
20   PROGRAM-ID.  firstprog.
30*  This is a very small COBOL program
40*  that displays one message
50*
60*  Author  Rich Yorke
70*  Date  January 1996
80*
90*
100  ENVIRONMENT DIVISION.
110  CONFIGURATION SECTION.
120  SOURCE-COMPUTER.  IBM 9370.
130
140  DATA DIVISION.
150  WORKING-STORAGE SECTION.
160  01  first-message  PIC X(23).
170         VALUE "My first program works!".
180  PROCEDURE DIVISION.
190  Main-Paragraph.
200  DISPLAY first-message
210  STOP RUN.
```

Fig. B.1 COBOL coding form

2 A programmer cannot use a reserved word as a name for an area of memory. Why not?

3 Examine the example program in Fig. B.1. How many sentences are there in the PROCEDURE DIVISION?

4 How many character-positions in memory do you think the compiler would assign to hold the data defined in the DATA DIVISION?

5 No peripheral devices are mentioned in the program. On what device do you think the output from the program would be displayed?

6 There are two executable statements in the PROCEDURE DIVISION, the DISPLAY and the STOP RUN. Does the compiler itself execute these statements?

B2   Coding rules

Each line of the program in Fig. B.1 represents one line on a screen as it is keyed in, so that the numbers along the top of the form represent column positions 1 to 72. You can see that there is a definite pattern to where different parts of the program are coded, e.g. the DIVISION names all start in column 8. This is because COBOL does have strict rules on where different parts of a program should appear. The various areas within the 72-column range are:

Columns 1–6, the Sequence Number Area.

This is used for numbering the lines in your program. You can actually use any characters, not just numbers, but the latter are the most common. It is quite possible that the editor you will be using to key in your COBOL program will automatically provide these for you. If you are creating your program on special coding forms to be keyed in by a data preparation operator, you may want to indicate what sequence numbers to use, although normally default values would be provided by the editor he/she uses.

Column 7, the Indicator Area.

Its main use is to identify comments. An asterisk (*) placed in this column will cause the whole line to be treated as a comment. There are other uses for this area but we will not consider them for the moment.

Columns 8–11, Area A.

This is where division, section and paragraph names must start and it is conventional to begin the names actually in column 8. Division and section names must be followed by a space, the words DIVISION and SECTION, respectively, and a full stop. Paragraph names must be followed by a full stop. Also, in the DATA DIVISION, as in the example on line 160 with the 01 entry, certain **level numbers** also start in Area A.

Columns 12–72, Area B.

72 is the most common upper limit for Area B but the actual limit is dependent upon the particular input device you are using, e.g. you may be using a screen that is wider than the normal 80 columns. However, we shall assume column 72 is the upper limit. COBOL sentences are written in Area B and your sentences can flow freely from line to line as long as you stay in Area B. There must be at least one space between words in a sentence, although you can have as many spaces as you like. It is a good habit to write only one statement on each line, but this is not a limitation imposed by COBOL. If a sentence is too long to fit on one line, it is possible to split words from column 72 on the line to the beginning of Area B on the next line by putting a hyphen (-) in the Indicator area of the second line but it makes for easier reading if you avoid splitting a complete word between lines.

It is becoming increasingly common for compilers to accept source programs that are not laid out as described above and you may find it rather irksome to have to follow such strict formatting rules. The only problem with using a freer format is that you make your program less **portable**, i.e. your compiler may be happy with the non-standard source statements but when you want to compile your program on another machine its compiler may not be so lax. A better approach is to get your computer to help you, because on many computers there are **formatters** available, which allow you to key in your program in a free-format way and they convert them to the standard COBOL format. This may even be a feature of your compiler. However, unless you have such features available, we recommend that you stay with the standard layout of COBOL programs.

Exercises

1 How can the compiler tell where a division, section or paragraph ends?
2 If you are using a keyboard to input your COBOL programs, you may be able to set up tab-stops. At which columns do you think it would be good to have stops?
3 Examine the example program in Fig. B.1. How many sections and paragraphs are there?
4 Suppose you are writing a COBOL program and you mis-spelled ENVI-RONMENT DIVISION as

(a) ENVIRONMENTDIVISION.
(b) ENVIROMENT DIVISION.

In each case, would the compiler accept these entries?
5 You are at column 64 of a COBOL source program and you have to input TAX-ALLOWANCE as the last word of a statement. What would be your approach?

B3   Name formation and punctuation

Programmer-defined names to represent data areas can be made up from any of the alphabetic characters A to Z, a to z, the numbers 0 to 9 and the dash or hyphen ('-'), provided there is at least one alphabetic character and the hyphen is not first or last. If lower-case letters are used in names, they are equivalent to the corresponding upper-case letters, i.e. COBOL is not 'case sensitive'. Traditionally, however, COBOL programs have been written in upper case only, so some compilers, although accepting the lower-case letters, will convert them to upper case such that when you get an output listing of your program, everything is in upper case. One standard that some people adopt, and we will generally use here, is to have upper-case letters for reserved words and lower-case letters for programmer-defined words, e.g. ADD tax TO pay, so that reserved words are clearly distinguished from other words. However, you could write this as ADD TAX TO PAY and COBOL would see this as being exactly equivalent to the previous form. For illustration purposes in later sections, we will sometimes use single upper-case letters for variables but always lower-case in program examples.

Thus, ABC-2 and 1-xyz are legal names. However, they would not be classed as good names because they are probably meaningless in terms of the problem you are trying to solve. Better names are ones that reflect the data that is being stored, e.g.

Payroll-Number
TAX-CODE
Partnumber

Use of good names makes the program longer to write initially, but this is a small price to pay for clarity. Names may not exceed 30 characters in length.

The same rules apply to programmer-defined names for sections and paragraphs, except that such names may also be all numeric. The approach that is taken in this book is to use paragraphs only in the Procedure Division but it is possible to use both sections and paragraphs. It is a good habit to choose meaningful names. Here are some examples.

Initialise-Files.
WRITE-REPORT-HEADINGS.

The first example above is in the style we shall use in this book for paragraph names, i.e. to have an initial upper-case letter followed by lower-case letters. Where a name consists of several words, each word can start with an upper-case letter.

The full stop is used as terminator in several places – division, section and paragraph names and sentences. It is possible to put a full stop at the end of every statement, thereby making each statement into a sentence and this tended to be the approach with pre-COBOL 85 programs, but the suggestion now is to have one sentence per paragraph, only putting a single full stop at the end of each paragraph.

Commas and semi-colons may be used as in normal English, to improve the readability of programs, but only in particular places. However, you are advised not to use them anywhere, but rather achieve readability through use of spacing, new lines and indentation.

Exercises

1 In each of the following cases, say whether the COBOL name is legal or illegal for representing a data area. Give reasons for illegal cases.

   (a) 1234
   (b) zl
   (c) low-tide
   (d) working-storage

2 For (b) and (c) above, would you say they are good names?
3 On a coding form or a piece of paper, write a COBOL paragraph, containing one sentence, which will perform the following:

   add 'bonus' to 'pay' then subtract 'tax' from 'pay' then subtract 'pension premium' from 'pay'.

   Make up an appropriate, meaningful name for the paragraph.

B4   Literals and figurative constants

Data used in COBOL programs is described and given names in the DATA DIVISION. Where the value of the data in fields within the program can change, say, through reading a new record or doing a computation, such fields are called **variables**. As an example, if a program were going to number all the pages of a report to be printed, the page number would be a variable. At the end of each page, 1 would be added to the page number variable in the program so that the next time that variable was used, it would have its new updated value.

However, the 1 that is added each time is an example of a **literal** – its value remains constant throughout the program; 1, actually, is termed a **numeric literal** as it represents a number. In general, a numeric literal may be formed by any string of digits optionally preceded by a + or − sign and with a decimal point inserted if needed. For example, the following are all valid numeric literals:

1.0
+12
123.77
−5
−7.24612

The decimal point may not be the last character, e.g. 1. is invalid but 1.0 is valid. If no sign is given, + is assumed. Numeric literals may not exceed 18 digits.

Non-numeric literals are constant values but not ones with which you are going to perform arithmetic. Anything enclosed in quotation marks is a non-numeric literal, e.g.

"Freda Smith"
"Error in Code"
"10.45"
" "

Note particularly the last two. The contents of "10.45" are numeric in nature but because it is quoted, you could not use this literal for arithmetic. For instance, it may represent the time of day and you would not necessarily want to do arithmetic on such a value. If you did want to do arithmetic on the value, you would have to create it as a numeric literal. As we shall see later on, COBOL handles numeric and non-numeric literals quite differently in other ways as well. The last example is a single space. This emphasises the fact that a space within a non-numeric literal does count as a character.

The maximum size of a non-numeric literal is 160 characters. However, we mentioned in frame B2 that it is not good practice to split names between lines. In the same way, if you have a very large non-numeric literal that would spread over two lines, it is usually better to split into two smaller ones and have each separate complete literal on its own line. It is unlikely, therefore, that you will need to be concerned with this maximum-size figure.

Certain literals can be referred to by names called **figurative constants**. These are special reserved words and some examples are:

ZERO, ZEROS, ZEROES   one or more zeros
SPACE, SPACES   one or more spaces
QUOTE, QUOTES quotation marks
HIGH-VALUE, HIGH-VALUES   the highest possible value
LOW-VALUE, LOW-VALUES   the lowest possible value

An example of their use is:

MOVE SPACES TO employee-surname

which would fill the memory area denoted by the name employee-surname with blank characters, the number of characters being determined by the size of that area. Whether the plural or singular version is used does not affect the value assumed by the compiler, e.g. MOVE ZERO TO cost would fill the variable denoted by the name 'cost', with a string of zeros, even though the figurative constant used was in the singular.

The highest and lowest values are used in situations where you want the highest possible or lowest possible value to be represented. We will see examples of their use later on.

A slightly different figurative constant is ALL which is used to repeat a character or string of characters, e.g.

ALL "*"

represents a string of asterisks, the actual number of asterisks being determined by the context in which it is used.

Exercises

1 For each of the following numeric literals, say whether it is valid or invalid, giving reasons for the invalid cases.

  (a) +1.0
  (b) −782.
  (c) .7
  (d) "18"
  (e) £19.25

2 For each of the following non-numeric literals, say, with reasons, whether it is valid or invalid.

  (a) "Frd Smith"
  (b) "ZEROES"
  (c) "END OF JOB
  (d) "18"
  (e) QUOTE""QUOTE

3 Why is it, do you think, COBOL does not allow a decimal point to be the last character in a numeric literal?

4 Rewrite the following using the ALL figurative constant,

  MOVE SPACES TO error-message

Answers – Section B

Frame B1

1 A full stop indicates where one sentence ends and another begins.
2 Reserved words have a special meaning and it would be confusing to allow these same names to be used to represent data areas. It is best to choose names for data areas that reflect their use (e.g. tax, pay) and so you are unlikely to want to use reserved words like SUBTRACT and ADD anyway.
3 One. There is a paragraph name Main-Paragraph and two statements, DISPLAY and STOP RUN within that paragraph – frame B2 will

explain how you can tell the difference between paragraph names and statements/sentences.

4 Twenty three – one for each character between the quotation marks and hence the number 23 on the previous line. More details of describing DATA DIVISION entries will come in Section E of this book.

5 The most likely output device would be the screen on a microcomputer. However, if the program were executed on a large mainframe computer, the output could be displayed on the operator's console in a separate computer room. Notice that the program does not explicitly state which peripheral device should be used – DISPLAY is a statement that assumes the 'standard' output device for a particular computer system and this would normally be a Visual Display Unit.

6 No. The compiler creates the object program and it is the latter that the computer executes. If you are unsure of this, refer back to frame A6.

Frame B2

1 Division – when a new division name or the end of program is met.
Section – when a new section or division name or the end of program is met.
Paragraph – when a new paragraph, section or division name or the end of program is met.

2 Column 7 – for indicating comments. This may well be your initial starting position if sequence numbers are supplied for you by your editor or compiler.
Column 8 – as the start of Area A.
Column 12 – as the start of Area B.

3 1 section (CONFIGURATION) in the ENVIRONMENT DIVISION.
1 section (WORKING-STORAGE) in the DATA DIVISION.
1 paragraph named PROGRAM-ID in the IDENTIFICATION DIVISION.
1 paragraph named SOURCE-COMPUTER in the ENVIRONMENT DIVISION.
1 paragraph named Main-Paragraph in the PROCEDURE DIVISION.
01 at line 160 in the DATA DIVISION is not a paragraph name although it does start in Area A – the next frame will give you more details of how you can tell the difference.

4 (a) No, as it will see the entry as one long name.
(b) The N in ENVIRONMENT is missing so probably no.
There are some 'intelligent' compilers that allow for slight spelling mistakes so if you have one of these, it may forgive you the missing N!

5 Put the whole name on the next line in Area B to avoid having to split the word. Preferably start the name at, say, column 15 of the continued line to emphasise it is part of a statement on the previous line.

Frame B3

1 (a) Illegal as no alphabetic character
  (b) Legal
  (c) Legal
  (d) Illegal as it is a reserved word. COBOL treats lower-case and upper-
    case identically.
2 z1 is not likely to be a good name although it does depend upon the
  problem area. 'low-tide' sounds a better name as long as it does reflect
  appropriate data. There have been some interesting cases of programmers choosing meaningful names and then using them to represent
  other data (say, putting high-tide information into the location denoted
  by low-tide!!). This is to be avoided at all costs.

3 `Calculate-Net-Pay.`
```
    ADD bonus TO pay
    SUBTRACT tax FROM pay
    SUBTRACT pension-premium FROM pay.
```

You may also have used upper-case letters and this would be fine.

Frame B4

1 (a) Valid.
  (b) Invalid – there is a decimal point at the end.
  (c) Valid.
  (d) Invalid – you cannot have quotes in a numeric literal.
  (e) Invalid – monetary symbols are not allowed.
2 (a) Valid – COBOL will not check for spelling mistakes!
  (b) Valid – its value is just the string of letters Z, E, R, O, E,
        S. COBOL will never try to interpret anything meaningful
        from characters between the quotes.
  (c) Invalid – missing closing quotes.
  (d) Valid – there is numeric data between the quotes but the whole
        entry is a non-numeric literal.
  (e) Valid – you may think that the resultant string consists of the two
        characters "" but in fact, what we haven't told you yet is
        that to provide a single set of quotes from within a string,
        you must specify 2 sets together! This is so that COBOL
        can distinguish between quotes within strings and quotes
        starting and terminating strings. Therefore, in the exam-
        ple, the outer figurative constant QUOTE pair specify the
        limits to the string and the two characters within the
        string are interpreted as the single character".
3 There might be confusion between the terminating decimal point of a
  numeric literal and a terminating full stop of a sentence. There is a good
  example of ambiguity within natural language which causes compilers

problems. Essentially, we have two different concepts, a decimal point and a full stop which are denoted by the same symbol. Some compilers are a little more intelligent and do allow you to transgress the rules in this situation, determining the meaning from the context.

4 MOVE ALL " " TO error-message.

However, the other version is clearer to someone reading the program and so is preferable.

C The Arithmetic Verbs

C1 The PROCEDURE DIVISION – ADD and SUBTRACT

Although the PROCEDURE DIVISION is physically last in a COBOL program, it is helpful to learn some of its features before looking at the other divisions. It is the division where you specify what processes should be performed, e.g. reading records, writing data, doing calculations. We have already met the PROCEDURE DIVISION statements ADD, SUBTRACT and MOVE. Here is a formal description of the ADD statement.

$$\underline{ADD} \begin{Bmatrix} \text{identifier-1} \\ \text{literal-1} \end{Bmatrix} \dots \underline{TO} \{\text{identifier-2 } [\underline{ROUNDED}]\} \dots$$

These formal descriptions provide concise and precise definitions for acceptable COBOL. Underlined words in capitals, e.g. ADD, are keywords and must be present if not surrounded by any brackets. Square brackets, [ ], indicate that the surrounded contents are optional, but if included, they will change the meaning of the statement. When items are stacked one above another, a choice must be made of one of the items in the stack. Curly brackets or braces, { }, indicate that a choice **must** be made from the surrounded contents. The ellipsis ... indicates that the preceding bracketed item can be repeated as often as required. 'Identifier' is a name for a variable and 'literal' is a literal of some kind.

This formal method is universally used for COBOL so it is worthwhile understanding it. However, individual COBOL constructs can be quite lengthy so we will often not provide complete descriptions in the main text, e.g. the above is a shortened description of the ADD statement – the full version is covered in frame C4. A complete formal description of COBOL is provided in Appendix D. Note that only the appearance (or **syntax**) of correct COBOL constructs is described by this method – the meaning (or **semantics**) of the constructs must be provided by accompanying English text.

The following are examples of correct ADD statements:

```
ADD bonus TO pay
```

```
ADD bonus TO pay ROUNDED
```

```
ADD 10.0
    first-mark
    second-mark TO total-mark ROUNDED
```

The result of any addition is placed in the variable after the 'TO', e.g. in the 'ADD bonus TO pay', the result of the calculation would be placed in the variable 'pay', thereby overwriting its previous contents. In general, for ADD, SUBTRACT, MULTIPLY and DIVIDE, the result is in the right-hand identifier unless the GIVING option is used (see below).

If, however, you wish to put the result in a separate variable, you need to use another version of the ADD statement:

$$\underline{\text{ADD}} \begin{Bmatrix} \text{identifier-1} \\ \text{literal-1} \end{Bmatrix} \dots \underline{\text{TO}} \begin{Bmatrix} \text{identifier-2} \\ \text{literal-2} \end{Bmatrix}$$
$$\underline{\text{GIVING}} \{\text{identifier-3 } [\underline{\text{ROUNDED}}]\} \dots$$

This introduces another feature of formal descriptions. Remember that underlined capital letters indicate compulsory words. Here, we have non-underlined capitals, which indicate optional words that may be omitted without changing the meaning of the statement. They are usually words to make COBOL read more like ordinary English. An example would be:

```
ADD bonus TO pay GIVING gross-pay
```

where the result of the addition would be in the variable 'gross-pay', and 'bonus' and 'pay' would contain the same values they had before the addition. To illustrate the difference between these two forms of the ADD statement, consider Fig. C.1 which assumes that you have three variables, A, B and C all defined in the DATA DIVISION, with A and B having three integer places and no decimal places, and C having three integer places and one decimal place. Note that the result of the addition depends upon the size of C as defined in the DATA DIVISION.

Fig. C.1 The effect of an ADD statement

Suppose instead that C had been defined in the same way as A and B, i.e. with no decimal place. After execution of the last instruction in Fig. C.1, the variable C would contain 145 only, the final .7 having been truncated. In general, COBOL will cause a result to be calculated and then try to fit it into the resultant variable, any excess digits being lost. The 145 is not as accurate a result as 146 would be, the latter being a **rounded** result. Thus, if the example had been:

```
ADD 12.7 to B GIVING C ROUNDED
```

and C were defined without decimal places, the result would have been rounded to 146 before being put into C. A half would be rounded up but less than a half rounded down. The same logic applies whenever the resultant variable has insufficient decimal places to hold the entire result. ROUNDED causes rounding of the least significant digit.

Exercises

1 For each of the following, state whether it is a legal or illegal ADD statement and for illegal cases, give a reason.

```
(i)     ADD X TO Y TO Z

(ii)    ADD X TO Y ROUNDED
                Z ROUNDED

(iii)   ADD X ROUNDED Y ROUNDED
              GIVING Z
```

2

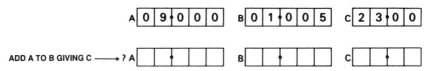

Fig. C.2 Exercise 2 – complete the drawing

3 The formal description of the two versions of the SUBTRACT statement is:

$$\underline{\text{SUBTRACT}} \quad \begin{Bmatrix} \text{identifier-1} \\ \text{literal-1} \end{Bmatrix} \dots$$

$$\underline{\text{FROM}} \ \{\text{identifier-2} \ [\underline{\text{ROUNDED}}]\} \dots$$

and

$$\underline{\text{SUBTRACT}} \quad \begin{Bmatrix} \text{identifier-1} \\ \text{literal-1} \end{Bmatrix} \dots$$

$$\underline{\text{FROM}} \quad \begin{Bmatrix} \text{identifier-2} \\ \text{literal-2} \end{Bmatrix}$$

$$\underline{\text{GIVING}} \ \{\text{identifier-3} \ [\underline{\text{ROUNDED}}]\} \dots$$

Which of these statements are legal?

```
(i)     SUBTRACT tax gross-pay
(ii)    SUBTRACT tax vat FROM gross-price
(iii)   SUBTRACT insurance
                 tax
                 union-fee FROM gross-pay
             GIVING net-pay
```

4 The entry after the 'FROM' in the simplest form of the SUBTRACT statement may not be a literal. Why?

5 Is the following statement legal?

```
ADD wholesale-price AND mark-up TO current-price
```

6 Remembering that A and B are variables that may take any value in the range allowed by their size, why is the ADD statement in Fig. C.2 unsatisfactory?

C2   MULTIPLY and DIVIDE

The basic structure of the MULTIPLY statement is:

$$\underline{\text{MULTIPLY}} \begin{Bmatrix} \text{identifier-1} \\ \text{literal-1} \end{Bmatrix} \underline{\text{BY}} \text{ identifier-2}$$

There are ROUNDED and GIVING options as with ADD and SUBTRACT. In the above version, the result of the multiplication would be placed in identifier-2, but if the GIVING option were used, the result would be in a separate variable.

The simplest form of the DIVIDE statement is similar:

$$\underline{\text{DIVIDE}} \begin{Bmatrix} \text{identifier-1} \\ \text{literal-1} \end{Bmatrix} \underline{\text{INTO}} \text{ identifier-2}$$

Again, there are ROUNDED and GIVING options, the latter allowing two forms:

```
DIVIDE A INTO B GIVING C
```

and

```
DIVIDE B BY A GIVING C
```

these two statements being equivalent.

In these two examples, the result, whether rounded or not, will be constrained by the size of the variable C. Sometimes with division, unless the result is exact, you are interested in the remainder, i.e. in the example, what is left over after you have obtained enough of a result for C. This is yet another option for the DIVIDE statement. An example is:

C = m D

```
DIVIDE 3.1416 INTO circle GIVING diameter ROUNDED
    REMAINDER diameter-rem
```

Here, the remainder from the division will be placed in the variable diameter-rem. The remainder is determined by COBOL in the following way:

1 It does the division and creates both a rounded result which is put into the quotient (diameter) and an unrounded result which is used to calculate the remainder. If ROUNDED were not specified, these two results would be the same.
2 It multiplies this unrounded result by the divisor (3.1416)
3 It subtracts the result of this multiplication from the dividend (circle) and puts this new result into the remainder field (diameter-rem). You must ensure that the remainder field has enough digits, both before and after the decimal point, to hold the remainder.

Exercises

1

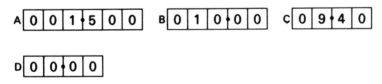

Fig. C.3 Exercise 1

Consider Fig. C.3. What would be the contents of A, B, C and D after each of the following statements? Assume the original contents of the four variables in each case.

```
(i)     MULTIPLY A BY B

(ii)    MULTIPLY A BY B ROUNDED

(iii)   DIVIDE B INTO A GIVING C
            REMAINDER D

(iv)    DIVIDE A INTO B GIVING C

(v)     DIVIDE A INTO B GIVING C ROUNDED
            REMAINDER D
```

2 What is wrong with this statement?

```
MULTIPLY radius BY 3.1416
```

3 Would execution of these two statements have the same or different effects?

```
DIVIDE A INTO B GIVING C
```

```
DIVIDE B BY A GIVING C
```

4 The cost of a meal, contained in raw-total, needs tax at 15% adding to it to produce a meal-cost figure. Meal-cost and raw-total can both hold three digits before the decimal point and two after the decimal point, i.e. they can hold a maximum value of 999.99. A variable int-total is available for intermediate results. The following COBOL statements attempt to solve this problem.

```
MULTIPLY 15 BY raw-total GIVING int-total
DIVIDE 100 INTO int-total
ADD int-total TO raw-total GIVING meal-cost
```

(i) If the result needs to be as accurate as possible, how many digits should int-total have both before and after the decimal point?

(ii) Should rounding occur in any of the three statements?

C3   COMPUTE

The COMPUTE statement allows for more complicated arithmetic. A formal description of its simplest form is:

<u>COMPUTE</u> identifier [<u>ROUNDED</u>] = arithmetic-expression

The expression to the right of the = sign is evaluated and the answer placed in the variable denoted by the identifier. An arithmetic expression is a series of numeric literals and identifiers with arithmetic operators placed between them. These operators are:

    +   addition
    −   subtraction
    *   multiplication
    /   division
    **   exponentiation (raising to a power).

For example, a legal expression would be:

```
COMPUTE alpha ROUNDED = beta - gamma / n * n
```

To human beings, this statement would be ambiguous. Would you do the subtraction or the division first? Thus

(beta − gamma) / n times n

is not the same as

beta − (gamma / n times n).

To avoid this ambiguity, COBOL works to a strict priority when evaluating operators, namely:

First **
Second * and /
Third + and −

For operators at the same priority level, evaluation takes place from left to right. You can always override these priorities by using brackets to contain the portion of the expression that you wish to be evaluated first, e.g. the COMPUTE example above without any brackets would be interpreted as follows:

beta − ((gamma / n) * n)

because the / and * have the higher priority and the / is performed first as it is the leftmost of the two. If you wished to perform the subtraction first and divide this by 'n times n', you would have:

```
COMPUTE alpha ROUNDED = (beta - gamma) / (n * n)
```

The use of brackets is recommended whenever the expression is complicated, even when they are not strictly necessary, because you are less likely to make a mistake and your statement will be easier for someone else to understand. At least one space should be left on either side of an operator.

Exercises

1 Is the following statement legal?

```
COMPUTE A = B ROUNDED
```

2 Recode question 4 of the C2 frame exercises using a single COMPUTE statement.
3 Assume that the area of a circle is 3.1416 times the square of the radius and you have declared suitable variables 'radius' and 'circle-area'. Provide COBOL statements to do this calculation

(i) without using the COMPUTE statement,
(ii) using a single COMPUTE statement.

Which is preferable?

4 Many compilers relax the rule about having a space on either side of arithmetic operators. However, an exception is the minus operator which always requires the spaces. Why?

C4   SIZE ERROR

We have considered the situation of rounding or truncating digits at the least significant (or right) end of result variables, but up to now we have always assumed that they are large enough at the most significant (or left) end to hold the result computed.

A **size error** occurs when there is overflow from the most significant digit within the resultant variable. In the example of 'ADD A TO B' in Fig. C.1, if A contained 920 instead of 120, the result of the addition would be 1053 but B only has room for 3 digits so 053 becomes the result in B and a size error occurs because the 1 has been lost.

To cope with this possible error situation, all the arithmetic statements have size error options we have not yet met. They are similar for ADD, SUBTRACT, MULTIPLY, DIVIDE and COMPUTE so we shall just use the first form of the ADD statement as an example. Its complete formal description is:

$$\underline{\text{ADD}} \ \begin{Bmatrix} \text{identifier-1} \\ \text{literal-1} \end{Bmatrix} \dots \underline{\text{TO}} \ \{\text{identifier-2} \ [\underline{\text{ROUNDED}}]\} \dots$$

[ON <u>SIZE ERROR</u> imperative-statement-1]
[<u>NOT</u> ON <u>SIZE ERROR</u> imperative-statement-2]
[<u>END-ADD</u>]

An 'imperative-statement', although always used in the singular in formal descriptions, actually indicates an imperative statement list, i.e. one or more imperative statements. We'll see later the exact definition of an imperative statement, but in its simplest form it is a single PROCEDURE DIVISION 'doing' statement, e.g. SUBTRACT, MOVE, ADD.

By the above definition, the following is a valid COBOL ADD statement:

```
Add bonus TO pay
ON SIZE ERROR
    DISPLAY "Bonus too large"
NOT ON SIZE ERROR
    ADD back-pay TO pay
    SUBTRACT tax FROM pay
END-ADD
```

Structured English to represent the logic is:

add bonus to pay
IF overflow error
    output "bonus too large"
ELSE
    add back-pay to pay
    subtract tax from pay
ENDIF

This illustrates that the ON SIZE ERROR and NOT ON SIZE ERROR clauses act like conditional statements.

In the COBOL code we have an ADD statement as part of another ADD statement. This is allowed because the 'inner' ADD is part of the imperative-statement list associated with the NOT ON SIZE ERROR option. You could also have SIZE ERROR and NOT ON SIZE ERROR options within these inner arithmetic statements, but for simplicity we will assume that the variable 'pay' is large enough to handle these latter calculations and it is only 'bonus' that could cause a possible size error.

The END-ADD is necessary to make it clear where the complete outer ADD statement ends and the next PROCEDURE DIVISION statement begins. However, if this ADD statement happened to be the last statement in a paragraph, there would be a full stop to terminate the sentence and this would automatically terminate the ADD as well so that the END-ADD would be unnecessary. However, it is always better to use the explicit terminator END-ADD when using ON SIZE ERROR or NOT ON SIZE ERROR or both.

The semantics or meaning of the above example is that an attempt would be made to add the contents of 'bonus' to 'pay'. If a size error occurred, the message 'Bonus too large' would be displayed on the screen and 'pay' would be left with its original value. If there were no overflow, the subsequent ADD and SUBTRACT statements would be executed. In either case, execution would flow on to the next statement.

As mentioned above, these size error options are similar for all arithmetic statements – the only difference is that each statement has its own END-SUBTRACT, END-MULTIPLY, END-DIVIDE AND END-COMPUTE.

Size error options need not always be used. If your result variable easily has enough digits to cope with the maximum possible answer that could be calculated, then the size error option would never be set so there is no point in using it. For example, if you had:

```
ADD A B GIVING C
```

and the variables A and B were both one integer digit in length and C was two digits long, then C would always be large enough – the maximum possible value from the addition is 9 + 9 giving 18 and this would fit into the two-digit C. However, in the earlier example in this frame, even if 'bonus' were smaller than 'pay', this statement could be executed many times so that in theory, if not in practice, 'pay' could overflow. Situations that cause overflow are often errors in data or the logic of the program, so using the SIZE ERROR option may give you useful information as to what is going wrong.

You may need to be wary in the use of the COMPUTE statement because even though the resultant variable is large enough to hold the maximum possible answer, an intermediate result may cause overflow, e.g. the division of a very large number by a very small fraction. The SIZE ERROR option will detect this condition so it is recommended that you always use it with complicated formulas.

Exercises

1 Using only ADD and SUBTRACT, produce COBOL statements to perform the calculation $A = B + C - D + E$ where all the operands have two decimal places and two integer places. Check for overflow and display an appropriate message if it occurs.

2 Is the following statement valid?

```
SUBTRACT tax FROM gross-pay ROUNDED
ON SIZE ERROR
    DISPLAY "Error in Pay Calculation"
    STOP RUN.
END-SUBTRACT
```

3 Taxable income is made up of Annual-Salary and Bonus less Allowances and a superannuation figure which is 5% of Annual-Salary. Tax is 30% of taxable income. Produce a single COBOL COMPUTE statement to calculate Tax, displaying a suitable message if overflow occurs.

4 (i)   What would happen when this statement is executed?

```
SUBTRACT A FROM A
DIVIDE A INTO B GIVING C
ON SIZE ERROR
    DISPLAY "Size error has occurred"
NOT ON SIZE ERROR
    DISPLAY "Divide OK"
END-DIVIDE
```

(ii) What would happen if no size error option were specified?

Answers – Section C

Frame C1

1 (i)   Illegal – 'TO' can only appear once.
  (ii)   Legal. N.B. ROUNDED must be coded after each variable that needs rounding.
  (iii) Illegal – 'ROUNDED' can only be applied to the final result field.
2 C contains 10.00, A and B are unchanged.
3 (ii) and (iii) are legal. (i) is missing a variable for the result, (ii) is legal by the first version and (iii) is legal by the second version.

  You may be wondering about positive and negative values – signs were not mentioned in Figs C.1 and C.2. These will be discussed fully in Section F but for the moment it is sufficient to know that COBOL can hold the sign of a value for a variable without affecting the variable's size.
4 The entry after the 'FROM' indicates where the result of the calculation will be placed and so must be a variable.
5 No. AND is not part of the valid syntax for an ADD statement even though you may want to express the addition with an 'and' in English. Though COBOL reads a little like English in parts, it is a long way from being a natural language.
6 The sum of A and B at maximum could be 199.998, which is larger than the size of C. C should be declared with 3 places before the decimal point. There may also be a rounding problem as the third decimal place is lost without rounding.

Frame C2

1 (i)   B contains 015.00, A, C and D are unchanged.
  (ii)   as (i)
  (iii) C contains 00.15, A, B and D are unchanged.
  (iv)   C contains 06.66, A, B and D are unchanged.
  (v)   C contains 06.67, D contains 00.01, A and B are unchanged.
2 You cannot store the result in a literal.
3 The same.
4 (i)   Five digits before and four digits after the decimal point. For the first multiplication by 15, int-cost must have two extra digits before the decimal point (think of the largest possible value here which would be 999.99 multiplied by 15). The division by 100 would then require two extra decimal places to preserve the required accuracy and this gives the total of five and four.
  (ii)   The first two statements are producing results without any truncation so rounding is not needed. The addition should have the ROUNDED option so that the most accurate final result is achieved. However, it may depend on whether you are the restaurant owner or a customer, as this will affect who gets the extra penny!

Frame C3

1 No, ROUNDED must appear after the result identifier A.

2 COMPUTE meal-cost ROUNDED =
raw-total + (raw-total * 15 / 100)

3 (i)   MULTIPLY radius BY radius
            GIVING circle-area ROUNDED
      MULTIPLY 3.1416 BY circle-area ROUNDED

  (ii) COMPUTE circle-area ROUNDED =
            3.1416 * radius ** 2

The second solution is preferable to the first in two ways:

(a) From a readability point of view, it allows you to state the formula in a natural way, whereas the double multiply solution is a little contrived.

(b) Solution (i) requires an intermediate variable. We have used circle-area as no special variable was provided in the specification; however, it is preferable to use an explicit intermediate variable so as not to confuse the use of circle-area. Also, you need to consider the rounding of the intermediate result. We have included it here, but it actually depends upon the size of radius and circle-area as to whether it is necessary.

4 Spaces are always needed either side of the minus sign to distinguish this arithmetic operator from a hyphen within an identifier name. We met a similar problem in frame B3 with a full stop, except that this time, COBOL is using the symbol '−' to represent two different things. Some computer languages do not allow hyphens within identifier names to get round the problem.

Frame C4

```
1 ADD B C E GIVING A
  ON SIZE ERROR
      DISPLAY "Overflow in addition"
  NOT ON SIZE ERROR
      SUBTRACT D FROM A
      ON SIZE ERROR
          DISPLAY "Overflow in subtraction"
      END-SUBTRACT
  END-ADD
```

Full stops were mentioned in frame B3. There are no full stops in the above code because the 'END-' phrases terminate the statements. However, in earlier versions of COBOL, the full stop was the only means of terminating conditional statements and this is still valid in COBOL 85. However, any full stops included in the above code would generate an error, probably on one of the 'END-' phrases, as the latter become superfluous to a terminated statement. The general recommendation for Procedure Division code is to have, for each paragraph, one full stop after the paragraph name and one full stop at the end of each paragraph.

2 This is a bit of a trick question because it's the little full stop that's the problem. The SUBTRACT statement is terminated by the full stop and this marks the end of a sentence. The END-SUBTRACT would be treated as a brand-new statement and by itself, would be illegal. The moral is to avoid full stops as much as possible – in the PROCEDURE DIVISION, they are only needed at the end of section and paragraph names and at the end of the sections and paragraphs themselves. Try sticking to this minimum requirement.

3
```
COMPUTE tax ROUNDED =
      ((annual-salary + bonus) - allowances -
          (annual-salary * 0.05)) * 0.3
ON SIZE ERROR
      DISPLAY "Overflow in Tax calculation"
END-COMPUTE
```

4 (i) 'Size error has occurred' would be displayed because dividing zero into any value will cause overflow.

   (ii) This is a little more difficult to predict as different machines may react in different ways. The most likely outcome is that the program will stop executing and the machine will produce a special 'divide by zero' message – not something you want to happen in one of your programs so it is always best to try to 'trap' such errors with your own COBOL SIZE ERROR option.

D Transfer of Control

D1 Simple conditional statements

The computer normally executes statements in the order in which they were coded. However, much of the power of the computer derives from its ability to branch away from this sequential flow, as for example when a decision is made within a program to follow one branch or another, depending on a condition.

This is achieved in COBOL by using the word IF, which introduces a conditional statement:

```
IF record-type = "1"
THEN
    ADD qty TO qty-in-stock
END-IF
```

If the condition is true (i.e. record-type contains the value 1) then the statement 'ADD qty TO qty-in-stock' will be executed; otherwise the program will simply pass on to the next statement. We might want it to take some alternative action if the condition is not true, and in that case we use the word ELSE:

```
IF record-type = "1"
THEN
    ADD qty TO qty-in-stock
ELSE
    SUBTRACT qty FROM qty-in-stock
END-IF
```

Incidentally, the word 'THEN' is optional in COBOL 'IF' statements, but we have chosen to use it throughout this book. The condition above was

one of equality, but we can use the operators 'GREATER THAN' ('>')
and 'LESS THAN' ('<'); we can also produce negative conditions by using
the word NOT.

```
IF no-of-items NOT > 100
THEN
    ADD amount TO item-total
    ADD 1 TO no-of-items
END-IF
```

Section I contains more details about conditions and conditional statements, e.g. 'nested' IF statements, COBOL's 'case' statement, EVALU-
ATE and compound conditions. You may wish to glance ahead now if
some of these terms are already familiar to you.

Exercises

1 Write a COBOL statement that will test the value of a signed variable
  called 'balance'; if it is greater than zero, add balance to a variable
  called 'total'.
2 Write a COBOL statement that will add 'stock-movement' to 'stock-
  total' if 'store-code' is equal to 1, and subtract it if 'store-code' is equal
  to anything other than 1.
3 Rewrite the following conditional sentence by introducing the word
  'NOT' into the condition (the result should be logically the same):

```
IF flag = "OK"
THEN
    MOVE "YES" TO end-flag
ELSE
    MOVE "NO" TO end-flag
END-IF
```

D2   The PERFORM verb

The PERFORM verb is one of the most useful in the COBOL language,
and a thorough understanding of both the concepts and the practical use
of the verb is essential. One of the simplest ways of using it is as follows:

```
PERFORM paragraph-name
```

We might include in a program a paragraph to which we have given the
name 'Calc-average'. The statement 'PERFORM Calc-average' would
transfer control to the statement immediately following the name 'Calc-
average', and when the end of the paragraph is reached, control returns to
the statement immediately after the PERFORM statement.

This type of PERFORM is called an 'out-of-line' PERFORM, because control deviates from its normal sequential path ('in-line') and goes away to another part of the program. But, having executed the out-of-line code as instructed by the PERFORM statement, control resumes its sequential path at the point where it broke off. Notice that the paragraph-name does not function merely as a label or point to branch to; the concept of the paragraph as a block of code is important, the block being terminated by a full stop, followed by a fresh paragraph-name (unless of course it happens to be the end of the program).

Typically, this version of the PERFORM statement is used to split the Procedure Division into separate parts (or modules) so that it is easier to understand.

It is also possible to PERFORM a number of paragraphs using the THRU clause, e.g.

```
PERFORM Initial-calculation THRU Main-calculation
```

All the paragraphs between, and including, 'Initial-calculation' and 'Main-calculation' are executed before control is passed on to the statement following the PERFORM. However, it is usually clearer to avoid such multi-paragraph PERFORMs and is mentioned here only for completeness.

Exercise

1 The out-of-line PERFORM is an instruction to execute a paragraph. Which of the following are valid paragraph names?

(a) PROC-1
(b) add
(c) 1234
(d) Procedure

D3   The PERFORM UNTIL

This second option of the PERFORM statement is used for looping and is COBOL's implementation of the *DO UNTIL* Structured English construct. Below is an example using an 'in-line' version of the PERFORM, i.e. rather than being in a separate paragraph, the code to be repeatedly executed is placed between the PERFORM statement and a matching END-PERFORM. The example is calculating the average (mean) for a set of numbers, the set being terminated by zero.

```
MOVE 0 TO accum howmany
ACCEPT num
PERFORM UNTIL num = 0
```

```
          ADD num TO accum
          ADD 1 TO howmany
          ACCEPT num
END-PERFORM
DIVIDE howmany INTO accum GIVING average
```

The three statements between the PERFORM and the END-PER-FORM are executed repeatedly until a value of zero is input. The UNTIL condition is tested **before** entering the loop.

This also illustrates the 'do ahead' principle, a general programming guideline for handling loops, whereby a loop is always entered with the latest new value ready for processing. In the above example, when the loop is entered for the first time, there will already be a value in 'num' and for subsequent entries the next value will be in 'num' through the ACCEPT at the end of the loop. This principle avoids the need for an IF statement within the main loop when a zero is accepted.

If we wish the condition to be tested **after** execution of the loop, this is specified with the PERFORM statement, e.g.

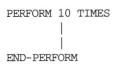

```
PERFORM WITH TEST AFTER
    UNTIL reply = "Q"
        |
        |
END-PERFORM
```

There is a WITH TEST BEFORE clause as well, but since this is the default it is usually left out.

An out-of-line PERFORM UNTIL can also be used e.g.

```
PERFORM Process-main-menu
    UNTIL reply = "Q"
```

Normally, this would only be where there are a substantial number of statements within the loop.

There is also a PERFORM option for executing a loop a fixed number of times, e.g.

```
PERFORM 10 TIMES
        |
        |
END-PERFORM
```

The statements within the loop are executed exactly 10 times. The number of times can be variable but it must contain an appropriate value when it is executed. Its use is fairly rare as most problems have variable amounts of data.

Exercises

1 Look at the following fragment of a COBOL program:

```
MOVE 0 TO num
PERFORM UNTIL num > 99
    ADD 2 TO num
END-PERFORM
```

Assuming that 'num' was a variable large enough to contain a value greater than 99,

(a) What would the value of 'num' be after executing these statements?
(b) What difference would 'PERFORM WITH TEST BEFORE' make?
(c) What difference would 'PERFORM WITH TEST AFTER' make?

2 What do you think would happen if 'num' was only a two-digit field, and so could not contain a value greater than 99?

D4   Nested PERFORMs

It is possible to include, within the statements being performed, another PERFORM statement, and within the statements performed by that, another PERFORM, and so on. This is called 'nesting' the PERFORMs, and it can be done with both in-line and out-of-line PERFORMs. The code that follows shows the Procedure Division of a program that calculates and displays the day number (i.e. 1 to 365 or 366) of a date (month-number and day-number) entered at the keyboard. This program may be said to be at three levels. The top level is the first paragraph, P1-Main; this contains a sequence of three out-of-line PERFORMs, and the paragraphs which they perform constitute the second level. The third, or bottom, level is represented by the paragraph P3-Find-days-in-month, which is performed from P2B-Calculate-days, which in turn is performed from P1-Main.

```
PROCEDURE DIVISION.
P1-Main
    PERFORM P2A-Accept-date
    PERFORM P2B-Calculate-days
    PERFORM P2C-Display-result
    STOP RUN.
P2A-Accept-date.
    DISPLAY "Enter month number" UPON CONSOLE
    ACCEPT month FROM CONSOLE
    DISPLAY "Enter day number" UPON CONSOLE
    ACCEPT days FROM CONSOLE.
```

```
P2B-Calculate-days.
    PERFORM P3-Find-days-in-month
    ADD days TO tot-days.
P2C-Display-result.
    DISPLAY "The day number is " tot-days
        UPON CONSOLE.
P3-Find-days-in-month.
    IF month = 1
    THEN
        MOVE 0 TO tot-days
    END-IF
    IF month = 2
    THEN
        MOVE 31 TO tot-days
    END-IF
```

(etc., for the rest of the months)

In the case of out-of-line performs of the PERFORM THRU type, or performs of sections, it is necessary to be careful; the paragraphs executed by a nested perform must either lie wholly within the range of the outer PERFORM or wholly outside it.

This is enough about the PERFORM statement at this stage but you may like to look at a further facility in frame I7 (the 'PERFORM VARYING').

Exercises

1 Pretend you are the computer executing the example program in this frame. List the paragraph names as you encounter them (this is called 'tracing' the program). Indent the list when you are executing a nested PERFORM.

2 The code within the paragraph 'P3-Find-days-in-month' in the above example uses a series of IF statements. Why might the logic of this code be questionable even though it produces the correct answer?

D5   The GO TO statement

Another way of causing a branch out of the normal sequential flow of control within a program is by using the GO TO statement. It should be said right away that many people frown upon the use of GO TO. This is because unwise and excessive use of this feature of the language results in programs that meander in a confusing way instead of exhibiting a satisfactory structure. In earlier versions of COBOL, such as COBOL 74, there were occasional situations in which it was necessary to use a GO TO, but in COBOL 85 it need never be used. We shall deal with the principles of program structure in Section K, and we shall have more to say about the GO TO then. For the present you should understand what it does, and how and how not to use it.

The format of the statement is simply:

```
GO TO procedure-name
```

'Procedure-name' can be a paragraph name or a section name, and the statement simply transfers control to the beginning of the specified paragraph or section. Thus, to transfer control to a paragraph that you have called 'Read-next-record' you would code:

```
GO TO Read-next-record
```

You may think it seems very like the out-of-line version of the PER-FORM statement, but there is an important difference. After a PER-FORM statement has finished executing its paragraph(s) or section(s), control returns to the point from which it branched, whereas after a GO TO statement the sequential flow continues from where it branched to; it has no memory of where it branched from.

There is a very important restriction to observe if you use a GO TO in conjunction with an out-of-line PERFORM. If the PERFORM is of a series of paragraphs (PERFORM-THRU, or a section) then those paragraphs must not contain a GO TO that branches out of the range of the PERFORM. It is permissible to branch forwards or backwards within the range of the THRU, or within the section, but if you GO TO a paragraph outside that range, then the PERFORM will lose track of where to return to afterwards.

There is no exercise for this frame.

Answers – Section D

Frame D1

```
1 IF balance > 0
  THEN
      ADD balance TO total
  END-IF

2 IF store-code = "1"
  THEN
      ADD stock-movement TO stock-total
  ELSE
      SUBTRACT stock-movement FROM stock-total
  END-IF
```

```
3 IF flag NOT = "OK"
   THEN
       MOVE "NO" TO end-flag
   ELSE
       MOVE "YES" TO end-flag
   END-IF
```

Frame D2

1 (a) and (c) are valid paragraph names; the other two are both reserved words.

Frame D3

1 (a) 100
  (b) and (c) – no difference.
2 The PERFORM would execute for ever, because 'num' would not be capable of storing the value 100; on reaching 98, the addition of 2 would set it to 0 and the cycle would repeat. Such a situation is called an endless loop, and it would normally require the operator to intervene and stop the program.

Frame D4

```
1 P1-main
       P2A-accept-date
       P2B-calculate-days
           P3-find-days-in-month
       P2C-display-result
   P1-main
```

2 When the correct month is reached, the appropriate MOVE is executed but any remaining IFs are also executed. A better solution would be to skip round remaining IFs once the correct one has been executed. This can be achieved using constructs we have not yet discussed – nested IFs and the EVALUATE statement. They feature in Section I.

E The DATA DIVISION

E1 Introduction

Figure E.1 illustrates the concepts underlying a COBOL program. A record in an input file can be read into an area of memory, under the control of the procedures of the program (a statement READ exists for this purpose). A record for an output file can be written from an output record area (WRITE exists for this purpose). Even if you wish just to write out the same record that was input, it is necessary to move the record internally in memory, i.e. from the input record area to the output record area – MOVE exists for this purpose. The arrows in Fig. E.1 show that the move could be made directly from the input to the output record area, or via Working-Storage. (ACCEPT and DISPLAY are also used for 'keyboard input'/'screen output' directly into/from Working-Storage but normally

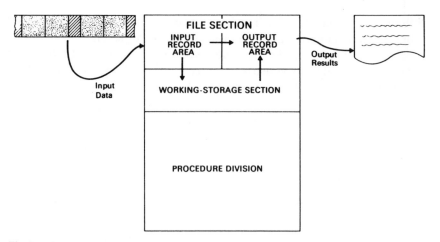

Fig. E.1 Contents of memory at execution of program

only where the amount of data is small – we shall look at these two statements in more detail later.)

The Data Division can be divided into five sections, each of which has a special purpose. However, simple COBOL programs need only two of these, the File Section and Working-Storage Section.

In the File Section, you define the files that are to be used by the program. The compiler uses this information to reserve the input and output record areas in memory. For example, say you had a file of records on a disk, each record consisting of one field that contained a two-digit number, and you wanted to find the total of all the numbers. (Records usually consist of several fields but for this introductory example, we will have just a single-field record.) When you define this disk file in the File Section, the compiler will allocate an input record area to hold the data for one record, i.e. a two-digit area. This is because the computer processes only one record at a time so that as the processing of one record finishes, the data from the next record can be read into the same input record area, thereby overwriting the previous contents.

The total you wish to accumulate from the records is not part of the file. Such variables which do not belong to any file are defined in the Working-Storage Section.

In the Data Division, therefore, you define memory areas for:

(i)   records, and fields within these records
(ii) independent data items

and give names (i.e. identifiers) for each of these areas. The compiler uses this information to map out the actual locations of data areas in memory so that when you refer to these areas by their names in the Procedure Division, it can link such names to where they are located. When your Procedure Division statements are translated into machine code operations, they can then operate on the correct locations. The term **data name** is also used in COBOL, and for simple data it is synonymous with the term 'identifier'.

Exercises

1 Refer to Fig. A.4. What data names must have been declared in the Data Division of the COBOL program?
2 The compiler will give you an error message, called a **fatal error**, if it cannot translate your program into machine code through some error on your part. If you referred to a variable in the Procedure Division but had failed to name it in the Data Division, do you think the compiler would give your program a fatal error?
3 If you named a variable in the Data Division but did not refer to it at all in the Procedure Division, would the compiler give a fatal error?

4 A program is to read in a disk file and, amongst other things, count how many records there are in it.

(a) In which section would you define the disk records?

(b) What other data element would you need and where would you define it?

E2   The FILE SECTION

You tell the compiler that you are starting the File Section by coding the section name immediately after the division name, i.e.

```
DATA DIVISION.
FILE SECTION.
```

Each file that is to be used by the program is then defined by two types of entry, a **File Description** (FD entry) and one or more **Record Descriptions** (01 entry).

File descriptions can be quite complex and certain compilers offer slight variations to the standard so it is worthwhile checking your particular language manual for full details.

An abbreviated standard form is:

FD file-name
        [BLOCK CONTAINS integer RECORDS]
        [RECORD CONTAINS integer CHARACTERS]

and the whole entry is terminated by a full stop. The letters FD, which signify a File Description, are coded within Area A, usually starting at the left-most position (column 8). Subsequent entries start in Area B and usually start in column 12. The file-name is made up by you in accordance with the rules for name formation (frame B3) and, of course, you should choose a meaningful name.

The optional BLOCK CONTAINS clause is used to specify, for magnetic tape and disk files, the number of records in a block (see frame A4). On microcomputers, this 'blocking factor' is often fixed and need not be specified.

The optional RECORD CONTAINS clause specifies the number of characters in one record. It is optional because the compiler can determine the size of a record from the size of the individual fields which comprise that record – these are specified after the FD entry for each file. However, it can act as a check that your later field descriptions are correct because with some compilers, if the total of all the individual fields is different from your RECORD CONTAINS figure, a **warning error** will be issued. A warning error is one that will not stop the creation of an object program (if there are no fatal errors!) but is given to draw your attention to a possible error situation.

Some FD entries have been made **obsolete** in the 1985 standard. 'Obsolete' means that they are still in the current standard but will be deleted from the next standard. Such items may well appear in programs that have been developed to the 1974 standard and so it is sometimes worthwhile being aware of their existence as much programming work involves updating of existing programs. Obsolete FD entries are:

LABEL RECORDS clause

VALUE OF ID clause

DATA RECORDS clause

Consult your particular compiler's language manual if you need details of these entries.

If there is more than one type of record in a file, each type is described in detail in a separate record description entry following the relevant File Description.

Example

A program reads records from two files, one a disk file and the other a magnetic tape file. The magnetic tape file has two types of 'transaction' record, Credits and Debits, both of length 60 characters. The records are stored in blocks of 20 records. The disk file, a 'master' file of customer records, has a fixed record size of 145 characters.

```
DATA DIVISION.
FILE SECTION.
FD transaction-tape-file
     BLOCK CONTAINS 20 RECORDS
     RECORD CONTAINS 60 CHARACTERS.
(here follows the record description for Credits)
(here follows the record description for Debits)
FD master-disk-file
     RECORD CONTAINS 145 characters.
(here follows the record description for a customer master record)
```

The **external name** of a file, i.e. the name by which it is known outside the program, is usually supplied either in the Environment Division or with operating system commands at the time of program execution. For example, the above file with **internal name** master-disk-file could have an external name 'CMV56.DAT' on a microcomputer. The rules for formation of an external name are determined by the operating system of the computer, not by COBOL.

Exercises

1 A disk file, which has fixed-size records of length 90 characters, has the records stored in blocks of 20. Each record contains information about a particular machine part. Write a suitable File Description.
2 A file to be called report-file is to be output on a line printer which can print 132 characters per line. Write the File Description.

E3   Data description entries

A data description entry specifies the characteristics of a particular item of data and its simplest form is:

$$\text{level-number} \quad \left\{ \begin{array}{l} \text{data-name} \\ \text{FILLER} \end{array} \right\} \quad \left\{ \begin{array}{l} \underline{\text{PICTURE}} \\ \underline{\text{PIC}} \end{array} \right\} \quad \text{IS picture-string}$$

A record description entry consists of a sequence of data description entries. A level number of 01 (which must be placed in Area A) shows that you are about to give a name to a whole record. Level numbers of 02 to 49 (placed in Area B) are used to describe the fields that are contained within the record. Thus, a level 03 could denote a field within a record and this could be split up into sub-fields by giving each sub-field a level number of 05, and so on. 03,05,07, etc., are used instead of 02,03,04 to allow for easier insertion of intermediate levels which may arise at some later time in the program's life. The actual numbers that are used do not have any special significance in themselves but their relative values are important – a higher number indicates a further breakdown of a field. Some people use 10,20,30, etc., and again this has the same meaning. The leading zero of a level number is optional but most programmers put it in to standardise level numbers as always having 2 digits.

The data-name is the name by which you wish to identify the data element. Sometimes you want to define data areas but not give them a name because you never want to refer to them individually. For these you can either leave this part of the description blank or use the reserved word FILLER. Leaving this part blank is recommended but FILLER was compulsory in the 1974 standard, so you may see it in lots of programs.

The PICTURE clause is used to describe the number and type of characters in a field. PICTURE 9999 would mean four characters of numeric data, PICTURE A would mean one character of alphabetic data and PIC-TURE XXX would mean three characters of any type – numeric, alphabetic or special characters like '&' and '?' – called alphanumeric. As

PICTURE X descriptions include alphabetic characters and most real data of an alphabetic nature tend to have the odd special character, PICTURE A descriptions are not used much. PICTURE XX99 would mean two alphanumeric characters followed by two numeric characters in the one field.

To avoid writing down long strings of characters for large items, a multiplier can be placed in brackets – the PICTURE will be interpreted as if the character before the multiplier had been repeated that number of times. For example, instead of writing PICTURE XXXXXXXXXX, you could write PICTURE X(10) and instead of PICTURE 999999, PICTURE 9(6). The word PICTURE can be, and often is, abbreviated to PIC.

Considering the example of frame E1; if we extended the size of each record to be 60 characters but we were still only interested in the first two characters for our particular problem, then a description of a suitable record area could be:

```
01 data-record.
   03  number-in   PIC 99.
   03              PIC X(58).
```

The compiler would glean from this that 'data-record' is the name of a record, that 'number-in' is the name of the first two characters in the record and their type is numeric, and that the next 58 characters cover the rest of the record but this field does not need to be referenced by a name.

A complete example of both file and record descriptions can now be given, assuming this is the first such description in the Data Division.

```
DATA DIVISION.
FILE SECTION.
FD data-disk-file
   RECORD CONTAINS 60 CHARACTERS.
01 data-record.
   03  number-in   PIC 99.
   03              PIC X(58).
```

Notice that 'data-record' itself is not given a PICTURE as the compiler can calculate the length of such **group items** from the total of the sub-fields. The type of a group item is always assumed to be alphanumeric, irrespective of the descriptions of the sub-fields (**elementary items**). Therefore, 'data-record' is a field of length 60 characters and is of type alphanumeric.

For files with different record types, a 01 record description can be given for each type. In such a case, they are all redefinitions of the one record area.

Exercises

1 A file called 'report-file' is to be written to the line printer which has a line length of 132 characters. Each line of print has six fields:

a 6-digit account number
a 3-character filler field
an alphanumeric 9-character name
a 3-character filler field
a 26-character address
a final filler field

Write a complete record description for this file.

2 Write the record description entries to describe this record layout.

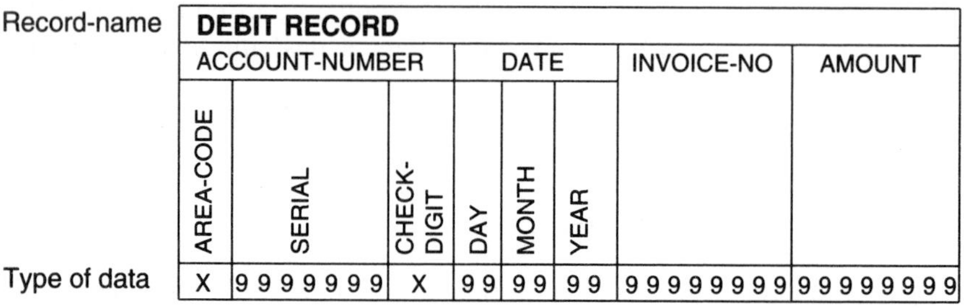

Record-name	DEBIT RECORD							
	ACCOUNT-NUMBER			DATE			INVOICE-NO	AMOUNT
	AREA-CODE	SERIAL	CHECK-DIGIT	DAY	MONTH	YEAR		
Type of data	X	9 9 9 9 9 9	X	9 9	9 9	9 9	9 9 9 9 9 9 9 9	9 9 9 9 9 9 9 9

Fig. E.2 Exercise 2

3 A record description entry appears as follows:

```
01 part-record.
    03 part-number.
        05 characteristics-code.
            07 material-code       PIC X.
            07 shape-code          PIC X.
        05 part-dimensions.
            07 part-length         PIC 99.
            07 x-section-area      PIC 9999.
        05 serial-number           PIC 9999.
    03 part-description            PIC X(10).
```

Draw a diagram similar to the one in Fig. E.2, to illustrate this record layout.

Answers – Section E

Frame E1

1 Total, number-in.
2 Yes.

3 No. Even though it may be wasteful not to use a variable that you have defined, it is not illegal.
4 (a) In the File Section.
  (b) A variable to count the records in the Working-Storage Section.

Frame E2

```
1 FD  parts-file
        BLOCK CONTAINS 20 RECORDS
        RECORD CONTAINS 90 CHARACTERS.
```

```
2 FD  report-file
        RECORD CONTAINS 132 CHARACTERS.
```

There is no blocking on a line printer.

Frame E3

```
1 01  report-record.
        03  account-number      PIC 9(6).
        03                       PIC X(3).
        03  account-name         PIC X(9).
        03                       PIC X(3).
        03  account-address      PIC X(26).
        03                       PIC X(85).
```

You may have used 'address' as the name of the final named field. Unfortunately, this would be illegal as **ADDRESS** is a reserved word. It is always safest to choose names which relate to the problem to avoid the more general reserved words.

```
2 01  debit-record.
        03  account-number.
            05  area-code        PIC X.
            05  serial-number    PIC 9(7).
            05  check-digit      PIC X.
        03  date-of-account.
            05  day-of-account   PIC 99.
            05  month-of-account PIC 99.
            05  year-of-account  PIC 99.
        03  invoice-number       PIC 9(8).
        03  invoice-amount       PIC 9(8).
```

Have you used any reserved words? Check against the list in Appendix C if you think you have.

3 See Fig. E.3.

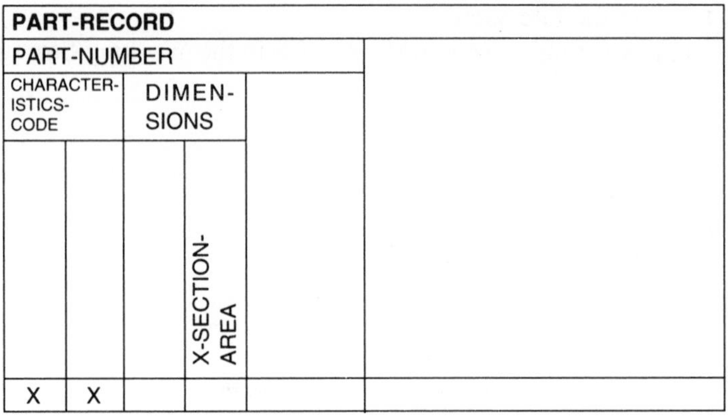

PART-RECORD					
PART-NUMBER					
CHARACTER-ISTICS-CODE		DIMEN-SIONS			
			X-SECTION-AREA		
X	X				

Fig. E.3 Answer to Exercise 3

F Further DATA DIVISION Entries

F1 The WORKING-STORAGE SECTION

Elements of data that do not form part of a file may be defined in the Working-Storage Section. Data items that are related to each other in some way, i.e. records, can be described in the same way as for the File Section. There is also a special level-number, 77, which indicates an independent data item, i.e. one that does not form part of a record. If you wished to accumulate a total in a three-digit field, you could write the following, assuming this was the first entry in the Working-Storage Section:

```
WORKING-STORAGE SECTION.
77  total-1       PIC 999.
```

The level 77s cannot be subdivided nor used to describe elementary items within a record. However, it is not illegal to use a lone 01 level entry to define an independent item and you can avoid the use of 77s completely by doing this. Therefore,

```
01  total-1       PIC 999.
```

is equivalent to the above 77 level description. However, the implication of an 01 level entry is that it is to be broken down into further subordinate items or is to be used for an input/output record. Therefore, some programmers avoid use of 77s by defining all their independent items together at the 03 level, under a single 01 level entry called, say, independent-items. By adopting this method, 77 levels are made redundant. It had been rumoured that they would disappear from the standard but this did not happen in the 1985 version and they are not on the obsolete list, so you may find both methods used in programs for some time to come. Both 77s and 01s can be written in any order within the Working-Storage Section although it is common practice to group 77 levels together.

You should never make any assumption about the initial value of an item in Working-Storage. If you wish to ensure that an item contains an initial value, say zero, you may specify this with the VALUE clause, e.g.

```
77  total-1      PIC 999    VALUE ZERO.
```

As another example, say you were wanting to number the pages of a report produced on a line printer, you might wish to start your page counter at 1. This could be written:

```
77  page-counter  PIC 99     VALUE 1.
```

A non-numeric literal can be used to initialise a non-numeric item. Consider the following example which assumes that the field being defined is part of a larger record and so is defined at the 03 level.

```
03                 PIC X(19)   VALUE "YEARLY SALES REPORT".
```

With such alphanumeric data items, if the non-numeric literal specified in the VALUE clause is shorter than the item, the literal is left-justified in the item and the remaining right-hand positions are filled with spaces. If it is longer than the item, you will lose some of the right-hand characters so you would try to avoid this.

The VALUE clause may not be used in the File Section as such data areas are associated with the flow of data to/from files and are not expected to be initialised in the same way as totals. However, especially for output report files, it is often useful to build up fixed parts of a record in Working-Storage. If the non-numeric literal example above were part of an 80-character print line, the whole record could be defined in the Working-Storage Section as:

```
01  page-heading.
    03             PIC X(30) VALUE SPACES.
    03             PIC X(19)
       VALUE "YEARLY SALES REPORT".
    03             PIC X(31) VALUE SPACES.
```

This record could then be moved through the File Section 01 record area (PIC X(80)) and out on to a printer unchanged. By including approximately the same number of spaces either side of the literal, the title would appear in the centre of the page.

As another example, this time using both constant and variable fields, suppose you wish to define a line of print like this:

salesperson no. : name : sales this month : sales to date

The colons and spaces are constants, the other items variables. It could be defined in Working-Storage as follows:

```
01  sales-detail-line.
      03  sales-person-number   PIC 9(4)
      03                        PIC X(5) VALUE " : ".
      03  sales-person-name     PIC X(20).
      03                        PIC X(5) VALUE " : ".
      03  sales-this-month      PIC 9(5).
      03                        PIC X(5) VALUE " : ".
      03  sales-to-date         PIC 9(6).
```

Exercises

1 What is wrong with this Data Division entry?

```
FILE SECTION.
FD  tape-file-in
      BLOCK CONTAINS 40 RECORDS
      RECORD CONTAINS 80 CHARACTERS.
01  tape-record-in            PIC X(80) VALUE SPACES.
```

2 Write Working-Storage Section entries to print the following heading in the middle of an 80-character print line:

PAYROLL ANALYSIS

– – – – – – – – – – – – – – –

The underline characters are hyphens, appearing on the line below, which should be specified in a separate record definition.

3 The date is to be printed out to the right of the words PAYROLL ANALYSIS in Exercise 2, after a gap of 20 spaces. This will take the form dd/mm/yy where dd, mm and yy are the two-digit day, month and year which will be inserted by Procedure Division statements. The oblique strokes are constants to be defined in the heading. Amend your answer to Exercise 2 to define this record (the date is not to be underlined).

F2   The PICTURE clause – numeric pictures

We have seen the Picture clause used to define simple numeric, alphabetic and alphanumeric items. We will now complete our knowledge of numeric pictures, then look at a special case of alphanumeric pictures – edited items.

Numeric pictures, in addition to the picture character 9, can also contain the characters S, V and P.

S shows that the number will have a sign, i.e. positive and negative values can be represented. S must be the first character in the picture and it does not add to the length of the item unless the optional phrase SIGN LEADING SEPARATE is added. For example:

```
03   tax-amount     PIC S999.
```

describes a three-digit numeric variable which may hold a positive or negative value, whereas:

```
03   tax-amount     PIC S999    SIGN LEADING SEPARATE.
```

describes a three-digit numeric variable preceded by a single character containing a + or − sign. In the former case, computers hold the sign as part of the number, which is why the length stays the same. In practice, the SIGN LEADING SEPARATE option is used when data is to be exchanged between different computers or is to be processed by programs written in different languages, because there is no official standard for how the sign is to be held when it is part of a number.

V shows the position of a decimal point within a numeric item and it does NOT add to the length of the item. The decimal point is **assumed** by the compiler to be in that position in the data specified by the V in the picture. An actual decimal point must not appear in the data. So

```
03   tax-amount     PIC S999V99.
```

defines a signed, five-digit field whose decimal point is assumed to be between the third and fourth characters, while

```
03   discount       PIC V99.
```

defines a two-digit unsigned field with an assumed decimal point at the beginning.

P is a scaling factor for handling either very small or very large numbers. In practice, it is rarely used, as normal commercial problems do not involve such data. It locates an assumed decimal point at some notional position to the left or right of the data item, e.g.

```
77   milliseconds  PIC VPPP999.
```

describes a three-digit numeric item which is to be treated in arithmetic as if it had .000 preceding it. In contrast,

```
77   round-millions  PIC 999P(6).
```

describes a three-digit numeric item which is to be treated in arithmetic as if it had six zeros following it. P does *not* add to the length of the item, so it allows such data to be stored in both memory and files without all the extra zeros.

Normally, numeric data is held in memory in character form, i.e. each digit is held as an independent character. On most computers it is possible to change this by specifying

USAGE IS BINARY

or

USAGE IS COMPUTATIONAL

after a numeric picture clause. BINARY states that the item will be held in binary format and COMPUTATIONAL (or COMP) states that the item will be held in some form defined by individual implementations of COBOL, but which usually is binary anyway. For example:

```
03  tax-amount    PIC S999V99  USAGE IS BINARY.
```

would cause the variable tax-amount to be held as a binary, rather than a decimal number. This can make a program execute more quickly, especially when there are a lot of calculations, because, in computers, arithmetic is usually performed in binary and it saves the program having to convert characters to binary form before doing such arithmetic. Also, less memory is needed to store large numbers in binary. The actual number of character positions allocated to a picture with usage BINARY or COMPUTATIONAL varies from machine to machine.

You may see COMPUTATIONAL or COMP in older programs only, as BINARY was a feature introduced in the 1985 standard and is likely to be the preferred option in the future.

Both the USAGE clause and the earlier SIGN LEADING SEPARATE clause may be used at group level, e.g. 01, in which case all subordinate items will be treated as having these characteristics.

Exercises

```
1 01  audit-record    SIGN LEADING SEPARATE.
      03  total-debits       PIC S9(8)V99.
      03  total-credits      PIC S9(8)V99.
      03  no-of-debits       PIC S9(6).
      03  no-of-credits      PIC S9(6).
```

How long is this group record?

2 What is wrong with this coding?

```
01   invoice          USAGE IS BINARY.
     03  gross-amount              PIC 9(8)V99.
     03  discount-rate            PIC V99.
     03  discount-amount          PIC 9(8)V99.
     ⋮
     COMPUTE discount-amount ROUNDED =
         gross-amount * discount-rate * (-1).
```

3 What is wrong with this coding?

```
01   order-summary     USAGE IS COMP.
     03  no-in-stock               PIC 9(8).
     03  backorders                PIC 9(8).
     03  free-items                PIC 9(8).
     03  next-delivery-date        PIC X(6).
```

4 USAGE BINARY may not be declared where SIGN LEADING SEP-
ARATE has been declared. Why not?

F3   The PICTURE clause – edited items

The picture clauses we have looked at so far hold data in a compressed
form, i.e. there is no room for characters like commas and decimal points
that make data more readable. This is acceptable for computers but not so
good for people. Therefore, when you are defining data areas that are destined for human consumption, e.g. for printed reports, COBOL provides
editing characters to allow you to make the data in such areas more readable.

Insertion editing characters used anywhere in a picture

```
,   comma
B   blank
0   zero
/   stroke
```

Use of any of the above in a picture string will cause that character to be
inserted in the appropriate place in the actual data. For example, the item

```
03   amount-out        PIC 99,999.
```

would always have a comma in the third character position. If you moved
the number 01276 to amount-out, it would contain 01,276 – note that the
insertion character does increase the length of the item, i.e. amount-out is
a six-character field. Furthermore, it is not a numeric item because the

comma is not a valid numeric character, and as such, amount-out may not be involved in arithmetic calculations. This rule applies to all edited items.

However, an edited item may be used in the GIVING option of arithmetic statements, as this is used for results only. Normally, therefore, you perform arithmetic with numeric variables, then, if a result is destined to be output to a report or a screen, i.e. for human consumption, you move it to an edited field via the GIVING option or by a separate MOVE statement.

Here are some other examples. Moving 051297 to

```
03   date-edited        PIC 99B99B99.
```

would give the eight-character item date-edited the value 05 12 97. Moving 1234 to

```
03   round-thousands    PIC 9,999,000.
```

would give this nine-character item a value 1,234,000.

Insertion editing characters used at fixed positions in a picture

- $,£   dollar or pound or any other currency symbol
- +   plus
- −   minus
- CR   credit
- DB   debit
- .   decimal point

The currency symbols work just like the characters already described, but they can only be inserted at the beginning of the data item. The plus and minus signs allow you to have a sign placed at the beginning of the data item but they work in a slightly different way. The + (plus) picture character will give a + sign if the data is positive or zero and a − sign if the data is negative. The − (minus) picture character will give a blank character if the data is positive or zero and a − sign if the data is negative, i.e. this latter case will only produce a visible sign if the data is negative, which is a requirement you sometimes want.

For example, if you moved −100000 to an item defined as

```
03   result-out         PIC -999,999.
```

it would contain −100,000 but if you moved +100000 to the item, it would contain _100,000 (the _ indicating a blank character). The signs, but not the currency symbols, can be used in the same way at the end of a picture string.

On financial statements, negative amounts are usually indicated by a CR or DB symbol. Which symbol is used depends upon whether you owe the money or you are owed money by someone else. In COBOL, CR and DB can only be used at the end of a picture and both are interpreted in the same way as the minus sign above, i.e. they will be inserted as two characters after the data item only if it is negative, otherwise two blank characters will be inserted.

A special insertion character is the decimal point. If an edited item's picture string contains a decimal point, the assumed decimal point within a numeric sending field (indicated by a V in its picture) will be lined up with the actual decimal point. For example, if an item were defined as

```
03  calculation-result    PIC 99V99.
```

and it contained 4735 (interpreted as having two decimal places) and if it were moved to an item defined as

```
03  result-out            PIC 99.99.
```

the value in result-out would be the five-character string 47.35. If the receiving field is larger than the data item sent to it, zeros will be placed in the unused positions, e.g. if the receiving item result-out had a picture of 999.999 rather than the one above, the value in result-out after the move would be 047.350.

Floating editing characters

These are used to replace (or **suppress**) leading zeros in the data by other characters.

Picture character	Leading zeros replaced by
Z	Spaces
*	Asterisks
$,£	Currency symbol
+	Plus sign
−	Minus sign

We have already met the last three as single insertion characters. When a number of these rather than just one appears in the picture string, they are interpreted as floating characters.

For all the floating characters, as soon as a non-zero digit is encountered in the data, all remaining positions are interpreted as if the picture character were a 9. For example, if an item were defined as

```
03  calculation-result    PIC 9(6)V99.
```

and it contained 00100879 (two decimal places) and a receiving field were defined as:

```
03  result-out            PIC ZZZ,ZZ9.99.
```

then after a move from calculation-result to result-out, the latter would contain _ _ 1,008.79. Note the use of an insertion comma with the floating Z characters. When the resultant data has fewer digits, the comma is also suppressed, e.g. if 0 were moved to result-out, it would have value _ _ _ _ _ _ 0.00.

The cheque protect character * works in the same way. If 0017v45 (small v indicating an assumed decimal place) were sent to an item with PIC*****.99, the resultant value would be ***17.45.

The characters plus, minus and the currency symbol are also repeated in the picture but their effect on the data is to 'float' the corresponding symbol to a position just to the left of the first non-zero digit. For example, sending data of 0012v34 to a field PIC $$$$9.99 will give a result of _ _ $12.34. When the floating symbols are used, an extra symbol should be placed at the left of the picture string to allow for the case where the data has no leading zeros.

If you want a field to contain all spaces when a zero amount is sent to it, use Z characters only in the picture. This also applies when commas and a full stop are used with the Z characters. For other picture characters, this is achieved by specifying BLANK WHEN ZERO after the picture clause. For example, if v50 is sent to an item defined as follows:

```
03  balance-out        PIC Z,ZZ9.99    BLANK WHEN ZERO.
```

it would contain _ _ _ _ 0.50, but if it were sent zero, it would produce eight spaces. The same effect could be achieved by Z,ZZZ.ZZ because an edited field with just Zs produces all spaces if zero is moved to it.

Data can be **de-edited** by moving from an edited item to an unedited item of the same type. More details of how de-editing is used are given in Section G.

Editing and de-editing work only when data is moved between elementary data items, i.e. those that have their own specific picture. When data is moved at a group level, e.g. from a 01 record name to another 01 record name, the move takes place as though the receiving area were plain alphanumeric even though it may contain subordinate edited fields. There are also more details of this in Section G.

Exercises

1 Rewrite the first record description of your solution to Exercise 3 in Frame F1, but this time using the insertion character '/' to separate the parts of the date.

2 In the following table, the data in the field described by the picture in the left-hand column is to be moved to the field with the picture given in the right-hand column. Write down the resulting contents of the receiving field. Use an underscore to show the presence of a space.

Sending Field		Receiving Field	
PICTURE	Data	PICTURE	Result
(a) AAA9	TSR2	AAAB9	
(b) 9(5)	00176	ZZ,ZZ9.99	
(c) 99V9	231	£££.99	
(d) 9	0	£££.99	
(e) S999V99	+12645	++++9.9999	
(f) 999	100	9PP	
(g) 9	2	$$$$$$9.99	

3 Here are a few more. Some of them were not specifically covered in the text so have a guess at what happens.

Sending Field		Receiving Field	
PICTURE	Data	PICTURE	Result
(a) 9999V99	123456	ZZ9.99	
(b) 999V999	234567	$ZZ9.99	
(c) 99V99	3456	$ZZ9.99	
(d) S99V99	−3456	−ZZ9.99	
(e) 999	100	9PPP	
(f) V99	01	VPP9	

4 Examine this picture string: PIC $,$$$,$$9.99. Can you see why it does not make sense (and will be illegal on some compilers)?

F4   Practical exercise Part 1

This is the first part of a practical exercise which will be completed when the statements OPEN, CLOSE, READ, WRITE and MOVE have been considered in the next section.

A file of 16-character records has four unsigned four-digit numbers recorded in each record. Each number has one decimal place. A program is to be written that will read each record, calculate the average of the numbers on the record and output the result together with the original numbers. The records are to be counted and the record number printed out along with the input numbers and the average.

The report is to be paged and the layout of the heading for each page is:

```
RECORD NO    NO 1  NO 2  NO 3  NO 4   AVERAGE
----------   ----  ----  ----  ----   -------
```

The format of each detail line is:

Field	Print positions
Record number	4–6 (maximum number of 999 records)
Number 1	14–18
Number 2	20–24
Number 3	26–30
Number 4	32–36
Average	39–45 (taken to 2 decimal places)

1 Obtain Identification Division and Environment Division entries from your tutor.
2 Write a complete Data Division for this program. Make sure that the page heading columns are lined up with the data fields beneath and edit the fields sensibly.
3 You will write the Procedure Division and run the program when the next section has been covered but you can compile the first three divisions to check that the COBOL you are using is valid. Again, details from your tutor.

Answers – Section F

Frame F1

1 The VALUE clause may not be used in the File Section.

```
2 01  payroll-title-line-1.
     03                           PIC X(32) VALUE SPACES.
     03                           PIC X(16)
          VALUE "PAYROLL ANALYSIS".
     03                           PIC X(32) VALUE SPACES.
   01  payroll-title-line-2.
     03                           PIC X(32) VALUE SPACES.
     03                           PIC X(16)
          VALUE ALL "-".
     03                           PIC X(32) VALUE SPACES.


3 01  payroll-title-line-1
     03                           PIC X(32) VALUE SPACES.
     03                           PIC X(16)
          VALUE "PAYROLL ANALYSIS".
     03                           PIC X(20) VALUE SPACES.
     03  day-out                  PIC 99.
     03                           PIC X     VALUE "/".
     03  month-out                PIC 99.
     03                           PIC X     VALUE "/".
     03  year-out                 PIC 99.
     03                           PIC X(4)  VALUE SPACES.
```

The second record description with the underline would remain the same.

Frame F2

1 36 characters.
2 There is a possibility of a negative result and discount-amount is an unsigned field. It should have an S at the beginning of the picture.
3 The alphanumeric item next-delivery-date cannot be declared as USAGE COMPUTATIONAL (same as USAGE BINARY).
4 The clauses are contradictory because USAGE IS BINARY is telling the compiler to produce a non-character representation of the number, including the sign, whereas SIGN LEADING SEPARATE is telling the compiler to make a character representation of the sign.

Frame F3

```
1 01   payroll-title-line-1.
       03                        PIC X(32) VALUE SPACES.
       03                        PIC X(16)
          VALUE "PAYROLL ANALYSIS".
       03                        PIC X(20) VALUE SPACES.
       03   date-out             PIC 99/99/99.
       03                        PIC X(4)  VALUE SPACES.
```

2 (a) TSR_2
  (b) ___176.00
  (c) £23.10
  (d) __£.00
  (e) _+126.4500
  (f) 1
  (g) _____$2.00
3 (a) 234.56
  (b) $234.56
  (c) $_34.56
  (d) −_34.56
  (e) 0
  (f) 0
4 The left-most comma appears to be the separator between the first digit and the second digit when the contents are over one million, but in fact the dollar symbol will always appear, even when the data cannot fit into the field. Therefore, the maximum value that can be represented is 999,999.99 thereby making the left-most comma redundant. The moral is always to allow an extra position for such floating symbols. In this example, the picture should be $$,$$$,$$9.99 to cope with single-digit million values.

G File Handling and Moving Data in Memory

G1 OPEN and CLOSE

Before you can read a record from a file or write a record to a file, the file must be **open**, either for input or for output as appropriate. A simplified form of the OPEN statement is:

$$\text{OPEN} \quad \left\{ \begin{array}{ll} \underline{\text{INPUT}} & \{\text{file-name-1}\} \dots \\ \underline{\text{OUTPUT}} & \{\text{file-name-2}\} \dots \\ \underline{\text{EXTEND}} & \{\text{file-name-3}\} \dots \end{array} \right\} \dots$$

Thus, if you wanted a program to read a file of unvalidated data, check it, write any errors to a print file and output the validated data to another file, you might code the following at the beginning of your Procedure Division:

```
OPEN INPUT    raw-data-file
     OUTPUT   validated-file
              error-file
```

The file names used would be the same ones you would have made up for your FD entry in the File Section. Opening causes a file to be located, if necessary, and set up for reading or writing. For example, opening the above raw-data-file, if it were held on a floppy disk, would cause the file to be located then set up for reading from the first record, though no actual data would be input. If the output validated-file were a magnetic tape file, then opening would cause a special header label to be written at the beginning of the tape and then it would be set up for writing at the beginning. If the error-file were a printer file, opening may simply cause a check that you have a printer attached to your computer but if you were in a multi-user environment, it may cause special header information to be written so that you would be able to distinguish your error report from that of any other users of the same system.

After you have processed all the records for a file (either reading or writing), the file must be **closed**, which usually happens at the **logical end** of the program, i.e. just before your program stops executing. For the above example:

```
CLOSE raw-data-file
      validated-file
      error-file
```

As with opening, CLOSE causes different things to happen depending upon the device being used, e.g. for a magnetic tape, a special trailer label would be written at the end of the file. In general, you should consult your tutor or your computer manufacturer's reference manual to find out the exact meaning of closing files on the system you are using. This is also true for some of the options for the CLOSE statement, e.g. WITH LOCK and WITH NO REWIND. For at least one compiler, if you do not close an output disk file WITH LOCK, it is assumed that the file you created in the program was only required temporarily and the file is deleted when the program terminates!

Sometimes, for disk or tape devices, you want to add records to the end of an existing file rather than at the beginning. This is achieved by specifying.

```
OPEN EXTEND file-name
```

rather than OPEN OUTPUT.

When handling the transfer of data from a keyboard or to a screen, such devices can be specified as files and READ and WRITE used as the input/output statements. However, it is more common, especially with microcomputers, to use ACCEPT and DISPLAY for keyboard input and screen output. For these statements, each data transfer operation is treated as independent of any other on the same device so that the data is not thought of as being records making up a file. Therefore, if you are using ACCEPT and/or DISPLAY, the keyboard and/or screen do not need to be specifically opened or closed. We have already seen the simple use of DISPLAY to output messages to the screen; a more complete discussion of both statements will be found in later sections.

Exercises

1 Once you have opened a file, can you open it again in the same program?

2 What is the difference between the logical end and the physical end of a program?

G2   READ and WRITE

Here is a simplified definition of the READ statement:

<u>READ</u> file-name RECORD
[AT <u>END</u> imperative-statement-1]
[<u>NOT</u> AT <u>END</u> imperative-statement-2]
[<u>END-READ</u>]

It causes the next record from the specified file to be read into the area described by the record description entry made for that file. You may wish to glance again at Section E, especially the diagram at the beginning, to see how data flows from files into memory.

An example might be:

```
READ raw-data-file
AT END
    CLOSE raw-data-file
    MOVE "EOF" TO end-of-file-flag
END-READ
```

Remember that an 'imperative-statement' in a syntax diagram actually indicates an imperative statement list so that the CLOSE and the MOVE above would both be executed when the end of raw-data-file is reached. An 'end of file' situation exists when an attempt is made to read beyond the last record in the file, i.e. you would have already processed the last record from a previous execution of the READ statement and you are now encountering something that is indicating the end of the file. For example, for a magnetic tape file, the special trailer label would be read and interpreted by the operating system as indicating the end of the data. For a disk file, the operating system keeps an account of the size of all files and would recognise when an attempt is made to read beyond the end of a file.

The statements associated with the AT END clause, therefore, are only executed once per program execution (unless you reopen and process the file a second time) and would be skipped over when normal data is read. In the above example, if it were not the end of the file, execution would continue with the statement after the END-READ. You can use the NOT AT END clause to have statements that would be executed every time you successfully read a record, but it is more usual just to pass on to the next statement after the READ.

After a record has been read into the data area associated with the file, you can get a copy of it transferred directly into working storage by using the INTO clause, e.g.

```
READ raw-data-file
    INTO data-checking-area
```

```
AT END
    CLOSE raw-data-file
    MOVE "EOF" TO end-of-file-flag
END-READ
```

This is equivalent to you having a separate MOVE statement, i.e. MOVE raw-data-record TO data-checking-area, assuming that raw-data-record was the level 01 name of the record area associated with raw-data-file in the File Section. However, INTO is not used very much because input record areas can be manipulated in the same way as working storage areas.

Writing to an output file is the opposite process. Data will be transferred from the record area associated with the file out on to a device like a disk or printer, e.g.

```
WRITE validated-record
```

would cause the data currently in validated-record to be copied out to the next record position in the file, probably called validated-file. For a print file, writing should also cause paper advancement but we will see more details of writing to a printer in the next frame.

In the same way that INTO causes a copy of data to be transferred into Working-Storage during a read operation, the clause FROM allows data to be written from Working-Storage, e.g.

```
WRITE validated-record
    FROM data-checking-area
```

would cause a copy of the data in data-checking-area to be transferred into validated-record then written out to the file.

Exercises

1 Give a single COBOL statement to read the next record from a file you have called input-tape. The record is called input-record at the 01 level. If the trailer label is encountered, you are to perform a paragraph called close-off and display a message indicating that the end of the tape has been reached.

2 You have a printer file called error-file with a record area called error-record. You also have two record areas defined in Working-Storage called error-heading-line-1 and error-heading-line-2. Ignoring paper control for the moment, i.e. assume that the paper will advance one line each time a record is written, give two statements to write out the current contents of the two heading lines.

3 A file may contain more than one type of record, in which case two or more record description entries may follow the file description in the File Section. Knowing this, can you explain why you READ file names but WRITE record names?

G3 Writing records to a printer

Additional facilities are given for controlling the line spacing when writing records to a printer, a shortened version of the format being:

WRITE record-name-1 [<u>FROM</u> identifier-1]
$\left\{\begin{array}{l}\text{AFTER} \\ \text{BEFORE}\end{array}\right\}$ ADVANCING $\left\{\begin{array}{l}\left\{\begin{array}{l}\text{identifier-2} \\ \text{integer-1}\end{array}\right\} \left\{\begin{array}{l}\text{LINE} \\ \text{LINES}\end{array}\right\} \\ \underline{\text{PAGE}}\end{array}\right\}$

This allows you to control line spacing on a page by specifying paper control either after or before the line is printed. For example, if you wanted to skip to the next line then print the next record, you could specify:

```
WRITE error-record
      FROM error-heading-line-2
      AFTER ADVANCING 1 LINE
```

which is using the 'integer' option from the ADVANCING clause. Assuming that the printer is currently positioned on a line from a previous WRITE, the paper will advance one line before printing the contents of error-heading-line-2 so that there would not be a gap between the two printed lines. You would need to advance 2 lines to give a blank line.

When the 'identifier' option is used, e.g.

```
WRITE error-record
      FROM error-detail-line
      AFTER ADVANCING no-of-lines-to-skip
```

the number of lines to advance is determined by the current contents of no-of-lines-to-skip, which will be a variable defined in the Working-Storage Section and probably given an initial value of, say, 2. This is a better approach than using the 'integer' option because if in the future you, or someone else, are required to change the number of lines to advance, you only need to alter the initial value for no-of-lines-to-skip, i.e. one change, whereas there may be lots of different WRITE statements in your program and you would have to alter the integer value in every one of them.

The PAGE option ensures that the printer skips to a new page when you want to do this in the program, e.g.

```
WRITF error-record
      FROM error-heading-line-1
      AFTER ADVANCING PAGE
```

would cause a skip to a new page, then the contents of error-heading-line-1 would be written at the top of this new page.

You can print a line then advance the paper by using the BEFORE option but you will generally find AFTER more useful and you certainly do not want to mix the two in the same program as it becomes difficult to avoid overprinting. For the time being, therefore, it is recommended that you use AFTER, so that you always know that you have paper advance first then the writing of the record. If you miss out the ADVANCING clause, the default is machine-dependent, so it is better to state it explicitly.

It may be that you do not have a direct link to a printer so that any files destined to be printed have first to be written to a disk file, say, then when the program has finished executing, you print the file created by using operating system commands.

Exercise

1 You count lines in a variable called number-of-lines-printed. Your print record area is called print-record and you have in Working-Storage an area called detail-line and an area called page-heading-line. You have to print a detail line unless 50 or more lines have already been printed, whence you should set the line counter to zero, print the page heading line on a new page and then print the detail line. In either case, if the detail line is printed, the line counter should be updated. The outline COBOL statements to do this are provided below (> = means 'greater than or equal to'):

```
IF number-of-lines-printed >= 50 THEN
    MOVE ZERO TO number-of-lines-printed
    <write-statement-1>
ENDIF
<write-statement-2>
ADD no-of-lines-to-skip TO number-of-lines-printed
```

Provide COBOL code for write-statement-1 and write-statement-2.

G4   MOVE

The MOVE statement is used to transfer a copy of the data in one area to another area. Its general form is:

$$\underline{\text{MOVE}} \quad \begin{Bmatrix} \text{identifier-1} \\ \text{literal-1} \end{Bmatrix} \quad \underline{\text{TO}} \text{ \{identifier-2\} } \ldots$$

Only a copy is moved so that the original data will still be in the sending field after the move.

As an example of the MOVE statement in the context of a realistic program, consider the following part program to list the contents of a disk file on to a printer. The first two divisions are missing but the Data Division and the Procedure Division are complete:

```
DATA DIVISION.
FILE SECTION.
FD disk-in-file
    RECORD CONTAINS 12 CHARACTERS.
01  disk-in-record.
    03  first-amount-in       PIC 9(4)V99.
    03  second-amount-in      PIC 9(4)V99.
FD print-out-file
    RECORD CONTAINS 80 CHARACTERS.
01  print-out-record          PIC X(80).
WORKING-STORAGE SECTION.
77  end-of-file-flag          PIC XXX VALUE SPACES.
77  no-of-lines-to-skip       PIC 9   VALUE 2.
01  detail-line.
    03  first-amount-out      PIC $$$$9.99.
    03                        PIC X(5) VALUE SPACES.
    03  second-amount-out     PIC $$$$9.99.
    03                        PIC X(63) VALUE SPACES.
PROCEDURE DIVISION.
Print-The-Disk.
    OPEN INPUT disk-in-file
         OUTPUT print-out-file
    READ disk-in-file
    AT END
        DISPLAY "empty disk file"
        MOVE "EOF" to end-of-file-flag
    END-READ
    PERFORM UNTIL end-of-file flag = "EOF"
        MOVE first-amount-in TO first-amount-out
        MOVE second-amount-in TO second-amount-out
        WRITE print-out-record
            FROM detail-line
            AFTER ADVANCING no-of-lines-to-skip
        READ disk-in-file
        AT END
            MOVE "EOF" to end-of-file-flag
        END-READ
    END-PERFORM
    CLOSE disk-in-file
          print-out-file
    STOP RUN.
```

The Procedure Division here consists of one paragraph named Print-The-Disk which contains a single sentence. As a simplification, no paging or report headings have been included. Note that an initial read is executed before the main loop. This is the 'read ahead' method and is a more common alternative to using NOT AT END.

The first MOVE statement is an example of moving a literal, in this case the characters 'EOF' to the variable end-of-file-flag. In the Working-Storage Section, this variable is initialised to spaces but when the end of the input file is detected, it gets set to 'EOF'. A **flag** in general is a variable that is set to a particular value in one part of the program because of a certain situation having happened (here, the end of the input file) so that it can be checked in another part of the program (here, to terminate the PERFORM statement). If, somehow, we could check for 'end of file' in the PERFORM statement itself, there would be no need for a flag, but this is not allowed in COBOL.

The two occurrences of the MOVE statement within the PERFORM are to transfer the input to the output so that there is spacing between the output fields (because of the description of the record area detail-line) and to make the data more readable (because of the edited output field descriptions).

If we were wanting an unedited listing of the contents of the disk file, i.e. with no spacing or individual editing of fields, then we could have written the print record directly from the input record area of the disk:

```
WRITE print-record
    FROM disk-in-record
    AFTER ADVANCING no-of-lines-to-skip
```

However, this would be very unusual, especially for print files that need spacing between fields, so you will find that you nearly always need the MOVE statement for the transfer and editing of individual fields.

Rules for the MOVE statement

Alphanumeric item to alphanumeric item
The data in the sending field is left-justified in the receiving field. If the receiving field is too large, it is right-filled with spaces. If the receiving field is too small, you will lose the right-most characters from the sending field. A group field always counts as an alphanumeric field.

Numeric moves

In the following rules, the 'assumed decimal point' means the position indicated by a V in a picture or the position to the right of the rightmost digit if no V is present, i.e. if it is an integer. The 'actual decimal point' means a '.' in the picture, or the position to the right of the rightmost digit if '.' is not present.

For numeric moves, if the receiving field is too large, leading or trailing zeros are added as required. If the receiving field is too small, you can get truncation at either end.

Numeric item to numeric item

The data in the sending field is aligned on the assumed decimal point in the receiving field.

Numeric item to numeric edited item

The assumed decimal point of the sending field is aligned to the actual decimal point of the receiving field, and the rules for editing are followed (frame F3).

Numeric edited item to numeric item

The actual decimal point of the sending field is aligned to the assumed decimal point of the receiving field and the data is de-edited in the receiving field, i.e. the reverse of the editing process. This is mainly used for interactive input/output where edited data displayed on a screen may need to be modified but then needs to be moved to an unedited field for further processing.

It is also legal, but rarely required, to transfer data between numeric and alphanumeric items but the programmer must ensure that the sending field, in either case, contains an integer.

When the sending field is a figurative constant, as mentioned in frame B4, the whole of the receiving field is filled with the constant specified. This is despite the use of the singular or plural version of a figurative constant, although it would be better programming practice to use the singular version, e.g. SPACE rather than SPACES, only when the receiving field is of length one character.

You have seen the use of ALL to repeat a character. When ALL is used with a string of length more than 1, and the string is shorter than the receiving field, the string is repeated, e.g.

```
MOVE ALL "-+" TO highlight-area
```

would fill the variable highlight-area with −+ pairs, say −+−+−+ if the variable were of length 6.

Exercises

```
1 03   alpha-1   PIC X   VALUE "1".
  03   alpha-2   PIC X(4).
```

What will be the contents of alpha-2 after

```
MOVE alpha-1 TO alpha-2 ?
```

```
2 03   num-1   PIC 9V9     VALUE 2.3.
  03   num-2   PIC 99V99   VALUE 0.
```

What will be the contents of num-2 after

```
        MOVE num-1 TO num-2 ?
```

```
3 03   num-1   PIC 99    VALUE 23.
  03   alpha-1 PIC X(4).
```

What will be the contents of alpha-2 after

```
        MOVE num-1 TO alpha-2 ?
```

```
4 03   num-1   PIC ZZ9.99.
  03   num-2   PIC 999V99.
```

What will be the contents of num-2 after

```
        MOVE num-1 TO num-2
```

if num-1 contained _23.48 before the MOVE?

```
5 03   alpha-1 PIC XXXX.
```

What would be the contents of alpha-1 after

(a) MOVE QUOTE TO alpha-1
(b) MOVE "*" TO alpha-1
(c) MOVE ALL "*" TO alpha-1
(d) MOVE ALL "ABC" TO alpha-1 ?

G5   Practical exercise Part 2

You are now in a position to complete the practical exercise started in frame F4. The general logic is similar to the example in frame G4 except that there is more processing, e.g. calculations for each detail record and paging. Here is the outline pseudo-code.

open files
write headings
attempt read of first record
IF no first record
   display an error message
   set the end-of-file flag
ENDIF

DO UNTIL end-of-file
  calculate the average
  IF new page needed
    write the headings
    reset line counter
  ENDIF
  write a detail line
  increment line counter
  attempt read of next record
  IF end-of-file
    set end-of-file flag
  ENDIF
ENDDO
close files

Therefore, you may wish to use this as a guideline to your logic and the G4 example as a guideline to some of the detailed COBOL.

Once you have successfully compiled the complete program, you will need to check that it executes correctly. Your tutor may supply you with a test file but if you are making up the test data for yourself, ensure that as a minimum you include:

a record with all zeros
a record with all 9s
a record with the first number being 0001 and all others zero

To test your paging, instead of constructing a really large number of test cases, you could set the number of detail lines per page to, say, 5.

Answers – Section G

Frame G1

1 To attempt to open a file twice would cause, for example, header labels to be written out twice, which is not allowed. However, if you have an intermediate CLOSE statement, say, for a period in your program's execution when you do not want to refer to the file, then you must reopen the file to use it again, so in this case, a second OPEN statement is quite in order.

2 The physical end is the last statement in the Procedure Division, i.e. physically the last line in a printed output of your program. The logical end is the last statement to be **executed** when a program is run and such a statement (usually STOP) is not normally placed anywhere near the physical end of the program.

Frame G2

```
1 READ input-tape
  AT END
      PERFORM close-off
      DISPLAY "End of tape file reached"
  END-READ

2 WRITE error-record
      FROM error-heading-line-1
  WRITE error-record
      FROM error-heading-line-2
```

3 A file may contain several different types of record. A READ statement causes the next record on the file to be input into memory, whatever type it is. When the READ is executed, the type of record that is next on the file is not known so it is impossible to state the specific record name into which the data is to be read. Therefore, READ uses the file name.

The various record descriptions for the file are actually alternative descriptions of the **same area**. It is then up to the program to discover which type the record is by inspecting the data read in.

When a WRITE statement is executed, the machine must be told which of the different record types is to be written out. Therefore, WRITE goes with the record name.

Frame G3

```
1 write-statement-1 is
      WRITE print-record
          FROM page-heading-line
          AFTER ADVANCING PAGE

  write-statement-2 is
      WRITE print-record
          FROM detail-line
          AFTER ADVANCING no-of-lines-to-skip
```

Frame G4

1 1___ where _ indicates one space.
2 0230 with an implied decimal place between the 2 and the 3.
3 23__ because the receiving field is alphanumeric and therefore fills with
   spaces.
4 02348 with an implied decimal place between the 3 and the 4.
5 (a) """""
   (b) *___
   (c) ****
   (d) ABCA

H Redefinition, Subscripts

H1 Redefinition

The REDEFINES clause is used in the Data Division and it allows you to give alternative names and pictures to areas already defined. The most common situation where it is needed is when individual fields in input data records can hold different types of data. Here is an example.

A file contains customer invoice records as follows:

Character positions	Field
1–6	Account number
7–25	Name
26–85	Address
86–165	Shipping address
166–169	Quantity ordered
170–171	Currency code (01 = sterling £, 02 = US $, etc.)
172–178	Amount (2 places of decimals if £ or $, none if lira, etc.)

The record layouts are identical for the different types of data except that the number of places of decimals in the amount field will vary with the currency code. If we considered just £, $ and lira for the moment, one way over this problem would be to give three completely separate record definitions in the File Section but this would be tedious considering that most of the layout is identical. A better solution would be to define just the amount field in three different ways, i.e.

```
01  invoice-record.
     03  account-number      PIC X(6).
     03  customer-name       PIC X(19).
     03  customer-address    PIC X(60).
     03  shipping-address    PIC X(80).
     03  quantity-ordered    PIC 9999.
     03  currency-code       PIC 99.
     03  amount-field.
          05  amount-sterling     PIC 9(5)V99.
          05  amount-US-dollar    PIC 9(5)V99
              REDEFINES amount-sterling.
          05  amount-lira         PIC 9(7).
              REDEFINES amount-sterling.
          ⋮
```

In the Procedure Division, if you refer to 'amount-sterling' or 'amount-dollar', the field will be assumed to have two decimal places, whereas if you refer to 'amount-lira', it will be assumed to be an integer amount. To decide which amount name is appropriate, you would have to check the currency code first. The redefined fields could have been at the 03 level, but using the subordinate 05 level emphasises the fact that all the definitions are alternatives for the more general 'amount-field'.

In general, therefore, REDEFINES is allowing you to refer to the same data area through different names and pictures. The redefining item must have the same field length as the redefined item.

Group items may also be redefined. For example, if the above account-number field contained a two-digit country code, a one-digit credit code and three-digit serial number for overseas customers, while home customers have a five-digit serial number following a special prefix 'H', you could define these variations as:

```
03  account-number.
     05  account-number-foreign.
          07  country-code          PIC 99.
          07  credit-code           PIC 9.
          07  foreign-serial-number PIC 999.
     05  account-number-home
          REDEFINES account-number-foreign.
          07  account-prefix        PIC X.
          07  home-serial-number    PIC 9(5).
```

Note that the two groups are the same length (six characters). Again, they are alternative ways of describing the same six characters of memory. REDEFINES may not be used at the 01 level in the File Section – it would be redundant anyway because multiple record definitions for a single file are assumed to be redefining the one record area.

Exercises

1   When using REDEFINES in the Working-Storage Section, you may use the VALUE clause with the item being redefined but you may not use the VALUE clause with the redefining item. Why is this?
2   A six-digit date field, to be used for interactive input of a date, is to be defined at the 03 level. The sub-fields within the date may be either European (DDMMYY), American (MMDDYY) or Julian (YYDDD). If the date is in Julian format, the sixth digit is not used. Write the Data Division entries to define the date with its sub-fields.

H2   OCCURS and subscripts

This clause may be used to describe a group of adjacent fields that have the same picture. Suppose a record contained 12 four-digit numbers, each with two decimal places. This could be described as:

```
01   payments-due.
     03 amount-due   OCCURS 12 TIMES   PIC 99V99.
```

In general, this is known as an **array** or **table** and it saves you from having to name each field. To refer to a particular field, you must place a *subscript* in brackets after the name associated with the whole set of fields, e.g. 'amount-due (1)' would refer to the first field in the record, 'amount-due (2)' to the second, and so on.

A group field may also be made to occur several times, e.g.

```
01   payments-due.
     03   payment-group   OCCURS 12 TIMES.
          05   month-of-payment      PIC 99.
          05   amount-due            PIC 99V99.
```

This would describe 12 group data items, each containing a two-digit month and a four-digit amount. You could access:

the first group with 'payment-group (1)';
the first data item in the first group with
'month-of-payment (1)';
the second data item in the first group with
'amount-due (1)';
and so on.

OCCURS may not be used at the 01 level.

You do not have to put a literal as the subscript. It may be a variable with an integer value in the correct range, e.g. in the range 1 to 12 in the above example. This is a very powerful feature.

Suppose in the above example we wished to total all the amounts in a field 'total-of-amounts'; we could write:

```
MOVE ZERO TO total-of-amounts
ADD amount-due (1)
    amount-due (2)
        ⋮
    amount-due (12) to total-of-amounts
```

but this is rather tedious. Using the following Working-Storage items

```
03  amount-subscript        PIC 99.
03  total-of-amounts        PIC 9(5)V99.
```

an improved version could be

```
MOVE ZERO TO total-of-amounts
             amount-subscript
PERFORM 12 TIMES
    ADD 1 TO amount-subscript
    ADD amount-due (amount-subscript)
        TO total-of-amounts
END-PERFORM
```

The general form of a subscript is

(integer) or
(variable ± integer)

so that if you use a variable, the resulting subscript can also be an offset of that variable's current value, e.g. (amount-subscript + 1).

If you wish to associate an initial value for each item within an OCCURS clause, there are two ways. First, by redefinition, e.g.

```
01  month-table.
    03  month-table-values.
        05          PIC XXX VALUE "JAN".
        05          PIC XXX VALUE "FEB".
        05          PIC XXX VALUE "MAR".
        05          PIC XXX VALUE "APR".
        05          PIC XXX VALUE "MAY".
        05          PIC XXX VALUE "JUN".
        05          PIC XXX VALUE "JUL".
        05          PIC XXX VALUE "AUG".
        05          PIC XXX VALUE "SEP".
        05          PIC XXX VALUE "OCT".
        05          PIC XXX VALUE "NOV".
        05          PIC XXX VALUE "DEC".
    03  REDEFINES month-table-values.
        05  alpha-month  OCCURS 12 TIMES  PIC XXX.
```

You could have specified a data name before REDEFINES but this is not necessary as 'month-table-values' is already a name referring to the whole area. In COBOL 74 programs, FILLER would be required between the 03 and the REDEFINES. Here, 'alpha-month (1)' would contain the three characters JAN, 'alpha-month (2)' would contain FEB, and so on.

Second, you can provide a value at the higher group level, e.g.

```
01   month-table
     VALUE "JANFEBMARAPRMAYJUNJULAUGSEPOCTNOVDEC".
     03   alpha-month   OCCURS 12 TIMES   PIC XXX.
```

You can use this latter approach only when the data is non-numeric or numeric with 'display' usage, i.e. if USAGE is BINARY or COMP, you can use only the first approach.

When you have a choice, there is an argument that the first approach is more professional since the program is easier to amend, but this is not so important with a very stable set of data like the names of months. If the table contents did change frequently, it would be better to store the initial values in a file and read the data into the table at the beginning of the program. The data could then be altered via an editor or some other software, before the program was run.

When a value is declared for a group item, there must not be a contradictory declaration, i.e. another value, for any subordinate items in the group. A VALUE clause and an OCCURS clause may appear in the same level definition, in which case all repeated data items will be initialised to the same value.

Exercises

1 (a) Different jobs in a company are paid at the following hourly rates:

Job code	Pay rate
A3	3.50
A7	3.75
G4	4.27
J4	5.20
L7	5.80
S3	5.95
etc.	

Provide a COBOL Working-Storage record description that could hold these values, given that there are a maximum of 11 different jobs.

(b) The actual values for the above table are held in the file 'pay-rate-file' which has the following record description:

```
01   pay-rate-record.
     03   job-code-in        PIC XX.
     03   pay-rate-in        PIC 9V99.
```

Also given are the following Working-Storage entries:

```
03   end-of-pay-rate-file    PIC XXX   VALUE "NO".
03   pay-subscript           PIC 99.
```

Provide COBOL Procedure Division code to read the values into your table defined in (a) above. You may assume that there are not more than 11 records on the file and that the file has already been opened.

(c) (i)   What would happen if there were more than 11 records in the input file?

    (ii)   How could you alter your code to catch this situation?

2   An input record area is described as

```
01   date-in
     03   day-in       PIC 99.
     03   month-in     PIC 99.
     03   year-in      PIC 99.
```

A generalised heading line for an output report has description

```
01   heading-line-1.
     03   general-report-title  PIC X(123).
     03   date-out.
          05   day-out       PIC Z9.
          05                  PIC X    VALUE SPACE.
          05   month-out      PIC XXX.
          05                  PIC X    VALUE SPACE.
          05   year-out       PIC 99.
```

For specific reports, you would move in your own version of 'general-report-title'. The following Working-Storage description is also provided:

```
01   month-table
     VALUE "JANFEBMARAPRMAYJUNJULAUGSEPOCTNOVDEC".
     03   alpha-month  OCCURS 12 TIMES  PIC XXX.
```

Provide Procedure Division code to create a correct output date from an input date, given that the output must be alphanumeric, e.g. JAN for the first month.

Answers – Section H

Frame H1

1 If a value were put on the redefining item as well as the redefined item, you would be asking the compiler to put two different values into the same area of memory. This is impossible.

```
2 03   european-date.
       05   european-day        PIC 99.
       05   european-month      PIC 99.
       05   european-year       PIC 99.
  03   american-date REDEFINES european-date.
       05   american-day        PIC 99.
       05   american-month      PIC 99.
       05   american-year       PIC 99.
  03   julian-date REDEFINES european-date.
       05   julian-year         PIC 99.
       05   julian-day          PIC 99.
       05                       PIC X.
```

Frame H2

```
1 (a) 01   pay-rate-table.
          03   one-job-rate   OCCURS 11 TIMES.
               05   job-code          PIC XX.
               05   pay-rate          PIC 9V99.
```

```
  (b) MOVE ZERO TO pay-subscript
      PERFORM UNTIL end-of-pay-rate-file = "YES"
           READ pay-rate-file
           AT END
               MOVE "YES" TO end-of-pay-rate-file
           NOT AT END
               ADD 1 TO pay-subscript
               MOVE pay-rate-record TO
                   one-job-rate (pay-subscript)
           END-READ
      END-PERFORM
```

Note here that as the job code and pay rate fields are next to each other in the input record **and** in the Working-Storage area, only one MOVE is required. It is certainly just as acceptable, and possibly more flexible, to have a separate MOVE for each of the elementary items.

  (c) (i) Eventually, 'pay-subscript' would have a value 12 and at the point the program tried to refer to the table, a runtime execution error would occur as there is no 12th item in the table.

(ii) Insert an extra check for the maximum value of 'pay-subscript' within the loop, e.g.

```
MOVE ZERO TO pay-subscript
PERFORM UNTIL end-of-pay-rate-file = "YES"
        READ pay-rate-file
        AT END
              MOVE "YES" TO end-of-pay-rate-file
        NOT AT END
              IF pay-subscript = 11
              THEN
                    DISPLAY "Too many pay rates"
                    MOVE "YES" TO end-of-pay-rate file
              ELSE
                    ADD 1 TO pay-subscript
                    MOVE pay-rate-record TO
                          one-job-rate (pay-subscript)
              END-IF
        END-READ
    END-PERFORM
```

The flag 'end-of-pay-rate-file' is used here to terminate the loop for the error situation as well. It would be better to have a separate flag for the error condition and test for the occurrence of either the end-of-file or the error at the beginning of the PERFORM – such constructs are introduced in the next chapter.

```
2 MOVE day-in TO day-out
  MOVE alpha-month (month-in) TO month-out
  MOVE year-in TO year-out
```

I More about Conditions and the PERFORM Statement

I1 Conditional expressions

In Section D we learned about conditional statements – the IF ... THEN ... ELSE ... construction. It is now time to look at these in more detail.

You will recall that IF statements generally consist of the word IF followed by a condition, and then two branches known as the 'true' branch and the 'false' branch. The true branch can start with the word THEN (though it does not have to) and the false branch always starts with the word ELSE; the whole statement ends with the word END-IF. You will also recall that an IF statement does not have to have an ELSE; in other words it may have a true branch but no false one. In fact there are many variations that we can encounter in the IF statement, and it is this variability that makes it necessary to tell the compiler where the end of the IF statement is, which we do with the word END-IF. This is known as a scope terminator because it shows how far the scope, or influence, of the condition in our IF statement extends. Without it we might find that the whole of the rest of the program depended upon the truth of the condition.

The branch of an IF statement (true branch or false branch) is not limited to a single statement; we can put as many statements as we like into the true branch and the compiler will know when it is complete by finding either the word ELSE or the scope terminator END-IF. If ELSE is there, then what follows is the false branch, and that, too, can contain any number of statements, until finally END-IF terminates the statement. For example:

```
IF record-number = saved-record-number
THEN
        ADD customer-balance TO customer-total
        MULTIPLY number-of-items BY order-cost
        ADD order-cost TO invoice-amount
```

```
ELSE
      MOVE customer-total TO output-total
      ADD  invoice-total  TO grand-total
END-IF
```

Exercises

1 Is this statement true?
  "A conditional statement in COBOL is introduced by the keyword IF,
  and contains the keywords THEN and ELSE."
2 Produce a COBOL sentence that will test the value of a variable called
  'valid-flag', and perform a paragraph called 'Error-para' if it does not
  contain the value 'OK'; however, if it does contain 'OK', then the paragraph 'Complete-invoice' is to be performed, followed by the paragraph
  'Print-invoice'. (Out-of-line PERFORMs are intended.)

I2   Simple and compound conditions

We said that IF is followed by a condition. The definition of a condition is
that it is an expression that can be evaluated to 'true' or 'false'. 'Expression'
in this context means a variable on the left-hand side being compared to
either another variable or a literal on the right-hand side. If we say

```
IF tax-code = 120 . . .
```

then, clearly, the condition 'tax-code = 120' can be evaluated to 'true' or
'false' depending on the contents of the identifier called 'tax-code' at the
time that that part of the program is being executed. This is an example of
a simple condition. Further examples are:

```
IF record-number = saved-record-number . . .

IF applicant-age > max-age-limit . . .

IF gross-stock < 1000 . . .
```

The '=', '>' and '<' in the above examples are called **relational** operators. There are also **class conditions** where a test can be made for an item
being within a particular class, e.g.

```
IF stock-ordered IS NUMERIC . . .
```

The full set of class conditions are:

NUMERIC – numeric data, including a possible sign
ALPHABETIC – both upper and lower case letters plus a space
ALPHABETIC-UPPER – upper case letters plus a space
ALPHABETIC-LOWER – lower case letters plus a space

It is possible to join simple conditions together with the **logical** operators AND and OR. For example:

```
IF sex = "F" AND age > 59 . . .
```

In this example we have two conditions which can each be either true or false independently of the other, but it is also clear that the condition as a whole will be either true or false. In fact it will be true only if both its parts are true – this is the implication of AND. If either part is false, or if both parts are false, then the condition as a whole is false.

By contrast, in the next example

```
IF tax-code < 120 OR marital-status = "S" . . .
```

we have a condition that will be true if either of its parts is true, or if both parts are true – this is the implication of OR.

We can make compound conditions by joining together any number of simple conditions, and the words AND and OR can be used in the same compound condition. For example:

```
IF tax-code < 120 OR sex = "F" AND age > 59 . . .
```

This could almost be part of an English sentence (as with so much of COBOL) but if it were, would you be certain what it meant? If the tax-code is less than 120 would that be enough to make the condition true, or must the age be over 59 as well? If the tax-payer was female, aged 65 and had a tax-code of 130, would she be entitled to a refund? In the second case we can definitely say that the condition would be true (work it out) but in the first case we would have to say 'It all depends . . .' In other words, the condition is ambiguous in English, although it is not of course ambiguous to the COBOL compiler, which always evaluates first those conditions joined by AND, and then goes on to consider any linked by OR. The effect is as though there were brackets surrounding the parts linked by AND. Thus:

```
IF tax-code < 120 OR (sex = "F" AND age > 59) . . .
```

So we see that a tax code of less than 120 **is** enough to make the whole condition true, regardless of other factors, and also that if the tax code is not less than 120, then the sex must be 'F' and the age greater than 59, if the condition is to be true. It is worth remembering this rule about AND-linked conditions being evaluated first (some people remember it by saying 'AND unites, OR separates'), but if you are not certain of it then you can always put the brackets in, as shown above. And if, sometimes, you want a different interpretation, then you **have** to put brackets into the expression, as follows:

```
IF (tax-code < 120 OR sex = "F") AND age > 59 . . .
```

Make sure you understand how this changes the implication of this conditional statement.

Exercises

1 Which of the following are NOT valid conditions?

```
(a)   flag-1 = "YES"
(b)   35 > clients-age
(c)   (wage - tax) = net-wage
(d)   net-wage = (wage - tax)
(e)   area-1 < area-2
(f)   surname = ALPHABETIC
```

2 Look at the following COBOL code:

```
IF a = b AND c = d OR c > d AND a > b . . .
```

For each of the following sets of values, state whether the condition is TRUE or FALSE:

(a) $a = 1; b = 2; c = 3; d = 4;$
(b) $a = 3; b = 3; c = 5; d = 5;$
(c) $a = 1; b = 1; c = 1; d = 1;$
(d) $a = 15; b = 13; c = 11; d = 9.$

I3   Compound operators and negation

We have so far seen the relational operators '=', '>' and '<'. It is worth mentioning that if you wish, you can use the words IS EQUAL TO, IS GREATER THAN and IS LESS THAN. The words IS, THAN and TO are optional, though if you do not use them the statement loses much of its resemblance to ordinary English, so you might as well use the symbols. COBOL also allows you to combine IS and a symbol, as in IS>.

There are also the compound operators GREATER THAN OR EQUAL TO and LESS THAN OR EQUAL TO, and the equivalent symbols '>=' and '<='. For example:

```
IF distance IS LESS THAN OR EQUAL TO 50 . . .
```

Observe that OR in this case is not really making a compound condition; you should think of it as a simple condition but with a compound relational operator.

The three relational operators can be combined with the word NOT in order to negate the condition. Thus:

```
NOT =
NOT >
NOT <
```

Once again, the words can be used (i.e. NOT EQUAL TO, NOT GREATER THAN, NOT LESS THAN), but you cannot use NOT with the compound operators. Here are some examples:

```
IF error-count NOT = ZERO . . .

IF error-count IS NOT EQUAL TO ZERO . . .

IF age IS NOT LESS THAN 60 . . .

IF country-name IS NOT ALPHABETIC-UPPER . . .
```

Some programmers like to write negative conditions in the form

```
IF NOT (error-count = ZERO) . . .
```

on the grounds that NOT belongs to the same group of words as AND and OR (they are known as 'logical operators'), and the logical way to negate a condition is first to express it in its positive form and then apply the appropriate logical operator (NOT) in order to render it negative. This argument has some force, and it can occasionally be useful to try rewording a condition in this way as a check that what you are coding really has the meaning you want it to have, but it is generally not thought to produce such readable code.

Exercise

1 Of the five conditions below, four mean the same thing; which is the odd one out?

```
(a)   IF p NOT < q
(b)   IF q IS LESS THAN OR EQUAL TO p
(c)   IF p > q
(d)   IF p IS NOT LESS THAN q
(e)   IF p IS GREATER THAN OR EQUAL TO q
```

I4   The negating of compound conditions

When you use compound conditions (as in frame I2) you must do so with care, as it is easy to make an error in the logic, but never more so than when you introduce NOT into compound conditions. Suppose that we wish to express the negative form of the example

```
IF sex = "F" AND age > 59 . . .
```

If we are sure that the condition is correctly expressed, logically, in its positive version, then the safest way to produce the negative version is by the method above, that of applying the logical operator NOT. This produces

```
IF NOT (sex = "F" AND age > 59) . . .
```

(The brackets are not strictly necessary here, but they do make the statement clearer.) Most people would not consider this to be very readable COBOL code (even with the brackets) and would prefer the version:

```
IF sex NOT = "F" OR age NOT > 59 . . .
```

Did you notice how the AND had to change to OR this time? This is an example of de Morgan's law; it is also an example of common sense, though it is surprising how many times this situation leads to logic errors. It is not helped by the fact that many versions of the COBOL compiler allow you to abbreviate compound conditions in order to make them more readable. For example:

```
IF transaction-type = "1" OR transaction-type = "2"
OR transaction-type = "3" OR transaction-type = "4" . . .
```

can be abbreviated in various stages. The first stage is that 'transaction-type' (the subject) does not have to be repeated each time, neither does the relational operator '=', since they are always the same. Thus:

```
IF transaction-type = "1" OR "2" OR "3" OR "4" . . .
```

Since all the logical operators are the same ('OR') the next stage is to omit all except for the last one of these. This produces:

```
IF transaction-type = "1" "2" "3" OR "4" . . .
```

More readable? It is certainly more like English, but it has led many a programmer (and not just students) to produce statements similar to the following:

```
IF transaction-type NOT = "1" "2" "3" OR "4" . . .
```

and then to wonder why their program does not work.

Since a lot of problems can arise through the use of negative conditions it is probably a good idea to avoid them if possible. A little thought will often produce a way of coding the program that does not resort to them. For example:

```
IF age GREATER THAN OR EQUAL TO 60 . . . or

IF age > 59 . . . instead of

IF age NOT < 60 . . . etc.
```

Exercises

1 Take the example

```
IF tax-code < 120 OR sex = "F" . . .
```

and make it negative using the two ways described above.
2 Explain why the example

```
IF transaction-type NOT = "1" "2" "3" OR "4" . . .
```

is not capable of performing a useful function within a program. Rewrite it in a way that makes sense.
3 What is wrong with the following compound condition?

```
IF sex = "F" AND age > 59 OR IF sex = "M" AND age > 59
```

I5 Nested IF statements

We have seen how the two branches of an IF statement themselves consist of one or more statements. In the examples we have so far used, these statements have been imperative statements, such as

```
MOVE "YES" TO error-flag

ADD 1 TO loop-counter

PERFORM Refund-paragraph
```

However, it is quite legal for the branch to contain further conditional statements, in other words we can embed an IF statement within an IF statement. And these embedded, or **nested**, IF statements can contain within their true and false branches further IF statements, and so on. As you can imagine, this can produce quite complex programs, and so it is a technique that should be used with restraint. If you do use it, you can assist yourself and other readers of your program by indenting each IF statement and coding its corresponding ELSE statement underneath. An example of this technique is:

```
IF input-name = stored-name
THEN
    IF input-address = stored-address
    THEN
        PERFORM Address-Write
    ELSE
        PERFORM Get-Next-Record
    END-IF
ELSE
    PERFORM Record-not-found
END-IF
```

In the example above, the nested IF statement was in the true branch of the first IF statement. A common example of a nested IF statement being placed in the false branch occurs when an item such as a transaction type is being used to determine what sort of processing is to be done. This can give rise to a series of nested IF statements, each one in the false branch of its predecessor. For example:

```
IF transaction-type = "A"
THEN
    SUBTRACT quantity FROM current-balance
ELSE
    IF transaction-type = "B"
    THEN
        ADD quantity TO current-balance
    ELSE
        IF transaction-type = "C"
        THEN
            MOVE quantity TO current-balance
        ELSE
            DISPLAY "Transaction Error"
        END-IF
    END-IF
END-IF
```

Notice the succession of END-IFs at the end of this piece of code, and the way in which the indentation makes it much easier to see which END-IF goes with which IF, and also to check that you have put an END-IF with every IF. In the above example every IF statement had an ELSE branch, but as you know, COBOL IFs do not have to have ELSEs, and in a nested IF statement in which some of the IFs have ELSEs and others do not, the END-IF terminators establish which ELSE is to be paired with which IF. Thus:

```
IF input-name = stored-name
THEN
    IF input-address = stored-address
    THEN
        PERFORM Address-write
    END-IF
ELSE
    PERFORM Record-not-found
END-IF
```

There is no exercise for this frame.

I6   Introducing the EVALUATE statement

Consider again the example in the above frame, where we tested the value of a transaction-type. For such situations, where a data-item may have one of several values, and we want the program to select one of several branches depending on the value held in the data-item, there is an alternative to the IF... THEN... ELSE... IF... method that we used there. This is the EVALUATE statement, and if we used it in the transaction-type example, the resulting code would be as follows:

```
EVALUATE transaction-type
    WHEN "A"    SUBTRACT quantity FROM current-balance
    WHEN "B"    ADD quantity TO current-balance
    WHEN "C"    MOVE quantity TO current-balance
    WHEN OTHER   DISPLAY "Transaction Error"
END-EVALUATE
```

This is much more concise than the IF... THEN... ELSE... IF... version, and most people would feel it was easier to understand. Used in this way it is what in other languages is called a 'case' statement.

Another example is

```
EVALUATE TRUE
    WHEN ws-code IS NOT NUMERIC
        PERFORM C3-Char-Code
    WHEN ws-code = 2
        PERFORM C4-Code-2-Processing
    WHEN OTHER
        PERFORM C5-Error-Processing
END-EVALUATE
```

Here, the first WHEN clause that is TRUE is executed. EVALUATE is quite a wide ranging statement, and a full explanation of all its features will have to wait until frame R7.

Exercises

1 Suppose that a data-item called flag-1 has been declared as PIC 9, and can have a value of 1, 2, 3 or 4. Write an EVALUATE statement that will PERFORM paragraphs called Proc-1, Proc-2, Proc-3 or Proc-4, depending on the value in flag-1. If some value other than 1, 2, 3 or 4 is in flag-1, then the message 'Data error' is to be displayed.

2 Now do the same again, only this time use the IF... THEN... ELSE... IF... method.

3 Rewrite the paragraph P3-Find-days-in-month in the example program of frame D4 but using EVALUATE.

I7   The PERFORM VARYING

Suppose that we wish to read up to one hundred records from a file and store them in an array, using a subscript called 'record-number' which will run from 1 to 100. The 'PERFORM VARYING' statement allows us to do it like this (the example uses an in-line perform):

```
OPEN INPUT input-file
PERFORM
    VARYING record-number FROM 1 BY 1
        UNTIL record-number > 100
    READ input-file
    AT END
        MOVE 101 TO record-number
    NOT AT END
        MOVE in-record TO array-record(record-number)
    END-READ
END-PERFORM
CLOSE input-file
```

The code above will cause the statements that extend from 'READ input-file' down to 'END-READ' to form a loop which will be executed one hundred times, or fewer if the end of file is reached on the way. The word FROM is followed by the value at which we want 'record-number' to start (in this case we specify a literal, although it can just as well be an identifier), and the word BY is followed by the increment that we want to apply to 'record-number' on every subsequent time that the block of statements is performed. This, too, can be either a literal or an identifier, and can even take a negative value – 'decrement' instead of an increment. A PERFORM VARYING must have an UNTIL clause which specifies the condition that will bring the repeated execution of the performed block to a halt. (You have already met PERFORM UNTIL in Section D.) In this case the condition is that 'record-number' has a value greater than 100. Such conditions can be simple or compound, just as with IF statements.

Notice how, if the end of the file is encountered, the repetition of the block is conveniently brought to a halt by moving a value greater than 100 into 'record-number', thus causing the value of the UNTIL condition to become true.

An example of a PERFORM VARYING with an out-of-line PERFORM is shown below:

```
MOVE SPACES TO finish-flag
PERFORM Accept-data-para
    VARYING table-sub FROM 1 BY 1
    UNTIL table-sub > 60
        OR finish-flag = "stop"
END-PERFORM
```

The paragraph 'Accept-data-para' would contain some code such as:

```
Accept-data-para.
    DISPLAY "Please input value. Input 99 to stop"
        UPON CONSOLE
    ACCEPT input-value FROM CONSOLE
    IF input-value = 99
    THEN
        MOVE "stop" TO finish-flag
    ELSE
        MOVE input-value TO table-1(table-sub)
    END-IF.
```

You should note that the control item (such as 'record-number' and 'table-sub' in the two examples above) does not have to feature in the UNTIL condition; the loop can be stopped by something quite independent of the value of the control item. However, it is very common for the PERFORM VARYING to be controlling a loop in which the item to be varied is a counter or subscript, in which case you will probably want to keep going round the loop until the item reaches its maximum value. If you are performing the loop WITH TEST BEFORE (which is the default) then you will need to have an UNTIL condition which tests for the control item being **greater** than the maximum (see the example above, where the PERFORM VARYING goes on until 'table-sub' is **greater** than 60). This is because the control item is always incremented before the next iteration of the loop is embarked upon. If the test is made before, then an UNTIL condition that tests for **equality** with the maximum will omit the final iteration. If on the other hand you code WITH TEST AFTER, then you can safely specify that the repetition is to continue until the control item **equals** its maximum value. For example:

```
PERFORM Para-1 VARYING sub FROM 1 BY 1
        UNTIL sub = 100
```

will cause 'Para-1' to be performed 99 times, because it will not do it when 'sub' is equal to 100. On the other hand,

```
PERFORM Para-1 WITH TEST AFTER
                VARYING sub FROM 1 BY 1
                UNTIL sub = 100
```

will cause 'Para-1' to be performed 100 times.

Exercises

1 In the Ruritanian tax system employees are given a code in the range A to G which shows the allowance to be deducted from taxable income according to the following table:

Tax code	Deduction
A	0
B	100
C	200
D	350
E	550
F	800
G	1100

In Working-Storage these two tables are defined as follows:

```
01  tables.
    02  table-of-codes       VALUE "ABCDEFG".
        03  tax-code         OCCURS 7 TIMES PIC X.
    02  table-of-deductions VALUE
                    "0000010002000350055008001100".
        03  deduction        OCCURS 7 TIMES PIC 9(4).
    02  sub                  PIC 9 USAGE COMP.
```

An employee record has been read by the program. It contains a PIC X field called 'emp-tax-code' which has been checked to be in the range 'A' to 'G'. Write statements that will subtract the appropriate deduction from an item called 'taxable-pay'.

2 Items are defined in Working-Storage as follows:

```
01  checking-items    USAGE IS COMP.
    02  temp          PIC 999.
    02  weight        PIC 9.
    02  sub           PIC 9.
    02  sum-1         PIC 999.
01  acc-no.
    02  digit         OCCURS 6 PIC 9.
    02  check-digit   PIC 9.
```

Each digit is to be multiplied by a weight, giving a weighted digit. The weight is 7 for the leftmost digit, 6 for the next and so on down to 2 for the rightmost digit. The sum of the weighted digits is to be divided by 10 and the remainder from this division, subtracted from 10, is to be stored in 'check-digit'. Code this.

Answers – Section I

Frame I1

1 Not entirely. A COBOL conditional statement does not always have an ELSE branch, and in any case the word 'THEN' is optional.

```
2 IF valid-flag = "OK"
   THEN
        PERFORM Complete-invoice
        PERFORM Print-invoice
   ELSE
        PERFORM Error-para
   END-IF
```

Frame I2

1 (a)–(e) are valid; (f) is invalid.
2 (a) FALSE
  (b) TRUE
  (c) TRUE
  (d) TRUE

Frame I3

1 (c) is the odd one out.

Frame I4

```
1 (a)   IF NOT (tax-code < 120 OR sex = "F")

  (b)   IF tax-code NOT < 120 AND sex NOT = "F"
```

2 When the logical operator in a compound condition is OR, the condition will be true even if only one of its parts is true. If the transaction type is valid (i.e. equal to one of the four values), then it is not equal to any of the other three, so three of the four parts of the condition are true; if it is invalid (i.e. equal to none of the four values), then all four parts of the condition are true. Therefore the condition will always be true, whatever the value of 'transaction-type'.

It should be re-written as:

```
IF transaction-type NOT = "1" "2" "3" AND "4" . . .
```

or, for preference:

```
IF transaction-type NOT = "1"
AND transaction-type NOT = "2"
AND transaction-type NOT = "3"
AND transaction-type NOT = "4" . . .
```

3 The word IF has been repeated inside the condition. (IF introduces a condition; it is not itself part of the conditional expression.)

Frame I6

```
1 EVALUATE flag-1
      WHEN 1 PERFORM Proc-1
      WHEN 2 PERFORM Proc-2
      WHEN 3 PERFORM Proc-3
      WHEN 4 PERFORM Proc-4
      WHEN OTHER DISPLAY "Data error"
  END-EVALUATE
```

```
2 IF flag-1 = 1
  THEN
      PERFORM Proc-1
  ELSE
      IF flag-1 = 2
      THEN
          PERFORM Proc-2
      ELSE
          IF flag-1 = 3
          THEN
              PERFORM Proc-3
          ELSE
              IF flag-1 = 4
              THEN
                  PERFORM Proc-4
              ELSE
                  DISPLAY "Data error"
              END-IF
          END-IF
      END-IF
  END-IF
```

```
3 EVALUATE month
      WHEN 1 MOVE 0 TO tot-days
      WHEN 2 MOVE 31 TO tot-days
      ⋮
  END-EVALUATE
```

Frame I7

1 Many possible answers. A simple one is

```
MOVE 1 TO sub
PERFORM UNTIL emp-tax-code = tax-code(sub)
    ADD 1 TO sub
END-PERFORM
SUBTRACT deduction(sub) FROM taxable-pay
```

2 Again, many variations possible. Sample:

```
MOVE 0 TO sum-1
PERFORM Calc-and-add
    VARYING sub FROM 1 BY 1
    UNTIL sub > 6
DIVIDE 10 INTO sum-1 GIVING sum-1
    REMAINDER check-digit
SUBTRACT check-digit FROM 10 GIVING check-digit
:
Calc-and-add.
    SUBTRACT sub FROM 8 GIVING weight
    MULTIPLY weight BY digit(sub) GIVING temp
    ADD temp TO sum-1.
```

J IDENTIFICATION and ENVIRONMENT DIVISIONS

J1 The IDENTIFICATION DIVISION

The IDENTIFICATION DIVISION is the initial part of a COBOL program and, as its name suggests, is used to identify the program. Its general simplified format is:

```
IDENTIFICATION DIVISION.
PROGRAM-ID. program-name.
```

However, it is also the best place to offer other information about the program, e.g. who wrote it, when it was written. Here is a sample entry.

```
IDENTIFICATION DIVISION.
PROGRAM-ID. Monthly-Sales-Analysis-SA23.
*****************************************************************
* Author. Tanya Stephenson.                                    *
* Date Written. February 1995.                                 *
* Installation. Central Computer Services.                     *
*                                                              *
* This program provides an analysis of company sales           *
* for a monthly period and is just one of the SA               *
* series of sales analysis programs.                           *
*                                                              *
* INPUT : Accumulated Monthly Sales File - AS04                *
*         Product Master File - PMAS                           *
*         Company Regions File - CREG                          *
*                                                              *
* OUTPUT : Report RP23 - product type within region.          *
*                                                              *
* PROCESSING : Information from file AS04 is read then          *
* sorted into product type within region code order.          *
* The report is produced from this sorted file,               *
* product descriptions and regional names being               *
* obtained from PMAS and CREG files, respectively.            *
*****************************************************************
```

This identifying information is provided here within a commented block of asterisks. There are actually separate COBOL Identification Division entries for some of the above, e.g. AUTHOR, but they are to be deleted in the next standard so it is recommended that the above format is used instead.

Exercise

1 Write the Identification Division for a program CPG/16 which reads an input file, called IF/05, of 80-character records, sorts them into ascending order on the first six characters, then lists them in a report SRP/16.

J2   The ENVIRONMENT DIVISION

The Environment Division is where you specify the particular computer environment in which you are working. This allows the Data and Procedure Divisions to be independent of any one computer and therefore portable.

There are two sections, the Configuration Section to specify the characteristics of your computer and the Input–Output Section to specify a link between program file names and the external peripherals that will be accessed. A simplified format of the Configuration Section is:

CONFIGURATION SECTION.
[SOURCE-COMPUTER. computer-name.]
[OBJECT-COMPUTER. computer-name.]
[SPECIAL-NAMES. special-names-entry.]

The Source-Computer and Object-Computer entries allow you to state the names of the computers used for compilation of your source COBOL program and execution of your object program, respectively. These will nearly always be the same machine but sometimes, especially when computer time is restricted, different machines are used for compilation and execution. Even though the entries are optional, it is recommended that you always include them, as it is useful for program maintenance to know on which computers a program was first developed.

The Special-Names paragraph allows you to state a number of different entries that are mostly related to altering what would normally happen by default on a particular computer. Some examples are:

1 specifying that a comma is to represent a decimal point as is common in Continental Europe;
2 specifying a different collating sequence;
3 indicating a particular currency sign;
4 providing names that can later be used to detect the status of certain switches on the computer.

An example Configuration Section entry is:

```
CONFIGURATION SECTION.
SOURCE-COMPUTER. IBM 9370.
OBJECT-COMPUTER. IBM 9370.
SPECIAL-NAMES. CURRENCY SIGN IS "L"
              DECIMAL-POINT IS COMMA.
* Setting the program to allow Italian Lira (L) in
* PICTURE clauses and to allow a comma as well as a
* period to represent a decimal point.
```

You will find that most installations have a set of standard entries which you can just copy into your program.

A simplified format of the Input–Output Section is

<u>INPUT-OUTPUT SECTION</u>.
<u>FILE-CONTROL</u>.
    {<u>SELECT</u> file-name <u>ASSIGN</u> to $\left\{\begin{array}{l}\text{implementor-name}\\ \text{literal}\end{array}\right\}$

       [<u>RESERVE</u> integer <u>AREAS</u>].} ...

The File-Control paragraph is used to link each file you define in an FD entry in the Data Division to a particular peripheral device or external file name (an external file name is the name by which a file is known via a computer's operating system, whereas an internal name is the name you have chosen in your COBOL program). These device and external file names vary with the machine.

Each file has a certain amount of memory allocated to it, called a buffer, which is used to hold the block of data currently being processed. Normally only one buffer is allocated to the file concerned. If RESERVE 2 AREAS were specified, two buffers would be allocated to the file, a block being read into the second buffer while the first is being processed. If your program is I-O bound', i.e. execution is slow because it is always waiting for a particular device to read the next block, then increasing the number of buffers may help. You can reserve several buffers if you wish and you can reserve buffers for output as well as input files. The computer manufacturer's reference manual should be consulted for precise details of the effect of this clause on the computer you are using.

Here is an example Input–Output Section entry where the first three files could be on disk, the computer assuming by default that all literals refer to a disk and the output goes to a line printer which has the device name PRINTER on that particular computer.

```
INPUT-OUTPUT SECTION.
FILE-CONTROL.
    SELECT acc-monthly-sales-file ASSIGN TO "AS04".
    SELECT product-master-file ASSIGN TO "PMAS".
    SELECT company-regions-file ASSIGN TO "CREG".
    SELECT sales-report-file ASSIGN TO PRINTER.
```

Exercise

1 Rewrite the above Input–Output Section example but for your computer. You may already have been given example supplied code that may
help you.

J3   An example program specification

This example program specification is part of a series of programs to
update a customer file for a company, e.g. if a customer has a change of
address, a transaction would be created so that the customer's master
record can be amended. This particular program validates such transactions after they have been keyed by a computer operator on to a serial
disk file from a written document. Figure J.1 illustrates the Program Run
Chart.

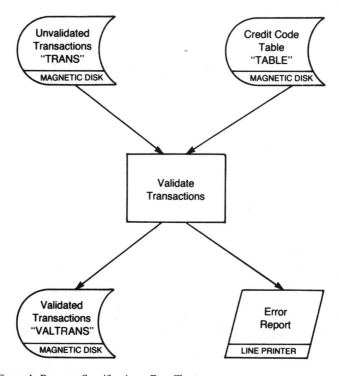

Fig. J.1 Example Program Specification – Run Chart

Input

1 TRANS has 136-character records in the following format:

Character Positions	Field	Type
1	Update Code	Should be one of 'A', 'D' or 'I'
2–6	Customer Number	Should be 5 digits
7	Credit Code	Should be an alphabetic character
8–16	Debit Balance	Should be 8 digits (£ & p), preceded by a sign
17–46	Customer Name	Should be 30 alphanumeric characters
47–136	Customer Address	Should be 3 lines of 30 characters each

The words 'should be' are used above because this TRANS file is unchecked data and so may contain errors.

2 TABLE has 8-character records in the following format:

Character Positions	Field	Type
1	Credit Code	One alphabetic character
2–8	Credit Limit	7 digits

There can be up to 26 records on the file, each one representing a particular credit limit (a monetary amount).

Outputs

1 VALTRANS, a file with the same record format as TRANS but it will contain only validated data.

2 An Error Report for those input records that are invalid in some way. Its format is specified in Fig. J.2.

The page heading must appear at the top of every page. For each input record that is invalid, three output lines are to be printed. The first line contains all the fields except lines 2 and 3 of the customer address, the second line contains an asterisk under the first character position of each field that is in error – there may be more than one error in a record. The right-hand part of this second line contains the second address line and line three contains the third address line. The customer address is not validated in this program so there is no asterisk position for these fields. All the data must be printed in an unedited form, i.e. in its raw form as it was read in. A group of lines for one invalid record must not be split across page boundaries.

The Report Totals are to be printed on a page by themselves after just the first page heading line.

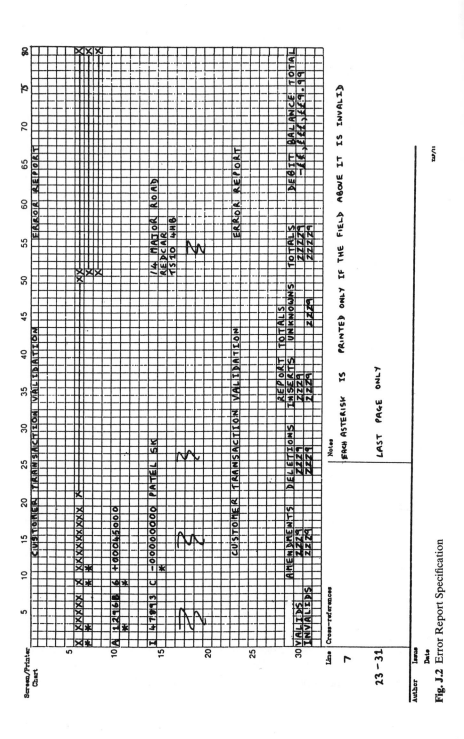

Fig. J.2 Error Report Specification

Processing

The TABLE file is to be read and stored in memory. There are meant to be 1–26 records on this file. If the file is empty or if more than 26 records are found, the program is to terminate abnormally with the message 'TABLE FILE EMPTY' or 'TABLE FILE INVALID' as appropriate.

Each record on TRANS is to be validated and valid records written to VALTRANS. If any field in a TRANS record is invalid, the record is invalid and is to be written to the Error Report as a group of lines. The validation checks are as follows:

The Update Code must be one of 'A', 'D' or 'I' (meaning Amend, Delete or Insert, to indicate whether the transaction is an amendment to current customer details, a deletion of a customer record or an insertion of a new customer). If this Update Code is invalid, of the remaining fields in the record, only the Customer Number is to be checked.

The Customer Number must always contain 5 digits.

For Amendments:
the Credit Code may be blank or must be an alphabetic character that is equal to one of the credit codes from the TABLE file;
the Debit Balance must be blank or a + or − sign followed by 8 digits;
the Customer Name can consist of any alphanumeric characters or be blank.

For Deletions:
all further fields to be checked must be blank.

For Inserts:
the Credit Code must be an alphabetic character that is equal to one of the credit codes from the TABLE file;
the Debit Balance must be +zero or blank;
the Customer Name must not be blank.

In addition, for valid records, a total of the debit balance figure is to be kept. This will be output on the last page of the report.

There are no exercises for this frame.

J4 Program debugging

Here is a revision list of the various stages of programming:

1 read and understand the program specification (by interacting with the person who wrote it, if necessary);
2 design, code and key in the program;
3 compile it until all source errors are removed;
4 test it to see that it performs as the program specification says it should, fixing any bugs that occur.

Notice that testing is a separate stage beyond compiling. Even though you may still be spending much time and effort in producing a program that compiles cleanly, as you become more familiar with COBOL, the time spent at this stage will reduce. However, testing is always a long and often complex process and in a typical commercial environment, will take longer than the initial design and coding of the program. Also, the above list is only for individual programs or modules. It is normal for programs to be tested with other related programs in a further 'sub-system' or 'system' test.

Once you start program testing, you will probably meet program bugs, at which time you enter the process of **program debugging**, i.e. diagnosing program faults and fixing them. The following notes may help you to do this methodically.

1 Study any runtime errors that may have been produced and check that you know how to determine exactly where they occurred in the program. You may need to look in a manual to find the meaning of such errors. Look carefully at a source listing of the program and inspect not only the offending line of code but also related areas.
2 Study any output that may have been produced and see precisely how it differs from expected output.
3 Check any input files to see that the data matches the format and contents that the program is assuming.
4 Check the program specification to see if it has bugs in it or if parts of it have been interpreted incorrectly.
5 The above four points involve sitting down and **thinking**, preferably away from the computer, especially when a bug is not found immediately. If you are still not successful, use a debugging aid that may be provided with your COBOL system. This will allow you to slow down the execution of the program and inspect the contents of any variables so that you can see when a program starts to vary from its expected path.
6 Ask someone else. Another person can often see a bug that you miss because program authors often interpret programs in the way that they **should** work rather than the way that they **are** working.

You would be wise to reinforce your knowledge of Sections A to J by further practical exercises before proceeding to Part 2. A selection of practical exercises is included in Appendix B and the first five can be completed using only the facilities learned so far.

There are no exercises for this frame.

Answers – Section J

Frame J1

1

```
IDENTIFICATION DIVISION
PROGRAM-ID. Sorted-Listing-Program-CPG16.
*****************************************************************
*                                                              *
* Author. Your name.                                           *
* Date Written. Current Month and Year.                        *
* Installation. Your computer installation.                    *
*                                                              *
* This program produces a report from the input file           *
* IF/05.                                                       *
*                                                              *
* INPUT : File IF/05 (80-character records)                    *
*                                                              *
* OUTPUT : Report SRP/16                                       *
*                                                              *
* PROCESSING : Information from file IF/05 is read              *
* then sorted into ascending order of the first six            *
* characters. The report SRP/16 is produced from               *
* this sorted file.                                            *
*****************************************************************
```

Frame J2

1 Your answer will depend upon your particular computer. Check with
  your tutor.

Part 2
Programming in COBOL

K Structured Programming Constructs

K1 Good program design

Most of this book so far has been about the syntax of the COBOL language, i.e. how to combine the language elements into statements that the computer will understand and that will do what you, the programmer, want them to do. But we have only been concerned with the individual building blocks of programming, things such as how to get the computer to add numbers together, read in data from the keyboard or move values from one data-name (or location) to another. This much you could glean from a manual of the type published by the software houses that market COBOL compilers.

But manuals normally only tell you about the smallest building blocks of programming. They offer no help on the best ways of combining these into complete programs; for there are many ways in which programs can be written, some good, some bad. During the comparatively short history of programming as a profession there have been different ideas about what makes a good program. Discounting the very early days, when to get the program to work at all was a considerable achievement, we have seen, over the years, different criteria held to be of greatest importance. At one time the main objective was to make the program execute ('run') as fast as possible; another objective was to get it to use the smallest possible amount of computer memory. Since these two objectives are almost always mutually exclusive, the quest for efficiency often resolved itself into a compromise between the two, biased towards one or other depending on how much memory you had at your disposal. But things change, computing power tends to get cheaper year by year, which is fortunate, while unfortunately labour costs tend to rise all the time, so that producing data processing systems doesn't necessarily get cheaper. What happens is that the cost factor represented by the computing machinery (hardware) diminishes when compared to the cost factor of the salaries earned by the programmers and analysts. This means that the most cost-effective program is no longer necessarily the one that uses the least computing power; it may be the one that uses the smallest amount of programmer time. And programmer time is not just involved in writing the original program; there is also the task of discovering and eliminating the logic errors ('debugging the program'); maintaining the program during its working life; and possibly modifying the program later on to cater for changes in the commercial environment.

Exercise

1 Place these programming objectives in the order you think they are most important in a commercial programming department.
(a) Minimising execution time and memory requirements.
(b) Minimising the amount of pencils and coding sheets used.
(c) Getting the results correct.
(d) Minimising the total effort spent on developing and testing the program to productive status.
(e) Minimising the total time spent on coding the program.
(f) Enabling someone else to understand your program so that he/she can:
   1 help you with a problem of logic
   2 take over if you leave or are absent
   3 amend the program after it is in production, to cater for an undiscovered fault or new requirements.

K2   Structured programming

The approach to good program design widely adopted in practice is that which is called structured programming. This is one of those terms that can mean a variety of things depending upon who is using it, but what it ought to mean is 'program design using the technique of top-down structure with stepwise refinement'. There is only room here for a brief explanation of that technique; whole books can be, and are, written about the subject.

Perhaps the best way to explain structured programming is to show how it could be applied to the design of one of the problems in Appendix 1. We will take Practical Exercise 1, the population explosion problem. At its highest level this could be represented diagrammatically by a box, labelled 'Population Explosion Program', thus:

Population Explosion Program

We shall call this level 0. We now have to 'refine' this by breaking it down into smaller and smaller components until at the end we have a set of program statements. These need not be COBOL statements; we are designing the program, not coding it at this stage, and good design ought not to be influenced by the language into which we are going to translate it. However, this is a book on COBOL, so we can say that we go on refining our design to lower and lower levels until we reach a level at which each component can be translated into a COBOL statement.

Now it is important to understand that in structured programming there are only three ways in which we can refine from one level down to the next. These three ways (usually known as 'constructs') are:

Sequence
Iteration
Selection

(The last one has a variation known as the 'case' construct, so you may sometimes see in books that there are four constructs, not three.)

In our example, the first stepwise refinement is to take the single box and turn it into a sequence. The sequence is simply several components being executed one after the other in a set order (or sequence). If we represented this by a program flowchart it would look like this:

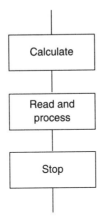

In our structure diagram (which is of a form sometimes known as a Nassi–Shneidermann diagram), we refine the original box as a sequence by dividing it horizontally into separate rectangles, so that it now looks like this:

Population Explosion Program

| Calculate surface area |
| Read and process the data |
| Stop |

We will call this level 1.

The first rectangle ('Calculate surface area') does not need any further refinement, because, by using the COMPUTE verb, we can realise it in COBOL; similarly, the third rectangle needs no further refinement, but the second one has a long way to go yet. We refine this first as in 'iteration'; the meaning of this construct is that we show that a component consists of a repetition of a sub-component, either a specified number of times or, more often, until a specified condition becomes true. (This should remind you of Section D, with its description of the 'PERFORM ... UNTIL' statement.) The program flowchart representation would be:

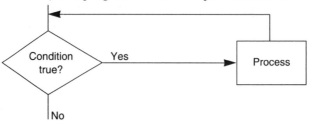

This is a 'DO WHILE' situation. You will sometimes encounter a slightly different form of this known as a 'DO UNTIL'. For this variation, see frame L4. We shall use 'DO WHILE' in this section, frequently in the form of 'DO WHILE NOT ...'. In our Nassi–Shneidermann diagram it is:

Population Explosion Program

Calculate surface area	
Do while not end of file	
	Read a record and process the data
Stop	

This is level 2.

The third construct is the selection. This means that a component is refined as being a choice between two possible sub-components. This should remind you of the COBOL 'IF ... THEN ... ELSE' statement and in a program flowchart it would be represented by:

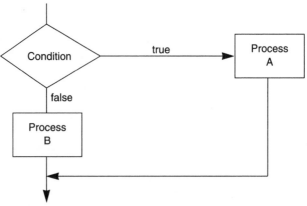

Adding this to the Nassi–Shneidermann diagram, we have:

Population Explosion Program

| Calculate surface area |
| Do while not end of file |

(Nassi–Shneidermann diagram:)

- Read record
- End of file? — Yes | No
- Process data (under No branch)
- Stop

This is level 3.

You will notice that there is actually nothing to do on the branch labelled 'Yes', and you may recall that an IF statement does not have to have an ELSE branch. In fact, what we have here is an IF statement that has an ELSE, or false, branch but no true branch. Conditions lacking an ELSE branch are perfectly valid examples of the selection construct; we can assume an empty, or dummy, component in the ELSE branch. The 'CASE' construct occurs where there are more than two possible paths to take, but still only one may be taken at any one time. For example, a program may read in a code that can have the value '1', '2', '3' or '4', giving four possible (and mutually exclusive) paths to take. (Five, if we include an ELSE path, to allow for the possibility of an erroneous (invalid) code.)

Of course it is not necessary to keep redrawing the whole diagram at each refinement to a lower level (though it is not a bad way to proceed until you have more experience of designing programs), but it is important to realise that at each stage the refinement can only be by one of the structured programming constructs, sequence, iteration or selection (or case). The virtue of the Nassi–Shneidermann diagram is that it only allows these constructs, and no others. We shall never see the words (or the concept) 'GO TO' in such a diagram, and it is worth emphasising that 'GO TO' is NOT a structured programming construct and cannot be used in a structured program to move from one level to another, because it cannot achieve the refinement of a component into sub-components. In a Nassi–Shneidermann diagram, if we follow the principle that, at each stage, refinement can only subdivide existing rectangles, then the top-down development will be guaranteed.

Figure K.1 shows the complete structure of the population explosion program, using Nassi–Shneidermann diagrams. Notice how the second diagram ('Print a Page of Results') is an expansion of the box in the first diagram, labelled 'Do: Print a Page of Results'. It is better to break a program down in this way, rather than to try to represent it all in one diagram.

There are no exercises for this frame.

Population Explosion (See Practical Exercise 1, Appendix B)

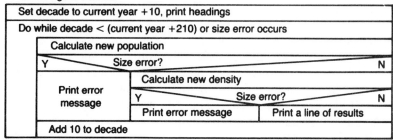

Calculate surface area			
Do while not end of file			
	Read growth rate		
	Y ⟋ End of file? ⟍ N		
		Calculate decade growth factor	
		Set starting population	
		Do: Print a Page of Results	
Stop			

Print a Page of Results

Set decade to current year +10, print headings			
Do while decade < (current year +210) or size error occurs			
	Calculate new population		
	Y ⟋ Size error? ⟍ N		
	Print error message	Calculate new density	
		Y ⟋ Size error? ⟍ N	
		Print error message	Print a line of results
	Add 10 to decade		

Fig. K.1 The structure of the Population Explosion Program

K3   The three basic control structures in COBOL

Sequence

This is obviously straightforward since all imperative statements in COBOL are executed in sequence. A sequence might consist of:

```
OPEN INPUT fa-input-file
MOVE ZERO TO wl-accumulator
READ fa-input-file
```

Iteration

The iteration is implemented either by PERFORM n TIMES or by PER-FORM UNTIL. In the Population Explosion example, the level 1 component 'Read and process the data' was refined to level 2 as an iteration. In COBOL this could be expressed as follows:

```
MOVE SPACES TO eof-flag
PERFORM UNTIL eof-flag = "eof"
```

   (statements to read and process the data
   – a component yet to be refined)

```
END-PERFORM
```

Selection

There are several ways in which the selection construct can be implemented in COBOL, but the basic one is the IF ... THEN ... (ELSE ...) statement. As an example of an IF statement without an ELSE branch consider the production of a printed report; each time we print one line of the report (usually known as a 'detail' line), we add 1 to a line-count. When the line-count reaches a predetermined value (say 20) we need to start a new page and we must print a heading before continuing with detail lines. The diagrammatic representation of this would be:

Is line count at maximum?		
No		Yes
	Re-set line count to 0	
	Print heading on a new page	
Print detail line		
Add 1 to line count		

In COBOL we would code:

```
IF line-count = 20
THEN
     MOVE 0 TO line-count
     WRITE aline FROM heading-line
         AFTER ADVANCING PAGE
END-IF
WRITE aline FROM detail-line
     AFTER ADVANCING 2 LINES
ADD 1 TO line-count
```

The example above would give a single blank line between detail lines; unfortunately it would only give us one blank line between the heading and the first detail line. A better arrangement would be to leave a number of blank lines (say five) after the heading before we print the first detail line. We could simply output some spaces; believe it or not, writing lines consisting entirely of spaces is a frequent activity in print programs, in order to achieve a pleasing format on the printed page. But we could also use an IF ... THEN ... ELSE ... construct, thus:

```
IF line-count = 20
THEN
     MOVE 0 TO line-count
     WRITE aline FROM heading-line
         AFTER ADVANCING PAGE
```

```
        WRITE aline FROM detail-line
             AFTER 6 LINES
ELSE
        WRITE aline FROM detail-line
             AFTER 2 LINES
END-IF
ADD 1 TO line-count
```

Exercises

1 Redraw the Nassi–Shneidermann diagram in the above frame to show the IF ... THEN ... ELSE ... version above.
2 How can we ensure that the page heading is printed on the top of the *first* page? (We shall not have had the opportunity to increment the line-count while printing detail lines as there won't have been any.) Suggest *two* ways in which we can ensure that the page heading gets printed the first time around.

K4   Other types of selection

The IF statement is not the only way in which the selection construct is implemented in COBOL. A number of COBOL verbs can have conditional phrases appended to them, an example being READ with the AT END clause (and sometimes also a NOT AT END clause). COBOL verbs usually introduce imperative statements, but when they have such conditional phrases appended to them, the effect is to turn the statement into a conditional one (not an imperative one), and so the logic from the condition onwards is a selection, not a sequence. (Another example is the WRITE with AT END-OF-PAGE, which gives us an alternative way of doing the page-heading example above.)

   We can illustrate this by returning to the example that we used for the iteration, and refining the component between the PERFORM and END-PERFORM as a selection, thus:

```
MOVE SPACES TO eof-flag
PERFORM UNTIL eof-flag = "eof"
     READ fa-input-file
     AT END
          MOVE "eof" TO eof-flag
     NOT AT END
          COMPUTE growth-factor ROUNDED = . . .
          MOVE 4000000000 TO population
             ⋮
          (further statements)
             ⋮
     END-READ
END-PERFORM
```

The basic verbs covered in Part 1 which have such conditional variants are:

arithmetic verbs with ON SIZE ERROR clause
(and NOT ON SIZE ERROR clause)
READ with AT END clause
(and NOT AT END clause)
WRITE with AT END-OF-PAGE clause
(and NOT AT END-OF-PAGE clause)

There are no exercises for this frame.

K5   The case construct

Another aspect of the selection is the variant known as the case construct. This is usually shown diagrammatically as follows:

This depicts a situation where a code is read which will have one of the values '1', '2' or '3' and one of three program components is to be selected according to the value of the code. Though this could be programmed in COBOL using three IF statements, or, better, a nested IF statement (IF ... THEN ... ELSE IF ... etc.), the most appropriate COBOL statement is the EVALUATE, which you met in frame I6. The following example shows how the above diagram might be translated into COBOL code, using EVALUATE. In this instance, out-of-line PERFORMs have been used for the three branches, although in-line code could have been used just as well.

```
EVALUATE trans-code
    WHEN "1"    PERFORM Trans-type-1
    WHEN "2"    PERFORM Trans-type-2
    WHEN "3"    PERFORM Trans-type-3
END-EVALUATE
```

Exercise

Imagine that there is no such convenient statement as EVALUATE. Code the example in frame K5 using a nested IF statement.

K6   Design for testing

Since the most important objective in programming is to get the results correct, the program should be designed so that testing can be achieved without too much effort. As it happens, programs that are designed with testing in mind can also take less time to develop to productive status and can be more maintainable, thereby satisfying other important programming objectives.

A remarkable trait shared by many programmers is their optimism. They write their programs as if they were going to be right first time. In practice, it is a very rare event that a program of any size is written correctly at the first attempt. We have seen experienced programmers code a large program in a matter of days and then spend weeks or even months trying to eliminate all the errors of logic. If they had spent a little more time on program design, their programs would have reached the stage of first compilation on a day or so later, but this delay would have been compensated for many times over by the reduction in the time needed for fault-finding and testing.

This also serves to encourage you to adopt a defensive attitude to programming. With such an attitude, programs are written in the expectation (which will almost certainly prove correct) that they will not work first time, and that much time and effort may be spent on finding errors.

As an example of how such an attitude can assist, consider the following. Possibly the most common error in programming, and certainly one of the hardest to find, occurs when intermediate data being used or manipulated by the program is incorrect or has been accidentally corrupted. Such errors are hard to spot because such data is 'invisible' when you have only the source code and the wrong results in front of you.

What usually happens is that at certain key points in a program, an assumption is made about the value of an intermediate result, e.g. a flag, a total or a subscript. These crucial assumptions are usually recognised by the programmer and are often asserted in a comment, e.g.

* The subscript now points to the last character of
* customer name

or

* The flag is always set to zero on first entry to
* this routine

This is very proper. However, as things stand, the only way of testing the truth of these assumptions is by mentally tracing through all the detailed logic of the program. This can be a demanding task to do without a slip, especially if one is being misled by one's own comment statements. A better approach would be to incorporate DISPLAY statements in the program at points such as these, when the program is first coded, to print out the important variables so that the assertions are tested. In other words, expect the worst. After a test execution, if all is well, the DISPLAY statements can be removed. Better still is the use of program debugging aids such as are provided by many of the software firms that market COBOL compilers. These allow the programmer to watch the program executing step by step, and to intervene at any time to query the value of variables. See also frame R2.

There is no exercise for this frame.

Answers – Section K

Frame K1

1 Most people readily agree that (c) is the most important and that (b) is least important; and that (d) is more important than (e). Our argument on objective (f) is that if the things listed cannot be done, objectives (c) and (d) will tend to be defeated. So we place it second most important. That leaves the relative merits of (a) and (d) to be discussed. The costs of developing a program are large enough to make (d) more important if (a) is not a pressing need. With that proviso, our list is: (c) (f) (d) (a) (e) (b).

Frame K3

1

Is line count equal to 20?	
Yes	No
Re-set line count to zero	Write detail line after advancing 2 lines
Print heading on a new page	
Write detail line after 6 lines	
Add 1 to line count	

2 If the line count starts at zero, we could use a flag ('first-time flag') to indicate that on our first entry to the write routine, a heading needs to be printed.

A simpler method is to start the program with the line count at 20.

Frame K5

```
1 IF trans-code = "1"
  THEN
       PERFORM Trans-type-1
  ELSE
       IF trans-code = "2"
       THEN
            PERFORM Trans-type-2
       ELSE
            PERFORM Trans-type-3
       END-IF
END-IF
```

This assumes that 'trans-code' cannot have any values other than '1', '2' or '3'. If this is not so, then the answer would have to be:

```
IF trans-code = "1"
THEN
     PERFORM Trans-type-1
ELSE
     IF trans-code = "2"
     THEN
          PERFORM Trans-type-2
     ELSE
          IF trans-code = "3"
          THEN
               PERFORM Trans-type-3
          END-IF
     END-IF
END-IF
```

L Structured Program Design

L1 Evolving the design

The previous section, in which the concepts of structured programming and good program design were introduced, dealt mainly with how to translate into COBOL code the structural constructs from which structured program designs are built, and the examples used there were on a comparatively small scale. This section deals with how to translate an entire problem into a structured program design, and then how to realise that design in COBOL code.

There are many books that go into the process of moving from the design to the code, and it is not appropriate in a book on COBOL to attempt to cover this area in great depth, so we will only illustrate two approaches to structured design and show the code that results from them. Though these are two approaches, they do have much in common; they share the concept that the problem is first defined at a high level, then progressively factored down to lower levels (top-down design) by the use of the constructs of sequence, selection and iteration.

The main differences are that the first approach takes a hierarchical view of the design, and produces code that makes extensive use of out-of-line PERFORMs (hierarchical code), whereas the other approach 'nests' the lower-level components within their higher-level parents and the code that results is called nested code, characterised in COBOL by the use of in-line PERFORMs.

In what follows, the hierarchical approach (frames L2 and L3) is based on the method known as JSP ('Jackson Structured Programming'), and uses both JSP and Nassi–Shneidermann techniques for defining the structure; the nested approach (frame L4) uses a technique known as Structured English.

L2   Data structures and program structures

Michael Jackson in his book *Principles of Program Design* (Academic Press 1975) highlighted the relationship between data structures and program structures. In order to decide on the program structure the programmer must first comprehend the data structures involved in the program. The data structures referred to are usually the input and output files, although in rarer cases an internal table needs to be analysed. The approach therefore is:

1 analyse the data in the problem,
2 produce **data** structure diagrams from this analysis,
3 derive from these diagrams the **program** structure diagram,
4 produce the COBOL program from the program structure.

In commercial programs the data structures can normally be represented by a hierarchy of the three constructs, sequence, selection and iteration, although with data structures, 'repetition' is a better term for the third. Jackson's diagramming blocks for these three structures are illustrated in Fig. L.1, where a circle in the top right of a box indicates selection and an asterisk in the top right of a box indicates iteration.

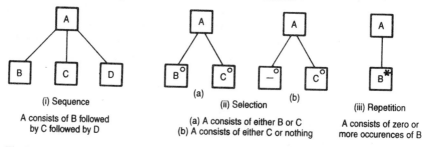

(i) Sequence

A consists of B followed
by C followed by D

(ii) Selection

(a) A consists of either B or C
(b) A consists of either C or nothing

(iii) Repetition

A consists of zero or
more occurences of B

Fig. L.1 Data Structures. By increasing the number of boxes in item (ii) we have a 'case' structure

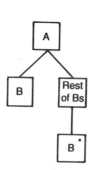

Fig. L.2a Illustrating the case where A is defined as being a repetition of one or more occurrences of B

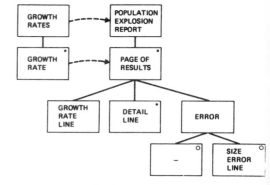

Fig. L.2b Population Explosion Problem

Notice how the repetition is defined as **zero or more** occurrences of the item. If we knew that there must always be at least one occurrence, then we would usually show it as in Fig. L.2a.

In Fig. L.2b you will see the data structures for the population explosion problem (Practical Exercise 1 in Appendix B). The curved dashed lines show the correspondences between the two data structures. These are important when it comes to deriving the program structure, which is built largely out of components that link input components to their corresponding output components. In this example the program produces a page of results (output) for each growth rate that it accesses (input).

Exercise

1 Draw the data structure diagram for the Student Attendance problem (Appendix B, No. 2).

L3   Deriving program structures – the hierarchical approach

We will take as a further example the validation program problem which you encountered in Section J. Sometimes, as here, a program consists of several phases, which can be considered independently. A phase is generally marked by the opportunity to close one or more files prior to opening others. Thus the storing of the 'table' file can be considered independently of the processing of the 'trans' file. This can be illustrated by representing the whole program, at the highest level, by a Nassi–Shneidermann diagram (Fig. L.3).

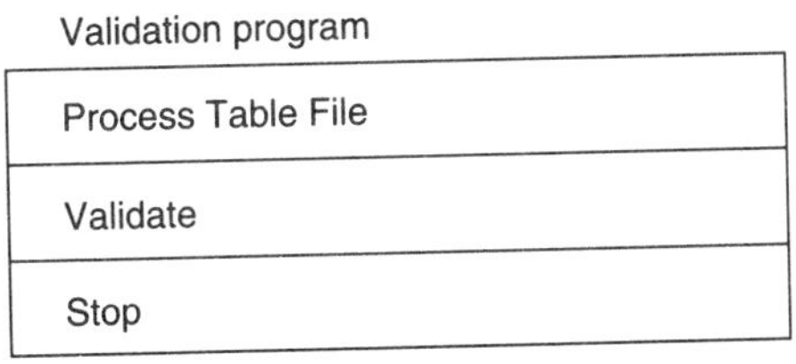

Validation program

Process Table File
Validate
Stop

Fig. L.3 Nassi–Shneidermann

For reasons of space, we will consider here only the design of the second phase, that which reads the transaction file and produces two outputs, a file of valid transactions and an error report containing messages about the invalid ones.

First we construct the input and output data structures; then identify and mark on the diagram the correspondences between components. This is shown in Fig. L.4. The three data structures do in fact correspond quite closely, as you would expect, though a clear difference is that the input transaction file contains both valid and invalid transactions, and therefore

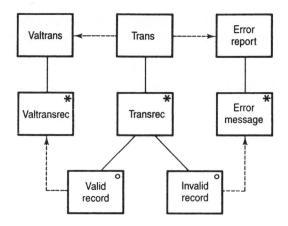

Fig. L.4

its structure contains a selection. The output file contains only valid transactions, and the error report deals only with invalid ones. To apply this
methodology fully it would be necessary to modify the defective structures
so that each of the three became effectively the same structure, in such a
way that by mapping them on top of one another we would produce a
combined structure. This in turn would become the basis of our program
structure. For example, the input and output transaction files can be
shown to have the same structure if we introduce a 'null' or dummy component into the output file to represent the missing invalid records. In a
similar way, we can supply the missing component in the error report data
structure by introducing a dummy in place of the valid transaction component. The relevant parts of the diagrams for each data structure are shown
in Fig. L.5.

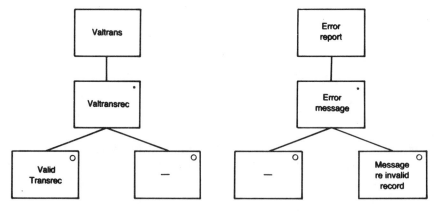

Fig. L.5

We shall probably want to develop the error message component as in
Fig. L.6, and the report footing will similarly be developed as a sequence
of four lines, but this causes no problems in matching the data structures;

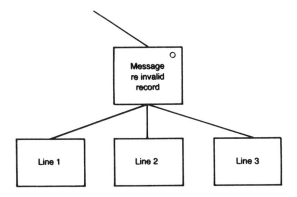

Fig. L.6

it is not necessary to introduce dummy components if there is no effect on lower levels of structure. We can now draw the complete program structure diagram (Fig. L.7)

The above is based on the methodology known as JSP (Jackson Structured Programming). We have actually taken a few short-cuts to arrive at the diagram above, but it should demonstrate the principle that there is a **logical** structure inherent in the data which forms the basis of the structure of the program that is going to process the data.

This progressive refinement of a program structure should be continued down to the point where each box on the diagram can be translated into a **sequence** of statements in the 'target' language (which in our case is COBOL). If, on examination, a box proves to need developing as a **selection**, or an **iteration**, then the process of refinement has not gone far enough, and further structural levels are required. When structural development has proceeded far enough the next stage is to translate the diagram into code. If the methodology has been followed rigorously and sufficient detail has been incorporated, it is actually possible to hand over the translation process to a piece of software called a JSP pre-processor which will produce the code automatically. However, since this is a book on COBOL programming, we shall be doing the translation ourselves.

To go on to this stage in our example, we need more detail than the program structure diagram contains at present. The full JSP method would develop the hierarchical diagram by adding conditions and actions at a detailed level, but for this example we shall do the next stage using the Nassi–Shneidermann technique. You will remember from Section K that this method uses the same standard constructs and is a useful design tool for stepwise refinement, or the progressive factoring of components from higher to lower levels. It suits both the hierarchical and the nested approach equally well. When used hierarchically it generally means that sub-components get developed as separate, subsidiary diagrams.

We left our program depicted by a high-level Nassi–Shneidermann diagram, in Fig. L.3. Remember that for this example we are only developing the 'VALIDATE' component, so taking this component first, we see from the

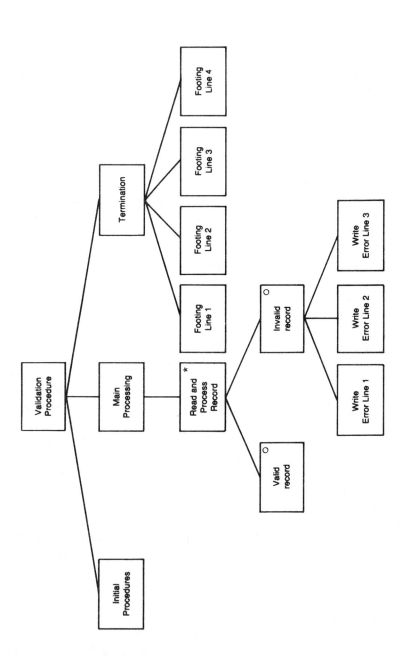

Fig. L.7 Program Structure Diagram

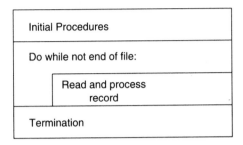

Fig. L.8

| Initial Procedures |
| Do while not end of file: |
| Read and process record |
| Termination |

Fig. L.9

JSP diagram that it is developed as a sequence (Fig. L.8). From the hierarchical diagram we see that 'Main Processing' is refined as an iteration, so that we obtain Fig. L.9. The final version of the structure diagrams for this program using the Nassi–Shneidermann approach is shown in Fig. L.10. Then, in Fig. L.11 you can see the resulting COBOL code – although we have omitted some of the more repetitious parts where the meaning is obvious.

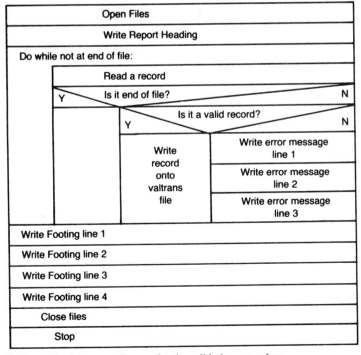

Fig. L.10 Nassi–Shneidermann diagram for the validation procedure

```
PROCEDURE DIVISION.
Program-control.
    PERFORM Process-table-file
    PERFORM Validate
    STOP RUN.
*
 Process-table-file.
```
(statements here to read and store the table)
```
*
 Validate.
    PERFORM Initial-procedures
    PERFORM Main-processing
    PERFORM Termination.
*
 Initial-procedures.
    OPEN INPUT transfile
          OUTPUT valtransfile errorfile
```
(statements here to write report heading)
```
*
 Main-processing.
    PERFORM Read-and-process-record
         UNTIL end-of-file-flag = "Y".
*
 Termination.
```
(statements here to write report footing lines)
```
    CLOSE transfile valtransfile errorfile.
*
 Read-and-process-record.
    READ transfile
    AT END
        MOVE "Y" TO end-of-file-flag
    NOT AT END
        MOVE "T" TO trans-rec-valid-flag
```
(statements to validate transfile record;
if invalid, set trans-rec-valid-flag to "F")
```
        IF trans-rec-valid-flag = "T"
        THEN
            PERFORM Valid-record
        ELSE
            PERFORM Invalid-record
        END-IF
    END-READ.
*
 Valid-record.
```
(statements to write record onto valtransfile)
```
*
 Invalid-record.
```
(statements to print out error message lines)

Fig. L.11 Outline COBOL code for the complete program

Exercise

1 Develop the outline program in Fig. L.11 along the lines shown in the structure diagrams in Figs L.7 and L.10 (refer also to the program specification in frame J3). For this exercise you need only develop the validation part of the program and you may leave the details of the record validation in outline form.

L4   The nested approach – Structured English

Another common method of representing the structure of a program is that called Structured English. This tends to look something like program code, especially the code of a PASCAL program, to which language it owes much of its inspiration. However, if properly handled it produces a design that is easy to understand (because it is in English) and which defines very precisely the structure of the program, while still remaining 'language-independent'. The latter point is important in the design of programs; it ought to be possible to translate a good design into any commonly used programming language. This is one of the benefits of using a restricted set of structured design constructs – modern programming languages all possess the ability to implement the standard constructs, both in hierarchical and nested code. Structured English can be used for designs that are going to be realised with out-of-line procedures, as with our hierarchical example, but it is just as suitable for the in-line or nested approach, and we are going to use it here to illustrate that approach to our validation program.

To write Structured English it is best if you use a sheet of paper with vertical rules ('music-ruled' computer listing paper turned through ninety degrees will do). Each vertical line, or margin, is used to denote the scope of the structured constructs. Sequence operations are written on successive (horizontal) lines against a margin. Selections are introduced by the keyword '*IF*', followed further down (if necessary) by '*ELSE*', rather like conditions in COBOL, and iterations are introduced by the keywords '*DO WHILE*' (or alternatively '*DO UNTIL*'). Both '*IF*' and '*DO WHILE*'/ '*DO UNTIL*' are followed by the appropriate condition, expressed in English. As long as operations are lined up vertically against a margin, the construct is a sequence. When an '*IF*' occurs, the operations dependent upon the condition are indented – i.e. they are lined up against the next vertical line to the right. The same thing happens with a '*DO WHILE*' or '*DO UNTIL*'. If in the course of these operations a further selection or iteration occurs, nested within the outer one, then there is further indentation, to the next vertical line. The layout of the operations on the page shows the scope of the constructs, but it is usual to make this even clearer with scope terminators, similar to those used in COBOL, namely '*END-IF*', '*END-WHILE*' and '*END-UNTIL*'. It is also common practice to begin the whole diagram with '*BEGIN-PROGRAM*' (or '*BEGIN-PROG*') and to show that it has come to an end by putting '*END-PRO-GRAM*' (or '*END-PROG*').

Look at Fig. L.12 below, which is an abbreviated Structured English design for the validation program.

One thing which should be explained concerns the two iteration constructs '*DO WHILE*' and '*DO UNTIL*', which can be represented on a Nassi–Shneidermann diagram as follows:

Do while <condition>
(process)

(process)
Do until <condition>

COBOL doesn't have a 'DO' verb, though it is fairly obvious that 'PERFORM' is the same thing. But although we have a 'PERFORM UNTIL', we don't have a 'PERFORM WHILE'. Instead, we have to code 'PERFORM UNTIL NOT <condition>', and either explicitly state 'WITH TEST BEFORE', or omit it since it is the default. To get the '*DO UNTIL*' version, we have to code 'PERFORM WITH TEST AFTER UNTIL <condition>'.

BEGIN-PROG
    Open files
    Write report heading
    DO WHILE not end of file
        Read record
        IF not at end of file
        THEN:
            IF record is valid
            THEN:
                Write record onto
                    valtrans file
            ELSE:
                Write error message line 1
                Write error message line 2
            Write error message line 3
            END-IF
        END-IF
    END-WHILE
    Write footing line 1
    Write footing line 2
    Write footing line 3
    Write footing line 4
    Close files
    Stop
END-PROG

Fig. L.12 Structured English for the validation program

Figure L.13 shows the COBOL code for the validation part of the program, this time using a nested approach with in-line PERFORMs. As with the Structured English, the code has been slightly abbreviated for reasons of space, but nothing vital to the structure has been omitted.

There are no exercises for this frame.

```
PROCEDURE DIVISION.
   ⋮
(First part of program reads and stores table.
Validation procedure follows:)
   ⋮
02-Validate.
      OPEN INPUT transfile
      OUTPUT valtransfile errorfile
         ⋮
      (statements here to write report heading)
         ⋮
*
*Main processing
      PERFORM UNTIL end-of-file-flag = "Y"
            READ transfile
            AT END
                  MOVE "Y" TO end-of-file-flag
            NOT AT END
                  MOVE "T" TO trans-rec-valid-flag
                     ⋮
                  (Carry out validation tests on record,
                  setting 'trans-rec-valid-flag' to "F"
                  if any errors found)
                     ⋮
                  IF trans-rec-valid-flag = "T"
                  THEN
*                 Valid record.
                        WRITE valtrans-rec FROM trans-rec
                  ELSE
*                 Invalid record.
                        MOVE trans-rec-details TO
                              error-line-details
                        WRITE print-line FROM error-line-1
                        WRITE print-line FROM error-line-2
                        WRITE print-line FROM error-line-3
                  END-IF
            END-READ
      END-PERFORM
*
*     Termination
   ⋮
(statements here to write report footing lines)
   ⋮
      CLOSE transfile valtransfile errorfile
      STOP RUN.
```

Fig. L.13 Outline COBOL code for the validation program, using the nested approach (compare Fig. L.12)

L5   The 'Do ... whenever'

If you look at the solution to frame 3 Exercise 1, you will see that when we wrote the error messages we included a test to see whether we had reached the end of a page ('AT END OF PAGE'), and if so, a paragraph was performed that would have output a page heading, after moving the paper to the top of the next page. This feature does not appear in either of the structure diagrams; strictly speaking it should, and it would certainly have been possible to include a 'page heading' component in the data structure diagrams from which the program structure evolved. It is, after all, a component of the error report data, but to have represented the condition upon which it depends would have made our diagrams considerably more complicated.

This problem can be overcome with a 'Do ... whenever' construct (this is not widely recognised as a structured programming construct). If we add the Page Heading component to the data structure diagram we shall revise Fig. L.6 to look like Fig. L.14.

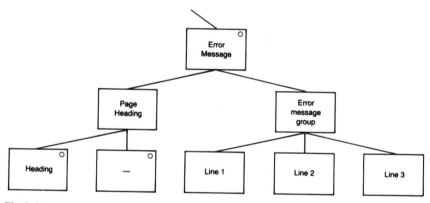

Fig. L.14

If we tick off all the data structure boxes as we convert them into components in our program structure or Structured English, we shall find that we have left unticked the page heading box because we have not yet defined the condition that governs its appearance. This is where the 'Do ... whenever ...' comes in. We consider the unticked box and ask the question 'I want to produce this output whenever I ... ?' The answer supplied should be a complete statement of all the conditions under which the output is to be produced.

If we express this idea in Structured English we will get something like this:

> *WHENEVER there is an error message to be produced*
>   *IF we are at end-of-page*
>   *THEN produce page heading*

This gives us the opportunity to consider whether we really have given a complete statement of the conditions. In fact there is probably another situation in which we need to produce the page heading, namely on the first page of the report. We can revise the above structured English thus:

WHENEVER there is an error message to be produced
    IF it is the first time OR we are at end-of-page
        THEN Produce Page Heading

We did not include this first time check in either version of our COBOL code. The most common way of doing so is to use a flag – we might call it 'first-time-flag' – which would initially contain the value 'T' (= true); we would test it each time we started to produce an error message and if it contained 'T' we would produce the page heading, and also reset it to 'F' (= false), which setting it would retain for the remainder of the program.

There is no exercise for this frame.

L6   Multiple input files

When there are multiple input files in a problem, draw the data structure and correspondences as before. Choose one file – the transaction file – to govern the procedure and derive the program structure that results from processing this file. If there are multiple transaction files, treat the problem as if it were two programs or two phases, the first to process the transaction files to produce a merged transaction file, the second to process the merged transaction file to produce the other outputs.

A typical problem calls for a transaction file to produce a report, to which corresponding master records also contribute. There may be many transactions for a given master, but only one master for a given transaction. The handling of the master may be outlined thus:

WHENEVER a transaction is to be produced
    IF the transaction identifier is not the same as the
                current master identifier
        THEN
            Get as current master the master with identifier
                    equal to the transaction-id
            IF there is no such master
        THEN

                . . .

If the master is a sequential one with records ordered in ascending identifiers, the transaction records being similarly sequenced, then the outline becomes:

WHENEVER a transaction is to be produced
   DO WHILE not eof master AND
        master-id less than trans-id
    Read master
   END WHILE
   IF eof master OR master-id greater than trans-id
   THEN
       . . .

It will be seen that both of these outlines give the clue as to where to put 'Process master' and thereby tick off an input master record box. As with transaction files, implementation of the second version is helped if one master record is read at the outset of the program; then 'Process master' is put under control of the 'DO WHILE', the last action of 'Process master' being:

```
READ master-file
AT END
    MOVE "T" TO eof-master-flag
END-READ
```

The case of the sequential input master being updated by transactions to produce a sequential output master (update by copy forward) can also be analysed with 'whenever' logic, e.g.

WHENEVER a master record is to be read in
       (not being the first master)
   Write out the current master

If the transactions include those that delete a record from the master file, we want to include something like:

IF transaction-type indicates deletion
THEN delete master-file record

When the master file is being updated by copying it forward, this operation is done by skipping over the output master with a second read. This is a case where the current master is **not** to be written out when a master record is to be read in, so the 'whenever' above needs to be modified:

WHENEVER a master record is to be read in
       (not being the first master)
       and it is not a read to effect a deletion
   Write out the current master

There is no exercise for this frame.

Answers – Section L

Frame L2

1 See Fig. L.15

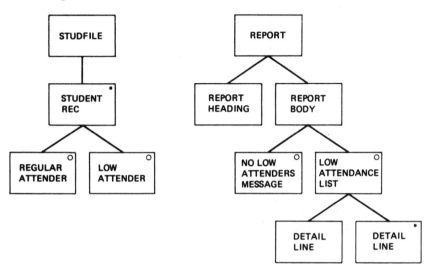

Fig. L.15

Frame L3

1 PROCEDURE DIVISION.

```
*
Program-control.
    PERFORM Process-table-file
    PERFORM Validate
    STOP RUN.
*
Process-table-file.
    :
```

(statements to read in the table file and
store the contents in an array)

```
    :
*
Validate.
    PERFORM Validate-initial-procedures
    PERFORM Validate-main-processing
    PERFORM Validate-termination.
*
Validate-initial-procedures.
    OPEN INPUT transfile
        OUTPUT valtransfile errorfile
    PERFORM Page-heading-routine.
```

```
*
 Validate-main-processing.
    PERFORM Read-and-process-record
        UNTIL end-of-file-flag = "Y".
*
 Validate-termination.
    PERFORM Page-heading-routine
    WRITE error-rec FROM footing-line-1
    WRITE error-rec FROM footing-line-2
    WRITE error-rec FROM footing-line-3
    WRITE error-rec FROM footing-line-4
    CLOSE transfile valtransfile errorfile.
*
 Read-and-process record.
    READ transfile
    AT END
        MOVE "Y" TO end-of-file-flag
    NOT AT END
        MOVE "T" TO trans-rec-valid-flag
        PERFORM validation-checks
        IF trans-rec-valid-flag = "T"
        THEN
            PERFORM Valid-record
        ELSE
            PERFORM Invalid-record
        END-IF
    END-READ
*
 Valid-record.
    WRITE valtrans-rec FROM trans-rec.
*
 Invalid-record.
    MOVE trans-rec-details TO error-line-details
    WRITE error-rec FROM space-line BEFORE
        ADVANCING 2 LINES
    AT END-OF-PAGE
        PERFORM Page-heading-routine
    NOT AT END-OF-PAGE
        WRITE error-rec FROM error-line-1
        WRITE error-rec FROM error-line-2
        WRITE error-rec FROM error-line-3
    END-WRITE
*
 Validation-checks.
    IF trans-update-code NOT = "I"
    AND trans-update-code NOT = "A"
    AND trans-update-code NOT = "D"
    THEN
        MOVE "F" TO trans-rec-valid-flag
    ELSE
```

```
        IF trans-update-code NOT = "D"
        THEN
            IF customer-name = SPACES
            THEN
                MOVE "F" TO trans-rec-valid-flag
            END-IF
        END-IF
    END-IF
```
⋮

(further validation checks, including
searching the table to check that the
credit code is valid).
⋮

*

```
 Page-heading-routine.
    WRITE error-rec FROM space-line BEFORE
        ADVANCING PAGE
    WRITE error-rec FROM heading-line BEFORE
        ADVANCING 5 LINES.
```

Note

You must be careful to avoid using reserved words as either data-names or
procedure-names. The word 'Validate' is not a reserved word at present,
but a 'VALIDATE' statement is under discussion, and may be introduced
in a future standard, in which case this program would have to be amended.

M Documentation

M1 Program documentation

Two main documents show in detail what a program does:

1 the Program Specification, i.e. file and record descriptions, procedure definitions in Structured English, decision tables or similar expressions of program objectives;
2 the Program Listing.

The first of these is more accurately a **design** document, prepared before coding commences. It is often prepared by a systems analyst rather than a programmer. Although nearly all installations require that the Program Specification be brought up to date to reflect the current status of the program, such updating is often done 'after the event'. In consequence, there may be discrepancies between the specification and the listing. The latter, therefore, is the only truly reliable statement of what a program does. It is to the listing that programmers turn when considering modification or correction of the detail of the program. For this reason, the front line of documentation should be the program listing. Not only is the listing the most credible of the available documents, it is also comparatively painlessly and automatically updated by the programmer.

Although it is easy to justify program documentation as an aid to later program modification, there is another more telling reason which is less obvious. A programmer who adopts consistent habits of documentation such as those described here will be working in a less error-prone fashion than one who does not. Since it is impossible fully to test a program after construction, it is vital that the development method should be robust. The documentation is an aid to maintaining integrity of purpose during the refinement of the problem into program code.

For small-to-medium-sized programs, a very good strategy for program development takes three steps:

1 Write a detailed definition in Structured English and have a colleague inspect and agree the detail of this specification.
2 Systematically code from the Structured English and have a colleague inspect and agree the detail of the coding.
3 Systematically test the program as explained in Section N and have a colleague inspect and agree the scope of testing and test results.

With large programs, it may be desirable to make a Structured English specification at an even higher level, perhaps defining programs that can be separately compiled and tested for later linking together (Section U). This also needs to be checked out before being systematically enlarged into the more detailed specifications.

A COBOL program written in a straightforward way does not alone produce a listing that adequately satisfies the additional **explanatory** requirements we are imposing. The following frames are concerned with suggestions for modifying the listing so that these requirements are met.

There are no exercises for this frame.

M2   Identification Division entries

As mentioned in frame J1, COBOL 85 has made many Identification Division documentation features optional so it is even more important that a programmer has the discipline to incorporate appropriate comments at the beginning. Some features to consider are:

(i)   identifying documentation
(ii) the place of this program in the suite of programs
(iii) the overall objectives of the program
(iv) the overall design of the program
(v)   the logic of the program in plainer language than COBOL code

The sample in frame J1 had examples of (i), (iii) and (iv), the overall design being provided in a narrative form. If there is a good standard of systems documentation in force, the first three of the above may be met by cross-referencing to other documents.

The overall design and logic can be illustrated by Structured English specifications, which in some cases may be taken from a design document or file produced for the programmer by the program designer. If some of the logic has been described by decision tables or state transition tables (see Section P), it is usual to include these as well. The hierarchy of Procedure Division paragraphs and sections can be illustrated with a 'Structure Chart' – see also frame M4.

When the process is composed of separately compiled programs (Section U), the name and purpose of each program should be listed in the main program.

Exercises

1 The programmer may direct the compiler to throw to the head of a new page of the listing by placing an oblique stroke '/' in column 7. Why is this useful when the documentation practice is to annotate the Identification Division as outlined here?
2 Most installations adopt a standard system of allocating program names. These systems usually aim at (a) ensuring that each program has a unique name and (b) identifying the system to which the program belongs. Why?
3 Of what practical value is it to record the program author and date compiled on the program listing?

M3   Data Division entries

Documentation in the Data Division centres around **name conventions** and **supplementary information**.

Name conventions have two objectives:

1 to aid location of the Data Division entry for a particular data item when it is referenced in the Procedure Division, e.g. so that its picture can be established;
2 to give meaning to a data item.

Of many possible schemes to achieve the first objective, a workable and consistent one uses a two-character prefix to each data name. This is an overkill on small programs, but it begins to make sense as programs get larger.

The first letter shows in which section of the Data Division the data item is defined:

F = File Section
R = Report Section
W = Working-Storage Section, etc.

The second letter of the prefix is used to identify the record in which the data item appears. The records are lettered in the sequence in which they are coded. If there are few data items in a section, the second letter of the prefix can be dropped. A complete example is given in Appendix A.

The suggested name conventions assume that the programmer has discretion to name the data items. In a well-organised data processing department, the systems analysts may have built up a dictionary or catalogue of all the data used in the system, and they may have defined the names of all the files, records and data elements. If this is the case, the programmer should use the same names in the File Section. If duplicate names arise when following this convention (e.g. when a sequential master file is to be updated by copying it forward) a reasonable way out is to add a suffix -I or -O to distinguish the input data items from the output data items.

In the Working-Storage Section, some records will arise naturally out of association with an input or output record type. The remaining data items need to be organised into records by the programmer. The following guidelines will help this process:

1 put into a common record all those data items that are meant to be globally accessible in the program, i.e. items that are used in the main procedure and subroutines;
2 put into a common record all those data items identified as being passed as parameters when a subroutine is called (i.e. one record for each PERFORM that passes a parameter);
3 put into a common record all those data items identified as being local to a subroutine, i.e. used only within the subroutine (one record per subroutine that requires any local data element).

Meaning is given to the data by the choice of good names, and it is largely a matter of common sense. This usually makes data names longer, but by any reckoning DUE-DATE-OF-NEXT-PAYMENT is to be preferred to DDONP.

A spin-off from prefixing is that accidental use of reserved words is avoided. A spin-off from meaningful names is that misspelling in the Procedure Division is less likely.

Supplementary information should aim to fill the information gaps that the COBOL language leaves. Thus, Data Division entries can tell you, of an item

1 its size and type (PICTURE)
2 its initial value (VALUE)
3 its internal storage format (USAGE)
4 its purpose (if you have picked a meaningful name)
5 the meaning of its values if it is a flag or code (if you use condition names – see frame R4)
6 what it is subscripted by if it is a table (if you use INDEXED BY – see frame Q1)

COBOL entries do not tell you:

1 its purpose (if this is not entirely clear from the name),
2 the range of values it can have (if this is less than the full range allowed by its PICTURE),
3 the meaning of its values if it is a flag or code and you have not used condition names,
4 what it is subscripted by if it is a table and you have not used

INDEXED BY.

This supplementary information should be given in a comment immediately following the date description entry. The skeleton of this comment would be:

* purpose
* RANGE range of values
* code MEANS meaning (as often as required)
* SUBSCRIPTED BY subscript name

The programmer should consider writing this comment after each data description entry, omitting irrelevant portions. This is a sort of quality control check, since if the programmer has chosen wisely a comment will rarely be required.

If a data dictionary exists in which the purpose, range, etc., of data items are recorded, there is not much point in repeating this information in the program.

Exercise

1 Write the data description entries and comment for a table of twelve three-character month names in working storage, to be used to translate a numeric month for printing out on a page heading.

M4   Procedure Division entries

The main suggestions for ease of reading are:

1 write one statement per line,
2 do not write on the same line as a paragraph name,
3 follow the indentation conventions for conditional statements,
4 if nesting more than about 3 or 4 deep, consider using an out-of-line subroutine instead, or consider documenting by comments the analysis that went into the deeply nested statements,
5 use blank lines to highlight the program blocks,
6 use paragraph names that describe the procedures in the paragraph,
7 use a procedure name prefix that will help location of the procedure.

A good prefixing system for procedures in a structured program uses a two-part prefix. The first part is a letter showing the level at which the paragraph, block of paragraphs or section is called. The main procedure is level A, and it PERFORMS level B procedures. A level C procedure is PERFORMed by a level B procedure, and so on. The second part is a serial number uniquely identifying the procedure and serving to help locate it in a large listing. The procedures should be coded in the listing in order of their prefixes. If a procedure block consists of a section or group of paragraphs, all the paragraphs in the block should have the same prefix.

Thus, in a program in which no procedures are reused in different places, the program control hierarchy will always be along the following lines:

A
   B1
      C1
      ⋮
      Cn
   B2
      Cn+1
      ⋮
      Cn+m
   B3
      Cn+m+1
      ⋮
   B4
   ⋮

When a procedure is reused, it is suggested that it is coded at a level corresponding to its highest-level use. The prefix that would have been allocated to it in its other use should be omitted from the procedures. This may sound a little complicated, but we are sure if you try it you will come to see that it makes a lot of sense.

There is an argument against reuse of procedures, as follows. A reused procedure is used in at least two different contexts. If it is modified in one of these contexts, the modification may corrupt it for use in the other context. Procedures should either be duplicated, or the documentation should make the reuse plain.

The hierarchy of control should be documented in the Identification Division comments to aid program maintenance. This can be done simply by listing out the names of the procedure blocks indented according to their level. It helps if in this list the prefixes omitted in the procedures on account of reuse are now included and cross-referenced to the block where the code appears.

Exercise

1 Derive procedure name prefixes for the program appearing as the answer to Exercise 1, frame L3.

Answers – Section M

Frame M2

1 The listing can be organised so that each major component of the com-

mentary and procedures appears on a fresh page. Splitting a Structured English specification or decision table over a page can be avoided. (No Structured English procedure should be longer than a page. Create more subroutines if necessary to meet this ideal.)

2 (a) Every program must have a unique name so that it can be entered in and retrieved from the installation's library of programs – see Section U.

(b) The other programs in the suite can be readily identified and located if the listings are filed in program-name order. This can be helpful in understanding the listing or in tracing the consequences of an amendment.

3 Author – might be handy to know who the original programmer was if the program goes wrong or needs amendment.

Date compiled – if more than one version of the listing has been filed, this will identify the current version.

Frame M3

```
1 01  wd-month-table.
       03  wd-table-contents.
           VALUE "JANFEBMARAPRMAYJUNJULAUGSEPOCTNOVDEC".
           05  wd-alpha-month  OCCURS 12 TIMES  PIC XXX.
 * Used to translate numeric months to alphabetic for
 * report headings.
 * Subscripted by numeric-month
```

Frame M4

```
1 A1-Program-control
    B1-Process-table-file
       -
       -
       -
    B2-Validate
       C1-Validate-initial-procedures
          D1-Page-heading-routine
       C2-Validate-main-processing
          D2-Read-and-process record
             E1-Validation-checks
                -
                -
                -
             E2-Valid-record
             E3-Invalid-record
                 D1-Page-heading-routine
       C3-Validate-termination
          D1-Page-heading-routine
```

N Program Testing

N1 Aim of functional testing

Testing of computer procedures may be considered from three points of view: the user's, the analyst's and the programmer's.

The user wishes to establish that the program is a good fit to his organisation's requirements. The user is the only one who can ultimately judge whether or not the program produces the desired results because he is the only one (we assume) who can conclusively decide what the 'desired results' are.

The systems analyst has tried to comprehend the desires of the user, but he may have done this imperfectly. He will seek to establish that the program matches up to the specification that he assisted the user to produce, and that it works as intended when run in a suite with other programs and human procedures.

The programmer has tried to comprehend the desires of the systems analyst and user, but he may have done this imperfectly. He will seek to establish that the program works in accordance with his understanding of the specification. If, at the program testing stage, it is found that the specification is at fault, it will be very much more expensive to correct the fault than if it had been detected at specification time.

The three parties may also have different viewpoints when it comes to formulation of test data. The test data is submitted to search out hypothetical faults in the program; each party has different reasons for these hypotheses, as follows.

The user may consider the whole computer system a black box. His choice of test data may come entirely from his understanding of what is important to him and the organisation. For example, he may choose data concerning his most important customer. Though the programmer may be unable to conceive of any reason why his program should behave differently for the most important customer, as opposed to any other customer, the user's test data should not be dismissed for this reason. His data probably covers the circumstances of greatest expected loss and this alone is a justification. The user may have other valid reasons for selecting test data, e.g. he remembers an event that caused difficulty with the old system last year and he thinks the same transaction should be tried with the new system.

The systems analyst may also consider the program a black box, but he probably has insights into computer programs in general and may hypothesise a different sort of fault to those imagined by user or programmer. For example, he may know that zero amounts or blank fields are often not processed as intended, or sometimes the intention for such cases is not clear from the specification. Test data conceived by the systems analyst can be a worthwhile addition to that of user and programmer.

The programmer considers testing in full knowledge of the processes of his program. Knowing the exact structure of the program, he is in a position to postulate faults that would escape the attention of analyst and user; for example, overflow on working storage variables, table overflow, incorrect arithmetic sign. The programmer's test data should be concerned with exploring the robustness of the program at its limits. If it works correctly with the limiting cases, it is very likely (especially with commercial programs) to work for all cases in between. The user should participate in certifying the correctness of the results, even those produced by the programmer's test data.

The aim of functional testing is to improve confidence in the program's functional correctness. Obviously all three parties should submit test data; the programmer's test data is just one step on the way to confidence. The programmer should concentrate on devising tests appropriate to his special knowledge of the program structure (and if the programmer is also the analyst or user, he should try to think like analyst or user in addition). Each test should explore some new facet of the program. Each test should be checked out to see if the results are correct. If the programmer succeeds in making each of his tests check something different, he will have an added incentive to verify all the results.

Testing a program is a necessary, but not sufficient, way to build confidence in it. A typical commercial program deals with hundreds of thousands of different possible input values, and it is out of the question to test them all. As important as the confidence that comes from testing is that which comes from using a robust method of program design (such as that of Sections K and L), from desk-checking, and from peer inspection of design and code (see frame M1).

Formal methods have been advanced for proving the correctness of programs, but these are difficult and expensive to apply in other than simple cases. In the absence of formal proof, close desk-checking inspection of the operations of the program, with a view to being informally convinced of its correctness, is called for. Experienced programmers have a knack of recognising which parts of their programs are not completely straightforward, and mentally tracing the program with test data that allows review of correctness.

There is a sound psychological basis for supposing that detailed inspection of a program by a fellow programmer may reveal faults which escaped the original programmer's attention, as well as experimental evidence to support this. The original programmer gets set or fixed on one particular interpretation of the program, which he has difficulty in standing back from. A fresh mind does not have the same constraint.

Exercise

1 Here is a question to think about. When a test exposes a fault in a program, and you fix the fault, should your confidence in the program be (a) increased, (b) reduced?

N2   Minimally thorough testing

The programmer cannot 'completely' test a program as if it were a black box, since that would imply that every possible combination of input data values, in every possible sequence, should be offered to it. This is a vast number even for quite trivial programs.

A target level of testing is required which is capable of being reached and which gives a reasonable degree of confidence – a 'thorough' test. Although we prefer to leave undefined exactly what is meant by a 'thorough' test, we can define a **minimally thorough** test and put forward other tests which should be considered for a given program. A thorough test may then be loosely defined as a minimally thorough test made by the programmer, together with selected other tests made by programmer, analyst and user.

A minimally thorough test is a test such that every simple condition in the program is executed in both its outcomes (true and false) where possible. 'Where possible' is stipulated because there may be conditions included in the program, one of whose outcomes cannot be made to happen with any possible input data. The reason for impossibility may be either logical contradiction or practical impossibility caused by the quantity of data that would be required. An example is where a defensive SIZE ERROR clause is added to a COMPUTE statement. There may be no known input value that will cause the size error; the SIZE ERROR clause results from following a belt-and-braces philosophy.

A similar position arises on rare occasions when there is a logic error on the programmer's part and some portion of the code is unreachable – an attempt to do minimally thorough testing will expose such errors. Another case occurs when a program is totalling fields in records that exist in undefined quantities in a file. The programmer may set the size of the total field such that he believes that there is no practical possibility of size error occurring; but since there is no size of total field that will eliminate the theoretical possibility of overflow, it is proper to include a SIZE ERROR clause, mainly to trap possible logic errors. The 'size error true' condition that results from admitting this clause might as well be considered as arising from an impossible set of input data. Neglecting such cases, minimally thorough testing as defined above ensures that there is no statement in the program which is not executed at least once during testing. Note that 'simple condition' in the definition includes conditional phrases such as SIZE ERROR as well as conditions in IF sentences.

If an identical condition appears in more than one place, every occurrence of it must be exercised. To create the set of test cases, place a T or an F against any defensive condition, showing which is the outcome for which no test can be created. Then specify a test input, and place a T or an F against each condition exercised by it, to show the branch that the test will cause the computer to take. Now look for any conditions that do not have both a T and an F, and specify a further test which will reach the condition and cause the untested branch to be taken. Again place a T or an F against all the conditions not already so marked which are now exercised by the tests. Continue until all conditions have both a T and an F. For each test case created, record your prediction of the result.

Sometimes a condition in a program cannot be exercised without more test data than you are presently prepared to supply, e.g. page overflow on a large page. An interim test can be made by suitably changing the condition, e.g. reducing the number of lines per page. Nevertheless, the program should be tested with the proper condition before it is finally accepted for production work.

Exercise

1 Specify minimally thorough tests for the procedure 'Validation-checks' of the validation program whose Procedure Division is outlined in the Exercise of frame L3.
2 How can you avoid creating 800-character records during the preliminary testing of the POEM program (Appendix B)?

N3   Other tests

Another idea for construction of test cases with knowledge of program structure is that of exploring the program with minimum and maximum values of input data and minimum and maximum values that exercise the conditions. The argument is that if the program works with these extreme values, it is likely to work for all cases in between, since most commercial programs have regular (technically, monotonic) processes.

In practice it is difficult to follow this idea to the limit and pursuing it does not always add to confidence. For example, size errors usually result in abnormal termination in commercial programs. If so, there does not seem much point in exercising the size error conditions with values that only just cause a size error and with values that will cause the largest possible size error. Nevertheless, it does seem a fair general rule to consider using maximum/minimum values and to judge each case on its merits.

To generate extreme test cases, inspect each numeric field in the input record layouts. Create tests in which each of these is given the smallest and largest values for which results are defined. Often these will be the values allowed by the PICTURE of the item (e.g. A PIC S99; smallest value of A −99, largest value of A +99). Sometimes results are specified to be 'undefined' when input values go outside a certain range (e.g. because a previous program has validated the data to be within the range). In this case, choose the smallest and largest values in the range for which the results are defined. Now inspect each relation condition comparing numeric data in the program and ensure that test cases are included that give rise to the smallest and largest values to exercise the condition in both its outcomes (e.g. IF A GREATER THAN 50; test cases for A = −99, A = 50, A = 51, A = +99). When the relation condition is 'equality', i.e. IF A = 50, there must be a test case where A = 50; the unequal outcome may be tested with minimum and maximum values of A.

When the condition is a loop terminator (e.g. a count) there is usually only one value that can be created to terminate the condition. So be it.

Other types of test to consider are those that would expose the following faults:

1 Zero faults. Test data in which numeric input is zero should be included. Consider also non-zero test data that produce a zero result, e.g. transactions that leave a zero account balance.
2 Overflow faults. Possible overflow of numeric fields, strings, tables or filespace.
3 Empty file faults. If the operating system permits input files to be empty of records, does the program handle this case correctly?
4 Case sequence faults. If the treatment of one input record may depend upon how the previous record was processed, or if different record types exist in the input, consider the permutations.
5 File mismatch faults. For example, a transaction for which there is no master.
6 End-of-file faults. Particularly when a master file is being updated by copying it forward, a test should be included to ensure that insertions before the end of the old master, and after the end of the old master, as well as insertions within the old master, are correctly handled. Similar consideration should be given to deletions, particularly a deletion of the last record on the old master. The same type of idea may apply to some table-handling operations.
7 Rounding faults. Particularly important with any sort of compound

interest calculation since insufficient precision in working storage variables may lead to error in a significant digit of the result. The test should cover the longest period of compounding and the results should be checked by hand or with a calculator (but beware, many cheap calculators are inaccurate when many digits of precision are called for).

8 Cycle faults. When an output file is to be re-input into the same program at next execution, this cycle must be tested at least once.

Exercise

1 Suggest the test data for the Population Explosion program (Appendix B).

N4   Self-auditing programs

An additional technique is to plan the program to be self-auditing. The idea is to arrive at the results by two different methods, as a check on the program logic. This is the same idea as that known to accountants as 'cross footing'. How it is done depends upon the exact nature of the program; here are a couple of examples.

Suppose a transaction file can add to or delete from a master file. Every time the program reads a transaction, it should add 1 to a transaction count, and similarly every time it reads or writes a master it should add 1 to an old or new master count. At the point where it determines that the transaction is an addition, it should add 1 to an addition count, while on the remaining path it should add 1 to a deletion count. At the end of the program it should check that

transaction count = addition count + deletion count

and that

new master count = old master count + addition count − deletion count

It is important that there is no branch instruction written between the instruction that adds to the count and the instruction that performs the operation it is counting.

For another example, consider a program that reads records containing a value and a code, and that is to accumulate totals of the values by code plus a grand total. You should add the value to the grand total as soon as the record is read (i.e. no branch instructions between the READ and the ADD – this may mean making the ADD conditional on the READ not having detected end of file) and then proceed to add the value of the appropriate total by code. At the end of the program, it should add up all the totals and check they agree with the grand total. (There would be little point in this particular check, though, if you were using very high-level facilities such as the SUM clause described in frame S3.)

This may strike you as overkill, considering that once the program is tested the self-audit procedures will be redundant. Remember, though, that commercial programs typically have lives of many years and are frequently revised and maintained. Your audit routine will tend to confirm that future amendments have been made satisfactorily.

There are no exercises for this frame.

Answers – Section N

Frame N1

1 Rationally, you could be influenced either way. The safest philosophy is to let each fault that you find **reduce** your confidence in the program. If you find more than two or three faults in a program, you should consider rewriting it from scratch, following a robust program design method.

Perhaps this answer surprises you; we have certainly met a lot of programmers who follow the converse philosophy. The point is that there is an enormous number of possibilities which are supposed to be correctly processed by the program. Any number of possibilities could be incorrectly processed, but your test data can consider only a relative handful of these. Before you do the testing, you have a certain level of belief (estimate of probability) that these untested possibilities are processed correctly. Each test **passed** by your program tends to confirm that it is robust and should increase your belief that the untested possibilities are correctly processed. Conversely, each test **failed** tends to confirm that the program is not robust and should reduce your belief that the untested possibilities are correctly processed.

This reduced confidence may be partly or wholly counteracted by the increased confidence that should be had when the bug is fixed. But there is a good chance that the programmer will let his confidence rise on account of this by more than is justified, so we think it better to err on the cautious side and neglect this aspect.

Frame N2

1 Test 1 A 'trans-update-code' value of 'Z' or some other value not equal to any of 'I', 'A' and 'D' would cover the first setting of the 'trans-rec-valid-flag' and covers the TRUE condition for each of the relations in the compound condition.

Test 2 A 'trans-update-code' value of 'I' with 'customer-name' of all spaces would cause the second setting of the 'trans-rec-valid-flag'.

Test 3 A 'trans-update-code' value of 'A' with 'customer-name' of all spaces would also cause this second setting.

Test 4 A 'trans-update-code' value of 'D' with 'customer-name' of all spaces should not cause the setting of the flag.

Test 5 A 'trans-update-code' value of 'A' or 'I' and 'customer-name'
not equal to spaces should not cause the setting of the flag.

2 Reduce the record size to a more convenient one, say 80 characters. To
prevent the possibility of the program dealing only with the special case
where the input record size was equal to the output record size, reduce
the line length to, say, 60 characters. A program that dealt satisfactorily
with 80 character input and 60 character output may be expected to
behave properly when these constants are changed to 800 and 80,
respectively; but this expectation will still need a final test, of course.

Frame N3

1 Test 1. Empty file.
Test 2. Three records,
0000
1001 (or any other data using the least significant digit; make a prediction of the final population and density)
9999 (expect size error)

Award yourself full marks if you deduced that one of the size errors (in
either population or density) must be impossible.

O String Handling Techniques

O1 String handling

A string, in a general computing sense, is a series of characters, e.g. the surnames of people are strings of different lengths. Until now, we have looked only at fixed-length data items so that variable-length strings, such as surnames, would normally be stored left-justified in a field and blank characters used to fill the field to the right. This often causes much wasted space on a file because even though an average surname size may be 7 characters, the field has to cope with the largest surname, perhaps 20 characters. Some systems try to save space by having a smaller surname field size, say 15 characters, in which case, larger surnames are truncated.

An alternative solution for saving space is to compress related strings into one fixed length field. For example, someone's name and address could be stored in a single field with a special character, say %, separating the different strings. The size of this one field would then be less than the size of all the separate fixed-length fields. An example is given in Fig. O.1 where the fixed-length separate fields total 77 characters, whereas the compressed field is of size 65 characters.

The process of combining such strings from several fixed-length fields into one field is an example of string handling. To perform this and other string operations, e.g. searching a string for a particular character, COBOL provides a separate set of special string handling commands:

Reference modification
INSPECT
STRING
UNSTRING

We shall look at each of these in this section, but first try the string handling exercise for this frame using only the COBOL you have covered so

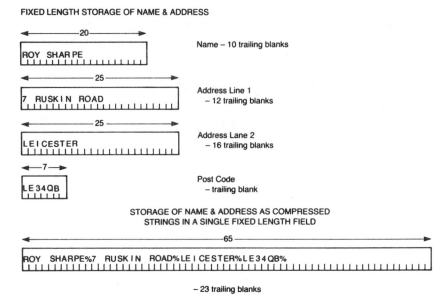

Fig. O.1 Fixed length and compressed string storage

far. This same exercise will be considered in later frames to illustrate how having special string handling operations simplifies solutions.

Exercise

1 A string of non-blank characters is left-justified within 'field1'. You are to transfer the string to 'field2' but making it right-justified with blank fill to the left. You may assume there will be at least one non-blank character in 'field1' and the maximum size of the string is 19 characters. Appropriate declarations are:

```
01  field1.
    03  field1-character   PIC X OCCURS 20 TIMES.
01  field2.
    03  field2-character   PIC X OCCURS 20 TIMES.
01  subscript-area.
    03  field1-subscript   PIC 99.
    03  field2-subscript   PIC 99.
```

O2   Reference modification

Reference modification allows you to refer to a string within a fixed-length data item. Its formal syntax is:

data-name (leftmost-character-position: [length])

As an example, assume you have 'surname-field' declared as PIC X(20), then a valid Procedure Division reference is:

surname-field (4:15)

which identifies a string starting at the fourth character in 'surname-field' and which is 15 characters long. The 'length' value must not cause the string to exceed the length of the data item. If the length is not mentioned, the end of the string is assumed to be at the end of the data item. For example:

surname-field (4:)

would identify a string of length 17 characters, starting from character position 4 within surname-field.

You may use variables or arithmetic expressions for both the 'leftmost-character-position' and the 'length', e.g.

surname-field (start-position:string-length)

would identify a string, the length of which is the current contents of the variable 'string-length' and the first character of the string within 'surname-field' is determined by the current contents of 'start-position'.

Normally, reference modification is applied to alphanumeric data items, but where a data item is declared differently, e.g. numeric, you can still use reference modification but the item will temporarily be interpreted as alphanumeric.

A string identified through reference modification can be used in exactly the same way as a normal fixed-length alphanumeric data item. As an example, given the following declarations:

```
01   surname                 PIC X(20).
01   initials-area           PIC X(10).
01   string-counters.
     03   initials-length    PIC 99.
     03   start-initials      PIC 99.
```

and assuming appropriate values have been assigned to 'initials-length' and 'start-initials', the following Procedure Division statement would copy a string from 'surname' and assign it to the defined part of 'initials-area', leaving the rest of 'initials-area' untouched:

```
MOVE surname (1:initials-length) TO
    initials-area (start-initials:initials-length).
```

For example, for 'surname' containing 'J.R. SMITH' and 'initials-length' containing 4, just the 'J.R.' would be extracted.

Exercise

1 Consider the same exercise as No. 1, frame O1 but now solve it using reference modification.
    Supplied declarations (OCCURS not now needed):

```
01  field1                  PIC X(20).
01  field2                  PIC X(20).
01  string-counters.
    03  current-position    PIC 99.
    03  string-length       PIC 99.
```

O3   INSPECT

The INSPECT statement is used to manipulate characters in a single data item. There are four options of INSPECT and each option has many variations. We will not attempt to cover all aspects but will introduce the main ideas behind each option.
    A simplified form of the first option, to count the occurrences of certain characters, is given below:

INSPECT identifier-1 TALLYING identifier-2 FOR

$$\left\{ \begin{matrix} \text{CHARACTERS} \\ \text{ALL} \qquad \text{identifier-3} \\ \text{LEADING literal-1} \end{matrix} \right\} \quad \left\{ \begin{matrix} \text{BEFORE} \\ \text{AFTER} \end{matrix} \right\} \quad \text{INITIAL} \quad \left\{ \begin{matrix} \text{identifier-4} \\ \text{literal-2} \end{matrix} \right\}$$

As an example, suppose you have a six-character alphanumeric field called 'num-field' containing values of the form _ _ _ _ 27, a numeric data item called 'space-count' and you wish to determine the number of leading spaces in 'num-field', Procedure Division code could be:

```
MOVE ZERO TO space-count
INSPECT num-field TALLYING space-count
    FOR LEADING SPACES
```

Note that the tallying identifier needs to be initialised.
    Here, the character to be searched for is a special form of 'literal-1', the figurative constant SPACES. We could have used SPACE or SPACES as they both denote a single space in this context, but the latter makes the code read more like ordinary English. However, we could have specified a longer literal, e.g. 'CAT', as the search string or the contents of 'identifier-3'.
    The 'ALL' variation will give you a count of all occurrences of the search string, not just the leading ones. You can further limit the part of the string over which tallying will take place, by using BEFORE/AFTER. For example, using the 'CHARACTERS' option, which tallies for every character found in the data item,

```
MOVE ZERO TO char-count
INSPECT char-field TALLYING char-count
     FOR CHARACTERS BEFORE INITIAL ".".
```

would count the number of characters in 'char-field' before the first full stop.

The second INSPECT option replaces characters in a data item. A simplified form is:

<u>INSPECT</u> identifier-1 <u>REPLACING</u>

$$\left\{\begin{array}{ll}\underline{\text{CHARACTERS}} & \\ \underline{\text{ALL}} & \text{identifier-3} \\ \underline{\text{LEADING}} & \text{literal-1}\end{array}\right\} \quad \underline{\text{BY}} \quad \left\{\begin{array}{l}\text{identifier-5} \\ \text{literal-3}\end{array}\right\}$$

$$\left\{\begin{array}{l}\underline{\text{BEFORE}} \\ \underline{\text{AFTER}}\end{array}\right\} \quad \text{INITIAL} \quad \left\{\begin{array}{l}\text{identifier-4} \\ \text{literal-2}\end{array}\right\}$$

Using the same 'num-field' as above, if you wanted to replace all leading spaces with zeroes, you could code:

```
INSPECT num-field REPLACING LEADING SPACES
     BY ZEROES.
```

The third INSPECT option is the combination of options 1 and 2, i.e. tallying and replacing. The full syntax description is given in Appendix D. An example is:

```
MOVE ZERO TO space-count
INSPECT num-field
     TALLYING space-count FOR LEADING SPACES
     REPLACING LEADING SPACES BY ZEROES
```

which is the above two problems combined.

There are many alternatives for all three options, e.g. tallies and replacements can be made both before and after a particular value in the data item concerned. An addition from COBOL 85 is to allow multiple entries of alternatives, e.g. you can have several BEFORE and AFTER phrases for one TALLYING/REPLACING.

The fourth option is also a COBOL 85 addition and it has the more specific purpose of converting a number of characters in a string to other characters. Its formal syntax is:

<u>INSPECT</u> identifier-1 <u>CONVERTING</u>

$$\left\{\begin{array}{l}\text{identifier-2} \\ \text{literal-1}\end{array}\right\} \quad \underline{\text{TO}} \quad \left\{\begin{array}{l}\text{identifier-3} \\ \text{literal-2}\end{array}\right\}$$

$$\left\{\begin{array}{l}\underline{\text{BEFORE}} \\ \underline{\text{AFTER}}\end{array}\right\} \quad \text{INITIAL} \quad \left\{\begin{array}{l}\text{identifier-4} \\ \text{literal-3}\end{array}\right\}$$

A good illustration for the use of this option is the problem of compatibility of data between different computers. Suppose you have received a large quantity of data created by a different computer. Usually, most of the characters have the same internal codes but some of the special characters may be different. For example, the code for '$' on the other machine might be the code for '£' on your machine so that, without conversion, all the '$' characters will be interpreted wrongly as '£'. You would need to convert '£' characters to '$' to get the correct interpretation. Assume the following mismatches occur:

Other computer	Interpreted by your computer as
$	£
@	~
~	@

A solution is to read the 'foreign' file and first execute the following statement so that your computer's initial interpretation can be corrected:

```
INSPECT input-record CONVERTING
    "£~@" TO "$@~"
```

Normal processing of the input record area could then continue.

INSPECT could also be used to convert from upper to lower case and vice versa but the FUNCTIONS UPPER-CASE and LOWER-CASE are now more appropriate – see Section W.

Exercise

1 The INSPECT CONVERTING option is actually a shortened form of a variation of INSPECT REPLACING. Provide an INSPECT REPLACING solution to the data conversion example given above.

O4   STRING

The statements STRING and UNSTRING, although at first sight seeming a bit formidable, provide sophisticated operations for the combining together and the splitting up of strings. We shall not attempt to provide a full description but rather, illustrate some of their potential.

A simplified formal description of STRING is:

$$\underline{\text{STRING}} \left\{ \begin{matrix} \text{identifier-1} \\ \text{literal-1} \end{matrix} \right\} \dots \underline{\text{DELIMITED}}\text{ BY} \left\{ \begin{matrix} \text{identifier-2} \\ \text{literal-2} \\ \underline{\text{SIZE}} \end{matrix} \right\}$$

$$\underline{\text{INTO}}\text{ identifier-3}$$

A full syntax description is provided in Appendix D. The ideal use of the statement occurs when you wish to collect together a number of strings to make one long string in a new field, as in the name and address situation described in frame O1. Another area where STRING is useful is in the displaying of messages on a VDU screen. Suppose you have the following input disk record with fixed-length fields:

```
01  part-record.
    03  part-number          PIC 9(4).
    03  bin-number           PIC 99.
    03  part-description      PIC X(20).
```

and you have an output record description for one line of the screen:

```
01  screen-line              PIC X(65).
```

A suitable output screen line with reasonable spacing could be created by the following Procedure Division code:

```
MOVE SPACES TO screen-line
STRING "PART: "
       part-number
       " DESCRIPTION: "
       part-description
       " BIN: "
       bin-number
    DELIMITED BY SIZE
    INTO screen-line
```

The DELIMITED BY SIZE clause applies to all the preceding identifiers/literals and means that the whole of each item is to be added to the resultant string. If 'part-number' contained 8076, 'bin-number' contained 16 and 'part-description' contained "TUBULAR STEEL._ _ _ _ _ _", then after execution of this statement, 'screen-line' would contain:

PART: 8076 DESCRIPTION: TUBULAR STEEL._ _ _ _ _ _BIN: 16

As with reference modification, there is no automatic space fill so you need the initial MOVE statement.

Suppose, now, that you would like to remove the full stop in the description and close the gap between the description and the bin number, this could be achieved by:

```
MOVE SPACES TO screen-line
STRING "PART: "
       part-number
       " DESCRIPTION: "
    DELIMITED BY SIZE
       part-description
```

```
DELIMITED BY "."
    " BIN: "
    bin-number
DELIMITED BY SIZE
INTO screen-line
```

When an explicit delimiter is used, as with the full stop above, the delimiter itself is not moved so that 'screen-line' would contain:

PART: 8076 DESCRIPTION: TUBULAR STEEL BIN: 16

The delimiter can be a string of characters. If a delimiter is not found, the whole of the sending data item is added to the string being formed.

When explicit delimiters are used, the length of the resultant string is not constant because it depends upon the length of the source strings. If you wish to know the resultant string length, you can use a POINTER option which references an elementary numeric data item that is automatically updated to point to the next available character position in the resultant string. For example, executing:

```
MOVE SPACES TO screen-line
MOVE 1 TO next-position
STRING "PART: "
        part-number
        " DESCRIPTION: "
    DELIMITED BY SIZE
        part-description
    DELIMITED BY "."
        " BIN: "
        bin-number
    DELIMITED BY SIZE
    INTO screen-line
    POINTER next-position
```

would have 46 in 'next-position', i.e. one more than the length of the string as this would be the next position for filling. As with reference modification, the initial value of the pointer indicates the start position of the string in the receiving data item.

If you now wanted to add to the resultant string in a subsequent operation, 'next-position' would hold the correct starting position. For example:

```
STRING " *OUT OF STOCK*"
    DELIMITED BY SIZE
    INTO screen-line
    POINTER next-position
```

would cause 'screen-line' to become:

PART: 8076 DESCRIPTION: TUBULAR STEEL BIN: 16 *OUT OF STOCK*

as long as 'next-position' had not been altered between the two STRING statements.

If the receiving data item is not large enough to hold the resultant string, an overflow condition occurs, causing the STRING statement to terminate. You can test for this explicitly in a similar way to SIZE ERROR with arithmetic statements. For example:

```
STRING " *OUT OF STOCK*"
    DELIMITED BY SIZE
    INTO screen-line
    POINTER next-position
    ON OVERFLOW
        DISPLAY "Overflow in stock screen line"
        STOP RUN
END-STRING
```

would cause the message to be displayed if the resultant string exceeded the size of 'screen-line', although as much of the string as possible would be created.

There is also a NOT ON OVERFLOW option to allow certain statements to be executed only if the resultant string did not overflow the receiving data item.

Exercises

1 Provide a solution to Exercise 1 of frame O2 using the INSPECT statement to find the string length in 'field1' and the STRING statement for the transfer.

2 Using the STRING statement, produce a solution to combine together the contents of the string within the four name and address data items in Fig. O.1. The resultant string should have % characters as separators, as illustrated in that figure. Assume that only one space separates the parts of each string in the sending fields, e.g. there is one space between '7' and 'RUSKIN' in the first address line. Appropriate declarations are:

```
01  fixed-name-and-address.
    03  fixed-name          PIC X(20).
    03  fixed-address-line1 PIC X(25).
    03  fixed-address-line2 PIC X(25).
    03  fixed-postcode      PIC X(7).
01  compressed-name-and-address
                            PIC X(65).
```

Display an appropriate message if overflow occurs.

O5   UNSTRING

The purpose of the UNSTRING statement is the opposite of STRING, i.e. to take a large string in a data item and distribute it as shorter strings to several receiving data items. A simplified form of its syntax is:

UNSTRING identifier-1

DELIMITED BY [ALL] $\left\{\begin{array}{l}\text{identifier-2}\\\text{literal-1}\end{array}\right\}$

INTO {identifier-3} ...

If we take as an example the name and address problem outlined in frame O1 and using the Data Division descriptions of Exercise 2 in frame O4, the unstringing of the contents of 'compressed-name-and-address' could be:

```
UNSTRING compressed-name-and-address
    DELIMITED BY "%"
    INTO fixed-name
        fixed-address-line1
        fixed-address-line2
        fixed-postcode
```

After execution of this statement, each of the four receiving data items would appear exactly as in Fig. O.1. For each string identified by the delimiter, a normal MOVE operation takes place for the next receiving field. Unused character positions are filled with spaces if the receiving data item is alphanumeric or alphabetic, or with zeroes if it is numeric. If a string were too large for a receiving data item, characters would be lost as for a normal MOVE but this does not cause an overflow condition.

An OVERFLOW condition does arise, however, if all the receiving data items are used and there are still characters to be sent. There is also a TALLYING option which allows tallying of the number of receiving data items into which some data has been moved. As an illustration of OVERFLOW and TALLYING, and if 'number-of-address-lines' had a PIC 9 declaration,

```
MOVE ZERO TO number-of-address-lines
UNSTRING compressed-name-and-address
    DELIMITED BY "%"
    INTO fixed-name
        fixed-address-line1
        fixed-address-line2
        fixed-postcode
    TALLYING IN number-of-address-lines
    ON OVERFLOW
        DISPLAY "Error overflow in address unstring"
        STOP RUN
END-UNSTRING
```

would cause 'number-of-address-lines' to have value four if the data in Fig. O.1 were used. The overflow message would appear only if a fifth string were identified in 'compressed-name-and-address'.

As with STRING, there is a pointer option and more than one delimiter can be specified by joining delimiters with OR. The delimiter itself can be saved separately by the DELIMITER IN clause. These features are illustrated in the next example, again based on Fig. O.1, but now we will assume that a postcode string may not be present in the compressed data item and the end of the compressed string is marked by an asterisk rather than a %, i.e. the initial value of 'compressed-name-and-address' could be:

ROY SHARPE%7 RUSKIN ROAD%LEICESTER*

or

ROY SHARPE%7 RUSKIN ROAD%LEICESTER%LE34QB*

Here, we will assume that 'next-position' has been declared PIC 99 and 'saved-delimiter' declared PIC X:

```
MOVE 1 TO next-position
MOVE SPACE TO saved-delimiter
PERFORM UNTIL saved-delimiter = "*"
    UNSTRING compressed-name-and-address
        DELIMITED BY "%" OR "*"
        INTO screen-line
        DELIMITER IN saved-delimiter
        POINTER next-position
    DISPLAY screen-line
END-PERFORM
```

This will cause the name and address to be displayed one line at a time. Note that the pointer is incremented for delimiters as well as string characters. When a pointer is used, in addition to running out of receiving fields, an overflow condition can be set by the pointer's value becoming greater than the size of the sending data item.

Other features of UNSTRING are:

a delimiter may be preceded by the word ALL, in which case several consecutive occurrences of the delimiter will be treated as a single occurrence;

if ALL has not been used and there are two consecutive delimiters, i.e. a null string is identified, the resultant receiving data item will be filled with spaces if alphanumeric, or zeroes if numeric;

the 'COUNT IN identifier' option allows you to count how many characters have been transferred to a particular receiving data item;

there is a 'NOT ON OVERFLOW' option to allow statements to be executed only if overflow has not occurred.

Exercise

1 A list of city names is stored in

```
03  city-name-list      PIC X(125).
```

Each name is separated from the next name by a comma and the string is terminated by an asterisk. There is also a table

```
01  city-table.
    03  city-name           PIC X(18)
            OCCURS 15 TIMES.
```

Provide code to fill the table with as many city names as possible, but do not overflow the table. Each table element should contain the name left-justified.

Answers – Section O

Frame O1

```
1 *
  * Find the length of the string
  *
        MOVE 1 TO field1-subscript
        PERFORM UNTIL field1-character (field1-subscript)
                                            = SPACE
            ADD 1 TO field1-subscript
        END-PERFORM
  *
  * Calculate the initial unloading point in field2
  *
        COMPUTE field2-subscript =
            20 - field1-subscript + 2
  *
  * Do the move
  *
        MOVE SPACES TO field2
        PERFORM VARYING field1-subscript FROM 1 BY 1
            UNTIL field1-character (field1-subscript)
                                       = SPACE
            MOVE field1-character (field1-subscript)
                TO field2-character (field2-subscript)
            ADD 1 TO field2-subscript
        END-PERFORM
```

There are other solutions, e.g. you could find the end of the string in field1 and move it from the back into field2.

Frame O2

1 One solution using reference modification:

```
*
* Find the length of the string
*
      MOVE 1 TO current-position
      PERFORM UNTIL field1 (current-position:1) = SPACE
          ADD 1 TO current-position
      END-PERFORM
      SUBTRACT 1 FROM current-position GIVING
          string-length
*
* Do the move
*
      MOVE SPACES TO field2
      MOVE field1 (1:string-length) TO
          field2 (20 - string-length + 1 : string-length)
```

Frame O3

1
```
INSPECT input-record REPLACING
      ALL "£" BY "$"
      ALL "~" BY "@"
      ALL "@" BY "~"
```

Frame O4

1
```
*
* Find the length of the string
*
      MOVE ZERO TO string-length
      INSPECT field1 TALLYING string-length
          FOR CHARACTERS
          BEFORE INITIAL SPACE
      COMPUTE current-position = 20 - string-length + 1
*
* Do the move
*
      MOVE SPACES TO field2
      STRING field1
          DELIMITED BY SPACE
          INTO field2
          POINTER current-position
```

```
2 MOVE SPACES TO compressed-name-and-address
  STRING fixed-name
         "%"
         fixed-address-line1
         "%"
         fixed-address-line2
         "%"
         fixed-postcode
         "%"
      DELIMITED BY "R"
      INTO compressed-name-and-address
      ON OVERFLOW
         DISPLAY
            "Overflow on name and address expansion"
  END-STRING
```

Note that two spaces are used as the delimiter. For simplicity, a single 'DELIMITED BY' has been used even though it is only appropriate to the first three data items. For the others, when the delimiter is not found, the whole of the string is moved anyway.

Frame O5

```
1 MOVE ZERO TO city-subscript
  MOVE 1 TO next-position
  MOVE SPACE TO saved-delimiter
  PERFORM UNTIL saved-delimiter = "*"
           OR city-subscript = 15
      ADD 1 TO city-subscript
      UNSTRING city-name-list
         DELIMITED BY "," OR "*"
         INTO city-name (city-subscript)
         DELIMITER IN saved-delimiter
         POINTER next-position
  END-PERFORM
```

P Programming Interactive Dialogues

P1 General guidelines

There is increasing direct user interaction with computers, and often such users are not experienced computing people. Therefore, there is a growing demand for 'user-friendly' interfaces where the dialogue between a person and a computer is such that the person will not be alienated. Two features of commercial interactive programming that make such an approach difficult to implement are:

(a) the input and output of information on VDUs is machine-specific,
(b) the choices a program has to make in response to input may be very complicated.

Unfortunately COBOL 85 offers no standard answer to (a). VDUs come with a wide variety of features such as reverse video, bold and underlined text, protected fields, X–Y cursor addressing, screen clear, flashing fields, audible signals, windows, etc. These features are usually invoked by outputting to the VDU, control symbols stored in the program, but the actual symbols vary from device to device. Different manufacturers also use a variety of COBOL statements to process VDU input/output. Some use READ/WRITE for simple line-by-line I/O, some use ACCEPT/DISPLAY for full screen I/O and some use the Communications module features (not discussed in this book).

There was much discussion prior to the announcement of COBOL 85 that 'screen management facilities' would be standardised, but this did not happen, mainly due to this great variety offered by different manufacturers. One new feature related to screen handling that did appear, however, was the ability to allow movement of data **from** an edited field. In earlier versions of COBOL, you could only move **to** an edited field. This now recognises the fact that screen input fields are often automatically edited, e.g. 0019 converted to _ _19, so you need to be able to transfer data **from** such a field. In addition, CODASYL are proposing a Screen Management Facility, part of which uses the commands SEND and RECEIVE for the transfer of data to/from a VDU, and this may well develop as a major part of the next standard. SEND and RECEIVE are currently part of the Communications module but they have different syntax and semantics within the Screen Management Facility.

As to (b), commercial interactive systems should react in an intelligent way to different input and this often makes processing quite complex. Frames P3 and P4 consider this complexity.

At the keyboard/screen level, there are two main types of interactive dialogues: 'menus' to allow easy selection of options by a user and 'form fill' where a screen is laid out like a form and data is entered into fields by the user. Most interactive systems have a combination of the two. Despite the variation of VDUs, there are some general guidelines to keep in mind when designing interactive dialogues.

1 Organise a large number of user selections into a tree of menus, i.e. a main menu allowing selection of sub-menus. About seven selections from any one menu is a realistic maximum, both from the screen presentation and user comprehension points of view.

2 Allow for case shift variants in replies, e.g. 'Y' or 'y' should both be allowable as valid user replies.

3 Give experienced users the chance to abbreviate or take short cuts, e.g. branch directly from a deep-level menu to the main menu.

4 Have a HELP option at each screen but also consider having different levels of HELP for users of different experience. The initial level can be determined by the user on entry to the system or the level can be adjusted by the system depending upon the progress of the user.

5 Keep the dialogue style consistent throughout the system, e.g. if 'Q' (for 'quit') is your menu exit selection, make sure 'Q' is used at all menu levels.

6 Allow an 'escape' option from 'form fill' screens so that a user can cancel a current entry. This is not necessary within menus as the 'exit' selection option plays this role.

7 Use single-key entry for menu options. Some people argue that this allows users to make mistakes too easily, but within menus a user can always exit from a wrongly selected option.

8 Give a quick response to each input, otherwise the user might start thumping the keyboard!

9 In menus, use single letters rather than numbers as selectors. The letters should relate to the various options, e.g. 'I' for Invoice.

10 Give as much thought to error conditions as the main dialogue and consider carefully how the system should respond to input errors.

11 For 'form fill' screens, completion of a field entry should be unambiguous, e.g. always use the TAB key no matter whether the field is full or not.

12 Avoid cluttered screens. You can always split your form into two screens.

13 Choose words carefully. If your spelling is poor, make sure you check all words.

14 Do not make the user rely on memory. All information relevant to a particular screen should be available at that screen.

15 Keep records of system and user responses for later improvements, e.g. numbers of transactions, frequency of different selections, frequency of errors.

Exercise

1 You are designing a menu-driven program which requires a user, initially, to select one of eighteen different geographical regions for further form-filling processing. What menu structure would you recommend?

P2   The menu dialogue

The menu is a relatively easy dialogue to program and is particularly suited to inexperienced users. Its main disadvantage is that it may be slow compared with other dialogue styles, especially if the terminal device is slow in operation.

Here is a short example. Suppose we have a main menu as follows:

Menu 1

Do you want to
 [T] enter a Transaction
 [F] print a File
 [H] get Help
 [E] Exit

A response of 'T' prompts the further menu:

Menu 2.1

Select type of transaction
 [I] Invoice
 [P] Payment
 [M] change Master file detail
 [H] get Help
 [E] Exit

while a response of 'F' to the main menu results in:

<u>Menu 2.2</u>
Select file to be printed
    [I] Invoices this month
    [P] Payments this month
    [C] Customer master
    [H] get Help
    [E] Exit

and so on. We are assuming here that Exit means transfer control to the menu above except at the top level, where it means exit the system. After successful completion of a lowest-level operation, the last menu offered is to be repeated. This hierarchical branching logic is a 'case' construction implemented in COBOL by the EVALUATE statement. In essence, the program is of the form:

Menu 1

Repeat until 'E' response
    Repeat until response valid
        Display menu
        Get response
        Evaluate response
            When 'T'
                Perform 'Menu 2.1'
            When 'F'
                Perform 'Menu 2.2'
            When 'H'
                Perform 'Menu 1 Help'
            When 'E'
                No action
            When Other
                Display error
                Response not valid

    Menu 2.1

Repeat until 'E' response
    Repeat until response valid
        Display menu
        Get response
        Evaluate response
            When 'I'
                Perform 'Enter invoice'
            When 'P'
                Perform 'Enter payment'

> *When 'M'*
> >*Perform 'Change master'*
>
> *When 'H'*
> >*Perform 'Menu 2.1 Help'*
>
> *When 'E'*
> >*No action*
>
> *When Other*
> >*Display error*
> >*Response not valid*

and so on.

With most computer systems, the dialogue text is better stored on secondary storage accessible to the program rather than embodied as constants in the program. This is because it is usually easier to edit a data file than to change a program and recompile it, and dialogue wordings often need successive refinements while they are being tried out with users. One possibility is to have each menu as a record on a file and use direct access (see Section T) to access each record, while another is to have each menu as a file and each selection as a record on that file.

The latter approach is more general and makes it easier to build a general-purpose menu-handling system where only one program handles the display of menus and the gathering of responses. With such a system, each menu item record includes the message to be displayed for the item and the action that is to be taken if that item is selected. This will be either presentation of a further menu (naming the menu file) or taking a 'leaf' action (naming a program), or both. With this strategy, the programming of a hierarchical menu dialogue is reduced simply to the creation of a set of data files for the menus and writing the leaf programs (the leaf programs can be executed by inter-program communication – see Section U).

Exercises

1 Complete the example given in this frame by providing a solution for Menu 2.2.
2 Amend the solution for Menu 2.1 so that the menu is not redisplayed when an invalid response occurs.

Practical

1 Write a Structured English specification of a general-purpose menu handler. Implement it. For simplicity of testing you may wish to restrict yourself to a small number of selections per menu.

P3   State transition tables

Interactive dialogues often involve the interpretation of strings of characters entered at the keyboard (this sort of problem more rarely arises with batch systems). Many of these problems can be solved with the UNSTRING and INSPECT facilities already explained. There is also quite a large class of problems that can be solved by state transition tables. The main advantage of these tables is that they help to clarify a complex problem prior to coding.

Suppose that in an interactive program a visual display operator is to enter a data item 'value of sale'. Further, although 10 character positions are to be allowed for the data item, the data can be of any length up to 10 characters, including an unspecified number of leading and trailing spaces. The amount may be arithmetically signed (+ or −). At least one digit must be present, and a decimal point may optionally be present. An integer is to be interpreted as 'dollars' unless it is followed by the symbol ¢, in which case it is to be interpreted as 'cents'. The symbol ¢ is not allowed when a decimal point is present.

To construct a state transition table for this case, identify all the characters or classes of character that are significant to the interpretation of the data – space, digit, decimal point, symbol ¢, any other character. These are the characters that cause a change of state as described later. All digits are lumped together in the class 'digit' because there is no different treatment required for any particular digit. Similarly, any character other than space, digit, decimal point and cent symbol will give rise to an error state.

In this case there is one other significant state of the input, namely the state where the field is completely full as a result of ten characters having been entered.

The input states and characters are used to label the columns of the table. Now, to construct the table, label the first row with the initial state (e.g. 'Before any significant digit') and enter in the table under each column an arbitrary number to represent the row of the new state. Use the same number, of course, if two different inputs lead to the same new state. Label the second row, and continue in this fashion until all entries are complete, except for those states considered terminal.

Figure P.1 shows the table that results.

In preparing the state transition table, there are likely to be states arising that were not clearly dealt with in the narrative specifications (e.g. can the decimal point be the last non-space character entered?). These points should be referred to the analyst or user for clarification.

In the example, to keep it short, states have been lumped together which could have been differentiated if called for. For example, there is only one 'error' state; different sorts of error could have been identified by having states 'Error – invalid character present', 'Error – embedded space', 'Error – blank entry', etc. (see also the next frame). Similarly, we

INPUT / CURRENT STATE	Space	Digit	Decimal point	Symbol "¢"	Any other character	End of data
1. Before any significant digit	1	2	3	6	6	6
2. Digits before decimal point	5	2	3	5	6	7
3. Expecting first digit after decimal point	5	4	6	6	6	7
4. Expecting second digit after decimal point	5	5	6	6	6	7
5. After end of entry	5	6	6	6	6	7
6. Error						
7. Finished						

Fig. P.1 State transition table showing the new current state that results from the specified input character or input state

would have had states like 'Finished and the field contains integer dollars', 'Finished and the field contains integer cents', etc.

Implementation of a program from a state table has straightforward possibilities, but which is the best approach depends upon the circumstances. An approach to consider is described below. This may seem a little complicated, but once understood we think you will not want to do it another way.

The columns are considered to be numbered 1, 2, 3, etc., and the states (= rows) are also numbered 1, 2, 3, etc. The state table is stored as data and the input character is converted, by means of a look-up table (see frames Q1 and Q5), into the column number. The procedure is then as follows.

Validate sale value
Set state to 1
Input (or index) first character
Repeat until state = 6 or 7
 Convert input character to column number
 Set state to table-entry (row = state, column = column number)
 If state not = 6 or 7
  Input (or index) next character

This approach leads to reasonably easy maintenance provided the maintaining programmer also understands the method, and the state transition table is documented.

Exercise

1 What change would you need to make to Fig. P.1 if the decimal point were not allowed to be the last non-space character in the input?

P4   State table to control dialogue progress

Cases often arise in interactive dialogues where it is desired to exercise control in a non-hierarchical way. For example, consider the following possible service to a user who wishes to consider investment choices.

Please respond to each of the following four questions. Respond
with a ? for the item you wish to find; enter the value of the
other three items. Only one ? is allowed in the answers.

Number of years of investment (whole years) = . . .
Amount of principal to be invested = £ . . . . . .
Annual rate of interest (compounded annually) = ...%
Maturity value of investment = £ . . . . . .

Press RETURN after each of your entries.
Press RETURN in answer to any question if you have made a
mistake and wish to start again at question 1.

zzzzzzzzzzzzzzzzzzzzzzzzzzzzzzzzzzzzzzzzzzzzzzz

The whole of the screen is to be presented at the outset (except the line of zs, which show the location of the result and error message area). The cursor is moved to the first dot of the first question. After the user's valid entry, the cursor is positioned at the first dot of the next question, and so on. After the last entry, a message is written, being one of these four corresponding to the '?':

Number of years required is ZZ9
Principal required is ££,£££,££9
Rate of interest needed is ZZ9.999%
Maturity value is ££,£££,££9

If a size error occurs, the message will be:

The answer is too large to report. Please enter new data.

If the user's data is not valid, a suitable error message is displayed in the message line and the cursor is repositioned at the first dot of the entry concerned. If the user's entry is empty (indicated by the entry of RETURN alone, with this particular equipment) the screen is re-presented and the cursor repositioned for question 1.

To rearrange this problem so that it is amenable to a hierarchical solution can be very pedestrian. In this example, it would require one menu offering four choices of query type, and for each query type there would be a different dialogue asking for the three values needed to answer that type of query.

The state table solution is similar in principle to that described in the previous frame, the only difference being that in addition to a new state being determined by an entry in the table, each current state/input combination also calls for an **action** to be taken before continuing to the next state.

Figure P.2 shows a state table for our problem. In addition to the new state, each item of the table has been labelled with an action number. This is only to help you understand the implementation of the state table; the action number is not included in the table stored in the program.

CURRENT STATE	INPUT CASE "?" 1	Valid numeric response to question 2	Any other case 3	Empty 4
1. Before no-of-years question	A1, 2	A2, 3	A3, 1	A4, 1
2. ? found, before principal question	A5, 2	A6, 4	A7, 2	A8, 1
3. ? not found, before principal question	A9, 4	A10, 5	A11, 3	A12, 1
4. ? found, before rate question	A13, 4	A14, 6	A15, 4	A16, 1
5. ? not found, before rate question	A17, 6	A18, 3	A19, 5	A20, 1
6. ? found, before maturity question	A21, 6	A22, 1	A23, 6	A24, 1

Fig. P.2 State transition table for the investment dialogue

Just as before, it is necessary to work methodically through the table, analysing the transitions from the current state to the next state, but in addition the action to be taken at each stage needs to be noted. For brevity the list of actions is omitted but has been incorporated into the Structured English specification of the program which follows:

Investment query program
Repeat until no-more-queries
          Display test on screen
          Cursor to number-of-years field
          Set state to 1
          Get input case
          Repeat until query-answered
                    Do 'Convert input case to column-no'
                    Do 'Carry out action' (state, column-no, query-answered)
                    Exit if query-answered
                    Set state to table entry (state, column-no)
                    Get input case
          Display "Do you have another query? Answer Y or N"
          If answer is "N"
                    No-more-queries

Convert input case to column-no
Evaluate user's response
When "?"
  Set column-no to 1
When space
  Set column-no to 4
When valid numeric response to question
  Set column-no to 2
Else
  Set column-no to 3

Carry out action (state, column-no, query-answered)
Evaluate state and column-no
When 1 and 1
  Set query-type to 1
  Cursor to principal field
When 1 and 2
  Cursor to principal field
When 1 and 3
  Write invalid data message
  Cursor to number-of-years field
When 2 and 1
  Write ? already entered message
  Cursor to principal field
When 2 and 2
  Cursor to rate field
When (2 and 3) or (3 and 3)
  Write invalid data message
  Cursor to principal field
When 3 and 1
  Set query-type to 2
  Cursor to rate field
When 3 and 2
  Cursor to rate field
When 4 and 1
  Write ? already entered message
  Cursor to rate field
When 4 and 2
  Cursor to maturity field
When (4 and 3) or (5 and 3)
  Write invalid data message
  Cursor to rate field
When 5 and 1
  Set query-type to 3
  Cursor to maturity field

When 5 and 2
> *Calculate maturity*
> *If size error*
>> *Write result too large message*
> *Else*
>> *Write maturity message*
> *Query-answered*

When 6 and 1
> *Write ? already entered message*
> *Cursor to maturity field*

When 6 and 2
> *Evaluate query-type*
> *When 1*
>> *Calculate years*
>> *If size error*
>>> *Write result too large message*
>> *Else*
>>> *Write years message*
> *When 2*
>> *Calculate principal*
>> *If size error*
>>> *Write result too large message*
>> *Else*
>>> *Write principal message*
> *When 3*
>> *Calculate rate*
>> *If size error*
>>> *Write result too large message*
>> *Else*
>>> *Write rate message*
> *Else*
>> *Program logic error*
> *Query-answered*

When 6 and 3
> *Write invalid data message*
> *Cursor to maturity field*

Else
> *Cursor to principal field*

State transition tables can be used to exercise larger control over dialogues, e.g. control over successive screen presentations. A complicated dialogue may call for control, at different stages or at different levels of analysis, by state tables, menus and structured constructs. The programmer who masters all three techniques is in a position to solve any commercial text-based dialogue problem.

There are no exercises for this frame.

Practical

1 Implement the investment query program on your equipment.

Answers – Section P

Frame P1

1 Following the guidelines of a maximum of seven options per screen, you might suggest an initial menu of three geographical groupings and then have three sub-menus, each having six options. However, it would depend upon the nature of the data because if the selections were particularly uniform and the screen not too cluttered, it may be acceptable to have two sub-menus, each having nine options.

Frame P2

1 Repeat until 'E' response
     Repeat until response valid
          Display menu
          Get response
          Evaluate response
               When 'I'
                    Perform 'Print invoices this month'
               When 'P'
                    Perform 'Print payments this month'
               When 'C'
                    Perform 'Print customer master'
               When 'H'
                    Perform 'Menu 2.2 Help'
               When 'E'
                    No action
               When Other
                    Display error
                    Response not valid

2 Repeat until 'E' response
     Display menu
     Repeat until response valid
          Get response
          Evaluate response
               When 'I'
                    Perform 'Enter invoice'
               When 'P'
                    Perform 'Enter payment'

> *When 'M'*
> > *Perform 'Change master'*
> *When 'E'*
> > *No action*
> *When Other*
> > *Display error*
> > *Response not valid*

The error actions would now have to include repositioning of the cursor at the data entry point.

Frame P3

1 Change the 5 in row 3, column 1, to a 6.

Q Table Manipulation

Q1 Table look-up

We have already met the concept of a table. It consists of repeated data items defined by an OCCURS clause. The example program specification of Section J3 refers to a file of credit codes which is initially read into memory as a table. The later searching of that table for particular credit codes is an example of table look-up.

As another example, let us assume that town names are stored in several files as two-character codes, e.g.

Town name	Stored as
Leeds	LE
Acton	AC
York	YO

but for reports we need to convert the codes to their full names. For simplicity, we will assume that we have a total of eight towns only and none of them is longer than five characters. For the conversion, we create a table of the two-character codes and their equivalent names.

Declarations for these tables are:

```
01  coded-town-table VALUE "DEYOAYACELTRCRLE".
    03  town-code      PIC XX OCCURS 8 TIMES
            INDEXED BY code-index.
01  full-name-town-table
        VALUE "DERBYYORK_AYR__ACTONELY__TRUROCREWELEEDS".
    03  town-name      PIC X(5) OCCURS 8 TIMES
            INDEXED BY name-index.
```

The use of 'INDEXED BY' defines a data item for use in referring to particular items in the table. It is the same concept as a separate numeric subscript but there are certain differences:

an index is named in the OCCURS clause rather than being declared separately; COBOL provides an appropriate declaration that suits the dimensions of the table and is usually more efficient than an equivalent subscript declared by the programmer;

an index is associated with a particular table whereas subscripts are independent of table declarations;

certain table-handling features (discussed later in this section) require indices, not subscripts;

indices may only be initialised or modified by the VARYING option of PERFORM, the separate statement SET (examples are given at the end of this frame) or the SEARCH statement (frame Q4).

The data for the above tables could have been on a file as the credit codes in the frame J3 program specification but it is just as valid for small tables to be initialised within a program. An advantage of having table data in a file is that if you wish to change the data in the table, only the file need be altered, not the programs.

Back to the above example. Assuming that a town code is part of an input record:

```
01   input-customer-record.
     ⋮
     03 town-code-in        PIC XX.
     ⋮
```

and we require the town name to be put into an output record:

```
01   output-customer-record.
     ⋮
     03 town-code-out     PIC X(5).
     ⋮
```

then appropriate Procedure Division code is:

```
PERFORM VARYING code-index FROM 1 BY 1
        UNTIL town-code-in = town-code (code-index)
          OR code-index = 8
    CONTINUE
END-PERFORM
IF town-code-in = town-code (code-index)
THEN
    SET name-index TO code-index
    MOVE town-name (name-index) TO town-code-out
ELSE
    DISPLAY "Town code " town-code-in " not found"
    MOVE SPACES TO town-code-out
END-IF
```

All the required processing for the search, i.e. initialising and increment-ing the index and testing for the terminating conditions, takes place in the heading part of the PERFORM. 'CONTINUE' is a dummy statement that has no effect but is required because you must have at least one statement within the body of a PERFORM.

In the search, either you find a matching code or you finish with the index pointing to the last item in the table. You cannot test beyond the end of the table, i.e. 'code-index > 8', because an index value of 9, when used in 'town-code-in = town-code (code-index)', would refer beyond the end of the table and, therefore, be illegal. A further test in a separate IF determines which condition terminated the search so that the appropriate statements can be executed.

Note the use of SET for manipulating indices – MOVE cannot be used. Other examples of the use of SET are:

```
SET code-index TO 1

SET code-index UP BY 1

SET code-index DOWN BY 1.
```

After execution of a SET statement, the value of an index item must lie within the range of its associated table.

Exercises

1 Provide an alternative solution to the above example by searching the code table from the end.
2 You are reading a file where the character '*' needs to be translated into three zeroes, all other characters remaining the same. The input record is 80 characters long and you are to build the translated data in a 240-character record (allowing for all asterisks in the input record). Any unused character positions in the output record are to be filled with spaces. Using the declarations below, provide Procedure Division code to translate one record:

```
01   input-record.
     03   in-char      PIC X OCCURS 80 TIMES
              INDEXED BY in-index.
01   output-record.
     03   out-char     PIC X OCCURS 240 TIMES
              INDEXED BY out-index.
```

Q2   Table organisation

When a large table is being searched for an item, and there are a great many items to be found, it is clear that there may be a great deal of pro-cessing time involved in the searching.

As an example, suppose the tables in frame Q1 contained 10,000 town codes and town names and the town codes were 5 characters long. Assuming each town code had an equal probability of being in the input data, an average of 5000 codes would be compared for each search and with 5-character codes, this is an average comparison of 25,000 characters for just one town code. Also assuming a typical input file of text had 1000 town codes to translate, this would be a total of 25,000,000 character comparisons, a large task even for a fast mainframe computer. When large tables and large files are involved, therefore, it can be desirable to find faster methods of searching.

When the items in a table are searched one after the other as in frame Q1, this is said to be a **sequential** search. One approach to speeding up sequential searching is to order the table items according to the frequency with which they are needed. Putting the most frequently encountered items at the beginning of the table will mean that, on average, fewer items will be inspected before the one needed is found. For example, if 'LONDON' were a frequently needed town name, it could be the first item in the town tables and this move alone could dramatically reduce the average search times.

Exercise

1 Assume that the town example had table and data item sizes as in frame Q2 above and it was estimated that the code for 'LONDON' appeared in the input data for 40% of the total number of town codes and the code for 'EDINBURGH' appeared for 20% of the total. What would be the average number of table items searched if the code and name for 'LONDON' were placed in the first position and the code and name for 'EDINBURGH' were placed in the second position of the respective tables?

Q3   The binary or logarithmic search

This is a technique of table searching which, if all items have equal frequency of being needed, guarantees that the fewest possible number of comparisons are made. The items in the table are sequenced in ascending (or descending) order of value. Using the town code and name example of frame Q1, and assuming ascending sequence, we have:

AC	AY	CR	DE	EL	LE	TR	YO

and the associated table of full names:

ACTON	AYR__	CREWE	DERBY	ELY__	LEEDS	TRURO	YORK_

Let the number of items in the table to be searched be N (8 in the above example) and assume we are searching for the code 'EL'. First, compare item N/2 (=the 4th, 'DE') from the beginning. As this is not the desired item, the search continues as follows; if the desired item is greater than the item just compared, this means that the whole of the left-hand side ('AC' to 'DE') of the table must be irrelevant. Compare item N/4 (=2) positions to the **right** of the last item compared (=the 6th, 'LE'). This means, for 'EL' which is less than 'LE', that the whole of the right-hand corner of the table is irrelevant. We now compare against the item N/8 (=1) positions to the **left** of the last item compared and finally get our match.

In general, the first comparison eliminates half the table, the second comparison a further quarter, the third a further eighth and so on. The maximum number of comparisons needed to locate an item in a table of N items is $\log_2 N$, whilst the average number is less than this as you always have a chance of finding the desired item earlier in the search, e.g. searching for 'DE' above would match after one comparison.

Exercises

1 One approach to implementing a binary search is to have a low boundary and a high boundary indicating the current part of the table in which the target data item can lie. Initially, the low boundary will be the start point of the table, usually 1, and the high boundary will be the maximum size of the table; the mid-point of the table for the first comparison will be the average of these two values. On each unsuccessful comparison, the low or high boundaries are adjusted appropriately and a new mid-point for the new range calculated. If the item is not in the table, the low and high boundary values will eventually point to the same table item.

Assume we have declarations as per frame Q1 except that the tables are now in ascending order and we have combined the two tables into one:

```
01   input-customer-record.
     ⋮
     03   town-code-in        PIC XX.
     ⋮
01   output-customer-record.
     ⋮
     03   town-code-out       PIC X(5).
     ⋮
01   code-and-name-town-table
        VALUE "ACACTON"
              "AYAYR__"
              "CRCREWE"
              "DEDERBY"
              "ELELY__"
              "LELEEDS"
              "TRTRURO"
              "YOYORK_".
```

```
03   one-code-and-name    OCCURS 8 TIMES
             INDEXED BY town-index.
      05   town-code        PIC XX.
      05   town-name        PIC X(5).
```

We also add declarations for constants to indicate the table size and for the boundary values:

```
01   table-constants.
      03   min-table-size  PIC 9   VALUE 1.
      03   max-table-size  PIC 9   VALUE 8.
01   search-boundaries.
      03   low-bound       PIC 9.
      03   high-bound      PIC 9.
      03   mid-point       PIC 9.
```

Provide COBOL Procedure Division code to convert 'town-code-in' to 'town-code-out' but using a binary search.

2 If the table size is not an exact power of 2, what will happen in the calculation of the mid-point?

Q4   SEARCH

COBOL provides an automatic method of searching one-dimensional tables – the SEARCH statement. You can use only indices, not subscripts, with SEARCH. Its simplified general form for sequential searching is:

<u>SEARCH</u> identifier
[AT <u>END</u> imperative-statement-1]
[<u>WHEN</u> condition imperative-statement-2] . . .
[<u>END-SEARCH</u>]

The identifier is a table name, i.e. a declaration, usually at the 01 level, that contains an OCCURS clause. The AT END clause allows you to provide statements to be executed if the item is not found in the table and the WHEN clause allows you to state the condition for finding the item. Here is a solution to the town code example of Frame Q1 but now with the SEARCH statement.

```
SET code-index TO 1
SEARCH town-code
AT END
     DISPLAY "Town code " town-code-in " not found"
     MOVE SPACES TO town-code-out
WHEN town-code-in = town-code (code-index)
     SET name-index TO code-index
     MOVE town-name (name-index) TO town-code-out
END-SEARCH
```

SEARCH does all the manipulation of the index after the programmer has set the initial value.

An automatic binary search is provided with the SEARCH ALL option. In this case, the data sequence has to be indicated in the declaration of the table. A solution to Exercise 1 of frame Q3 using SEARCH ALL is:

```
01   code-and-name-town-table
     VALUE "ACACTON"
              "AYAYR__"
              "CRCREWE"
              "DEDERBY"
              "ELELY__"
              "LELEEDS"
              "TRTRURO"
              "YOYORK_".
     03   one-code-and-name   OCCURS 8 TIMES
              INDEXED BY town-index.
              ASCENDING KEY IS town-code.
          05   town-code      PIC XX.
          05   town-name      PIC X(5).
              ⋮
SEARCH ALL one-code-and-name
AT END
     DISPLAY "Town code " town-code-in " not found"
     MOVE SPACES TO town-code-out
WHEN town-code-in = town-code (town-index)
     MOVE town-name (town-index) TO town-code-out
END-SEARCH
```

There are no exercises for this frame.

Q5   Multi-dimensional tables

These are found when a repeated item appears within another item which is itself repeated, i.e. when one OCCURS clause is subordinate to another OCCURS clause. For example, suppose a manufacturer supplies parts to overseas agents, area distributors and contractors with a different rate of discount, depending upon the nature of the part and the class of purchaser, as follows:

	Parts			
Purchaser	Motors	Panels	Wheels	Other
Overseas agent	35%	30%	30%	30%
Area distributor	30%	25%	20%	20%
Contractor	10%	5%	5%	0%

A program is to prepare an invoice for a customer from an order record which, apart from the gross cost of the order, contains two single-digit items coded as follows:

purchaser-code	part-type
1 = Overseas agent	1 = Motors
2 = Area distributor	2 = Panels
3 = Contractor	3 = Wheels
	4 = Other

A relevant table declaration for a program to apply the discount would be:

```
01   discount-table VALUE "353030303025202010050500".
   03   purchaser OCCURS 3 TIMES.
      05   discount OCCURS 4 TIMES PIC V99.
```

This describes a table of 3 rows and 4 columns. The first four items in the VALUE clause are the discounts for each column of the first row (Overseas agent) of the table, the next four are the discounts for each column of the second row, and so on.

An individual item can be located with two subscripts/indices, the first for the row and the second for the column. Wheels for Overseas agents have the discount in the first row, third column, i.e. 'discount (1,3)'. Panels for area distributors would have 'discounts (2,2)'. The contents of the VALUE clause can be imagined to be split up as in Fig. Q.1. Within a row, each item can be imagined as the first row below (see Fig. Q.2).

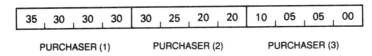

Fig. Q.1 Contents of 'discount-table'

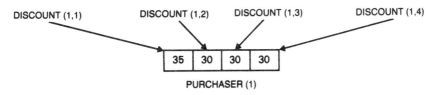

Fig. Q.2 Contents of purchaser (1)

In the above example, the 'purchaser-code' correctly describes a desired row and the value of 'part-type' describes the desired column. If these were used directly as subscripts, they could pick out the appropriate discount. An example Procedure Division statement might be:

```
MULTIPLY gross-cost BY
    discount (purchaser-code, part-type)
    GIVING discount-amount ROUNDED.
```

You can refer to a complete row of four discount values by using just one subscript, e.g. 'purchaser (3)' refers to the four discount values for a Contractor.

You may declare indices for some or all of the dimensions within a multi-dimensional table; therefore, a reference to an individual item in a table may have a mixture of subscripts and indices. You are allowed up to **seven** dimensions in COBOL 85, although most applications would not go beyond two or three.

Exercises

1 Suppose, in the example in the text, 'purchaser-code' took the values 0,1,2,3. How would you have to amend the program?
2 In the same program as the example in the text, assume that there is an output table declared:

```
01  discount-print-table.
    03  purchaser-print OCCURS 3 TIMES.
        05                      PIC XX VALUE SPACES.
        05 discount-print    PIC 0.99B OCCURS 4 TIMES.
```

There are also two subscripts, 'row-sub' and 'column-sub', each declared as PIC 9. Provide Procedure Division statements that will move each 'discount' value into the corresponding 'discount-print' field. (Hint: consider having a PERFORM within a PERFORM, the outer one to control the row subscript and the inner one to control the column subscript.)

Answers – Section Q

Frame Q1

```
1 PERFORM VARYING code-index FROM 8 BY -1
        UNTIL town-code-in = town-code (code-index)
            OR code-index = 1
    CONTINUE
  END-PERFORM
  IF town-code-in = town-code (code-index)
  THEN
      Set name-index TO code-index
      MOVE town-name (name-index) TO town-code-out
  ELSE
      DISPLAY "Town code " town-code-in " not found"
      MOVE SPACES TO town-code-out
  END-IF
```

2 With indices, you have to be careful that the result of a SET statement does not create a value outside the range of the table, i.e. 'out-index' cannot be set to 0 or 241. As it is possible to have a complete input record of asterisks, the solution below, without the initial IF statement, would have attempted to set out-index to an illegal 241 after translation of the last input character. When indices are manipulated within a PER-FORM, they are allowed to have a value one less/more than the range of the table, as with 'in-index' below.

```
IF input-record = ALL "*"
THEN
     MOVES ZEROES TO output-record
ELSE
     MOVE SPACES TO output-record
     Set out-index TO 1
     PERFORM VARYING in-index FROM 1 BY 1
                UNTIL in-index > 80
          IF in-char (in-index) = "*"
          THEN
               PERFORM 3 TIMES
                    MOVE ZERO TO
                            out-char (out-index)
                    SET out-index UP BY 1
               END-PERFORM
          ELSE
               MOVE in-char (in-index)
                    TO out-char (out-index)
               SET out-index UP BY 1
          END-IF
     END-PERFORM
END-IF
```

An alternative solution would be to use subscripts that do not have the same restrictions on holding values within the range of a table. In general, however, indices offer more protection because if a subscript did contain a value outside the range and it was used to refer to a table item, it could cause a runtime error.

Frame Q2

1 40% of searches would require 1 comparison (London). 20% of searches would require 2 comparisons (Edinburgh). The rest (40%), would require 2 + (10,000 − 2)/2 = 2 + 4,999 = 5001 comparisons. The overall average number of comparisons would, therefore, be:

$$(40 \times 1 + 20 \times 2 + 40 \times 5001)/100$$
$$= 2001.2 \text{ comparisons.}$$

Frame Q3

```
1 MOVE max-table-size TO high-bound
  MOVE min-table-size TO low-bound
  COMPUTE mid-point = (high-bound + low-bound) / 2
  SET town-index TO mid-point
  PERFORM UNTIL town-code-in = town-code (town-index)
              OR high-bound = low-bound
      IF town-code-in < town-code (town-index)
      THEN
          SUBTRACT 1 FROM mid-point GIVING high-bound
      ELSE
          ADD 1 TO mid-point GIVING low-bound
      END-IF
      COMPUTE mid-point = (high-bound + low-bound) / 2
      SET town-index TO mid-point
  END-PERFORM
  IF town-code-in = town-code (town-index)
  THEN
      MOVE town-name (town-index) TO town-code-out
  ELSE
      DISPLAY "Town code " town-code-in " not found"
      MOVE SPACES TO town-code-out
  END-IF
```

2 There would be truncation of the mid-point value calculated. This is not necessarily a problem but you would have to check that no items in the table are missed. Another approach is to make the table have size equal to the next power of 2 and pad-out unused items with HIGH-VALUES.

Frame Q5

1 The discount table would have four rows. If 'purchaser-code' were used as a subscript, you would have to add 1 to it first to refer to a table row. This can be achieved by **relative** subscripting, i.e. a subscript can be any item plus or minus an integer, e.g.

```
MULTIPLY gross-cost BY
    discount (purchaser-code + 1,part-type)
    GIVING discount-amount ROUNDED.
```

You can also have relative indexing.

```
2 PERFORM VARYING row-sub FROM 1 BY 1
            UNTIL row-sub > 3
    PERFORM VARYING column-sub FROM 1 BY 1
            UNTIL column-sub > 4
        MOVE discount (row-sub,column-sub)
            TO discount-print (row-sub,column-sub)
    END-PERFORM
END-PERFORM
```

Part 3
Further COBOL

R Further General Features

R1 COPY and the source library

For programs in the same application area, there are sometimes program parts which are identical, e.g. where different programs have the same input file, the FD and record descriptions could all be the same. Rather than repeating such code you can save one version in a file then copy that file into several programs at the appropriate point. The collection of all such COBOL files is called the source program library.

You may copy COBOL text into a program at any point and the simplest format is:

<u>COPY</u> file-name

where 'file-name' follows the rules for your operating system. For example, an input file of customers may have the following description:

```
FD   input-file
     LABEL RECORDS ARE STANDARD.
01   input-record.
     03   customer-id        PIC X(6).
     03   customer-name      PIC X(15).
     03   customer-details   PIC X(90).
```

If this were the complete contents of 'infile.cob', at the point in your program where you would have coded this, you can now put:

```
COPY "infile.cob"
```

and the compiler will temporarily switch to 'infile.cob' for its input source statements, then at the end of this file revert back to the main source program.

You can also replace certain characters at the time of copying so that general source library files can be made more specific to your program, e.g.

```
COPY "infile.cob"
    REPLACING input-file BY customer-file
              input-record BY customer-record
```

would become

```
FD   customer-file
     LABEL RECORDS ARE STANDARD.
01   customer-record.
     03   customer-id        PIC X(6).
     03   customer-name      PIC X(15).
     03   customer-details   PIC X(90).
```

as the copied code. You can make text substitutions of any kind but, for partial words, it is preferable to surround the text parts with == so that the previous example could have also been coded as

```
COPY "infile.cob"
    REPLACING ==input== BY ==customer==
```

Large applications will set up a source library at any early stage of development to reduce duplication. It also means that if any changes occur in the source library code, only one file need be altered rather than all the separate programs that use the code. It also reduces programming errors as you ensure that source libraries contain correct COBOL.

R2   Debugging aids

In frame J4, some guidelines for fault detection and correction were given. However, bugs can often be so obscure that it may be necessary to use special software, called debug aids, to help you. COBOL 74 standardised some of these features, but recognising that many manufacturers provide their own quite sophisticated debugging aids, COBOL 85 has made the debug module facilities obsolete so that they will be removed from the next standard. The only remaining standardised feature is the debug line.

Debug lines

These are lines of source code that are inserted into a program during testing but are not intended to be part of the finished program. Any line with a 'D' in column 7 is a debug line, which is normally treated as a comment by the compiler but which can be activated by the programmer by inserting

```
SOURCE-COMPUTER. computer-name WITH DEBUGGING MODE.
```

in the Environment Division. This will cause all lines with a 'D' in column 7 to be compiled as normal COBOL code. Typically, debug lines in the Procedure Division would be displaying:

(i)   the contents of critical variables (monitoring)
(ii) messages indicating the current point of execution (tracing).

Manufacturer-specific features

Nearly all compilers will offer their own monitoring and tracing facilities so that, for example, you can easily list out Procedure Division paragraph names or line numbers in the order in which they are executed.

However, there are also some very sophisticated features whereby you can 'watch' your program execute at various speeds, stopping and investigating the current contents of data areas at any point. These usually have part of the screen containing the current equivalent Procedure Division source statements for the object code being executed and, via the cursor, indicating exactly which source code statement is the current point of execution.

Such facilities usually require a 'monitoring' version of the program to be created via a special compilation.

R3   Operator communication

A message can be passed to the computer operator during execution of the program by the DISPLAY verb. This is simply the word DISPLAY followed by a string of variables and/or literals, e.g.

```
DISPLAY "NO OF RECORDS READ =" rec-count
```

If 'rec-count' contained 01273, the message

NO OF RECORDS READ = 01273

would appear on the 'display device', i.e. the peripheral device designated for displays. This is often the computer operator's console display or the display from which execution of the program was initiated. With some computers the display device can be explicitly stated.

Similarly, information can be obtained from the operator with the ACCEPT verb. This is the word ACCEPT followed by a single identifier of some element of data in the Data Division. The machine stops and whatever the operator types is entered in the variable, e.g.

```
DISPLAY "ENTER 2-DIGIT RUN NUMBER"
ACCEPT run-no
```

Again, with some computers, the device is explicitly stated. Whatever the operator keys is entered left-justified in the accepting field, so with numeric fields there may have to be some juggling with the data if the operator does not enter the full number of digits in the item.

The ACCEPT statement has a second format:

$$\underline{\text{ACCEPT}}\ \text{identifier}\ \underline{\text{FROM}} \left\{ \begin{array}{l} \underline{\text{DATE}} \\ \underline{\text{DAY}} \\ \underline{\text{DAY-OF-WEEK}} \\ \underline{\text{TIME}} \end{array} \right\}$$

If they are set properly, all computers hold the current date and time. As long as you ensure that 'identifier' has an appropriate format, it will hold the date/time as follows, all examples assuming 12 noon on Friday 2nd January 1998:

DATE –   six-digit date in the form YYMMDD, e.g. 980102
DAY –   five-digit Julian date in the form YYDDD, e.g. 98002
DAY-OF-WEEK – one digit representing 1 for Monday through to 7
                   for Sunday, e.g. 5
TIME –   eight-digit time in hours (24 hour clock), minutes,
                   seconds and hundredths of a second, e.g. 12000000

For example, if you had the declaration:

```
01   input-date-area.
     03   input-year          PIC 99.
     03   input-month         PIC 99.
     03   input-day           PIC 99.
```

in the Working-Storage Section and the statement

```
ACCEPT input-date-area FROM DATE
```

in the Procedure Division, you would have available the complete date via 'input-date-area' or the individual components via their appropriate name, e.g. 'input-day'. See also the date and time functions in frame W2.

R4   Condition names

A documentation aid that allows you to make your Procedure Division code more readable is the level 88 **condition name**. In the Data Division, a name made up by the programmer is associated with a value or values that could appear in an elementary item, e.g.

```
03   error-flag             PIC X.
     88 input-record-is-invalid  Value "I".
```

It must be stressed that this is not initialising 'error-flag' (see SET below) but rather associating the name 'input-record-is-invalid' with a possible value 'I' in error-flag.

Condition names and testing

For the above example, in the Procedure Division, the use of 'input-record-is-invalid' will give value **true** if 'error-flag' contains 'I' but value **false** if 'error-flag' contains anything other than 'I'.

Here is some sample Procedure Division code first without using a condition name:

```
PERFORM Validate-Input-Record
IF error-flag = "I"
THEN
    PERFORM Process-Invalid-Record
ELSE
    PERFORM Process-Valid-Record
END-IF
```

Here, now, is the same logic but with a condition name:

```
PERFORM Validate-Input-Record
IF input-record-is-invalid
THEN
    PERFORM Process-Invalid-Record
ELSE
    PERFORM Process-Valid-Record
END-IF
```

A good choice of condition names provides more problem-oriented information to the reader of a program and can result in fewer comments in the Procedure Division.

You can have several values within one 88 level and several 88 levels for one elementary item. Also, a range of values can be assigned by the THRU option, e.g.

```
03  transaction-type       PIC X.
    88  valid-transaction-type  VALUE IS "A" "I" "D".
        |
        |
03  quantity-ordered       PIC 9(4).
    88  small-quantity-ordered  VALUE IS 0 THRU 100.
    88  large-quantity-ordered  VALUE IS 101 THRU 9999.
```

Condition names and moving values

A condition name value can be put into its associated elementary item by using SET, e.g. for the first example above

```
SET input-record-is-invalid TO TRUE
```

would cause 'error-flag' to have value 'I'. This is exactly equivalent to

```
MOVE "I" TO error-flag
```

although, again, the former makes the code more self-documenting. You cannot use FALSE in this context.

   If more than one literal or a range of values is specified with a condition name, the first-mentioned literal is used, e.g. for the second example above

```
SET small-quantity-ordered TO TRUE
```

would cause 'quantity-ordered' to become zero, as 0 is the first-mentioned literal in the range 0 THRU 100.

R5   STOP RUN

We have used this statement without explanation up to now because its purpose is reasonably plain. In addition to stopping execution of a program, it also causes any open files to be closed.

   There is also a 'STOP literal' statement but this will be deleted in the next version of the standard.

R6   INITIALIZE

The INITIALIZE statement provides the ability to set data areas to predetermined values. It acts like the VALUE clause of the Data Division but as it is a Procedure Division statement and can be placed anywhere in that Division, it also gives you the flexibility to reinitialize areas at any point.

   In its simplest form, numeric areas, both edited and unedited, are initialized to zero and alphabetic and alphanumeric areas are initialized to spaces, e.g. given the following Data Division entries:

```
01   totals-and-flags.
        03   record-count        PIC 999.
        03   end-of-file-flag    PIC XXX.
```

the Procedure Division statement

```
INITIALIZE record-count
           end-of-file-flag
```

would set 'record-count' to zero and 'end-of-file-flag' to spaces. You can initialize group items which causes subordinate items to be initialized appropriately, e.g.

```
INITIALIZE totals-and-flags
```

would have the same effect as above.

The REPLACING option allows you to initialize to other values, e.g.

```
INITIALIZE totals-and-flags
    REPLACING NUMERIC DATA BY 100
            ALPHANUMERIC DATA BY ALL "*"
```

would set all numeric fields to value 100 and all alphanumeric fields to asterisks. In the above example, 'record-count' would be set to 100 and 'end-of-file-flag' to asterisks. If 'totals and flags' contained other data items that were not numeric or alphanumeric, e.g. numeric edited, they would be unaffected. The various categories of data for the REPLACING option are:

ALPHABETIC
ALPHANUMERIC
NUMERIC
ALPHANUMERIC-EDITED
NUMERIC-EDITED

Only the simple INITIALIZE affects all items if a group item is specified.

R7   Further use of EVALUATE

The simplest form of EVALUATE was introduced in Section I as an implementation of the structured programming 'case' statement. It has, however, a more complicated form consisting of multiple subjects and corresponding objects and which can be a direct implementation of a truth table. As an example, assume we want to increment appropriate counters for adolescent males and females, otherwise we want to add to an 'adult' counter irrespective of the sex of a person. This could be coded in one statement as follows:

```
EVALUATE person-age ALSO     TRUE
    WHEN 0 THRU 18  ALSO person-sex = "M"
        ADD 1 TO young-males
    WHEN 0 THRU 18  ALSO person-sex = "F"
        ADD 1 TO young-females
    WHEN   OTHER    ALSO     ANY
        ADD 1 TO adults
END-EVALUATE
```

The first line contains the subjects 'person-age' and TRUE, separated by the reserved word ALSO. Each object line has a similar list of entries separated by ALSO and each object entry must match the type of its subject, e.g. 'person-age' must be an integer field that can hold at least two digits. For the first WHEN that has all its objects true, the equivalent statement is executed then control passes to the statement after the EVALUATE. Where an individual object value is irrelevant, as in the third case above, the reserved word ANY can be used. WHEN OTHER is the 'catch-all' object at the end whose statement will be executed only if no other object lines are selected.

There is no limit to the number of subjects and object lines and the statement at the end of each object line can actually be a series of imperative statements.

There are no exercises in this section.

S The Report Writer

S1 Background

The Report Writer feature employs concepts that are quite different from most other COBOL concepts. For this reason, COBOL courses often omit any mention of it, and the result is that many COBOL programmers do not learn how to use it.

The main difference is that the Report Writer is mainly a **declarative** language, i.e. the programmer declares what results he wants and lets the machine worry about how to achieve these. Other aspects of COBOL are mainly **procedural**, i.e. the programmer has to stipulate exactly **how** the results are achieved. Although it may seem obvious that the declarative style is desirable, in practice it is not very flexible. The Report Writer is very good for straightforward reports, but it tends to get rather complicated for anything out of the ordinary.

There are so many facilities in the feature that to cover them all in detail would be like learning a new programming language. Our aim here is to provide a foundation on which the student can build from the reference manual if desired.

The aim of the Report Writer is to make it easier to produce reports on the line printer. Its value rests in the fact that many reports take the same shape. They start off with **headings**, followed by lines of **detail** with **total** lines at some **control break**. To write the report in conventional COBOL requires standard procedures like numbering the pages, counting the lines, repeating the headings on each fresh page, making sure there are spaces between the data items. The Report Writer handles all these things automatically, with only the minimum of procedural statements by the programmer.

There are no exercises for this frame.

S2   A typical report: FD of a report file

Suppose your task is to prepare a Sales Analysis report from sales records
which contain the following information

Col	1	Area code
	2–5	Salesman number
	6–11	Date of sale DDMMYY
	12–17	Value of sale 9(4)V99.

The file of records for a month is held in ascending salesman number
within area. The desired report has the following appearance:

	MONTHLY SALES ANALYSIS		PAGE 1
AREA	SALESMAN	DATE OF SALE	AMOUNT
1	1001	01 01 83	27.46
1	1001	07 01 83	100.00
SALESMAN TOTAL		127.46	
1	1002	01 01 83	50.00
1	1002	21 01 83	100.00
SALESMAN TOTAL			150.00
AREA TOTAL			277.46
	⋮		
	⋮		
GRAND TOTAL			9900.46

There are three control breaks in this report – change of salesman number, change of area number and end of report.

If the report is to be produced by the Report Writer, the File Section of
the program will be

```
FILE SECTION.
FD   sales-file
     RECORD CONTAINS 17 CHARACTERS.
01   sales-record.
     03   area-code       PIC 9.
     03   salesman-no     PIC 9999.
     03   sale-date       PIC 9(6).
     03   sale-value      PIC 9(4)V99.
FD   print-file
     REPORT IS sales-analysis.
```

There are no exercises for this frame.

S3   The REPORT SECTION

The report layout and control breaks are defined in the Report Section, which is the last section in the Data Division. The description comprises an RD clause (report description), which specifies the control breaks, followed by level 01 entries to describe the lines of the report.

The report description for our example could be:

```
REPORT SECTION.
RD   sales-analysis
        CONTROLS ARE FINAL
              area-code
              salesman-no
        PAGE LIMIT 55 LINES.
```

The CONTROLS ARE clause defines the control breaks in major-to-minor order, i.e. the most significant control break first (the one that prints last) and the least significant control break last (the one that prints first). FINAL is a keyword for the control break that occurs at the end of the report. PAGE LIMIT tells the Report Writer to throw to a new page and print out heading lines when the line number specified is reached.

The RD entry is followed by 01 entries for the lines. These differ from the usual 01 entries in several respects:

1 They can be given a TYPE. TYPE PAGE HEADING means the line is a page heading to be printed automatically on each new page. TYPE DETAIL means the line is a detail line, to be printed under the control of the Procedure Division. TYPE CONTROL FOOTING followed by a control break data-name means the line is a total line, to be printed automatically when the control break occurs.
2 Names of records and fields can be omitted. Only the detail line usually needs a name.
3 The LINE clause specifies how the paper is to be advanced. LINE 1 means print on the first line, LINE PLUS 1 means print one line after the previous line, LINE PLUS 2 means print with double spacing, and so on.
4 The fields in the record are specified to start in a particular column of the page by a COLUMN clause. Fillers are not needed; the Report Writer automatically inserts spaces between the fields.
5 It is not necessary to move data to the fields. The SOURCE clause is used to state where the data comes from.
6 Totals can be accumulated in a field by the SUM clause.

The entries for our example will show the use of these features in practice.

```
01   TYPE PAGE HEADING.
     03   LINE 1.
          05   COLUMN 11        PIC X(22)
                    VALUE "MONTHLY SALES ANALYSIS".
          05   COLUMN 40        PIC X(4)    VALUE "PAGE".
          05   COLUMN 45        PIC Z9      SOURCE PAGE-COUNTER.
     03   LINE 2.
          05   COLUMN 1         PIC X(4)    VALUE "AREA".
          05   COLUMN 10        PIC X(8)    VALUE "SALESMAN".
          05   COLUMN 20        PIC X(12)   VALUE "DATE OF SALE".
          05   COLUMN 36        PIC X(6)    VALUE "AMOUNT".
01   sales-line
     TYPE DETAIL
     LINE PLUS 1.
     03   COLUMN 2         PIC 9
             SOURCE area-code.
     03   COLUMN 11        PIC 9(4)
             SOURCE salesman-no.
     03   COLUMN 20        PIC 99B99B99
             SOURCE sale-date.
     03   COLUMN 34        PIC ZZZ9.99
             SOURCE sale-value.
01   TYPE CONTROL FOOTING salesman-no
     LINE PLUS 1.
     03   COLUMN 9         PIC X(14)
             VALUE "SALESMAN TOTAL".
     03   COLUMN 33        PIC Z(4)9.99 SUM sale-value.
01 TYPE CONTROL FOOTING area-code
     LINE PLUS 1.
     03   COLUMN 9         PIC X(10)
             VALUE "AREA TOTAL".
     03   COLUMN 32        PIC Z(5)9.99 SUM sale-value.
01 TYPE CONTROL FOOTING FINAL
     LINE PLUS 1.
     03   COLUMN 9         PIC X(11)
             VALUE "GRAND TOTAL".
     03   COLUMN 31        PIC Z(6)9.99 SUM sale-value.
```

In this example:

1 PAGE-COUNTER is a reserved word for the page counter which is automatically updated by the Report Writer.
2 The first record describes two lines which are to be printed on the page heading.
3 The second record describes the detail line, which is printed under the control of statements in the Procedure Division (see next frame).
4 The last three records describe the lines to be printed out at the control break specified, i.e. change of salesman, change of area and final.

The SUM clause means that the total of all the preceding 'sale-value's which have been printed out is to be accumulated in the field concerned, i.e. every time a detail line is printed, 'sale-value' is added in the fields in columns 33, 32 and 31, respectively, in the last three records. This breaks the usual rule about not using an edit-picture item for arithmetic, but the Report Writer caters for this. These fields are automatically cleared back to zero when the lines they are in are printed out.

Exercise

1 The SUM clause can also be used with the name of a total field accumulated for a less significant control break – provided, of course, that field has been given a name. This can save the machine doing a lot of additions when accumulating the higher-level totals. Amend the example in this frame so that the area total is summed from the salesman total and the grand total is summed from the area total. Also arrange for the total lines to come with double, triple and quadruple line spacing, respectively.

S4   Procedure Division entries

Three special verbs are provided to handle the report. These are

1 INITIATE report-name, which initialises the page counter and arranges for the heading to be printed before the first detail line.
2 GENERATE record-name, which arranges for the printing of the detail line (all other lines are printed automatically).
3 TERMINATE report-name, which arranges for the final control break to be handled. This counts as a control break for **all** the control fields.

Applying these to our example, the entire Procedure Division would appear as follows assuming the presence of an appropriate condition name eof-sales.

```
PROCEDURE DIVISION.
A1-Produce-Report.
    OPEN OUTPUT print-file
    INITIATE sales-analysis
    OPEN INPUT sales-file
    PERFORM UNTIL eof-sales
        READ sales-file
        AT END
            set eof-sales true
        NOT AT END
            GENERATE sales-line
        END-READ
    END-PERFORM
    TERMINATE sales-analysis
    CLOSE sales-file
        print-file
    STOP RUN.
```

These are all the statements required to write the report as described in frame S2.

N.B. There is no exercise for this frame, but it would be instructive to consider the coding needed to produce the identical results of this example without using the Report Writer feature.

Answers – Section S

Frame S3

```
1 01   TYPE CONTROL FOOTING salesman-no
       LINE PLUS 2.
       03   COLUMN 9              PIC X(14)
               VALUE "SALESMAN TOTAL".
       03   salesman-total  COLUMN 33   PIC Z(4)9.99
               SUM sale-value.
  01   TYPE CONTROL FOOTING area-code
       LINE PLUS 3.
       03   COLUMN 9              PIC X(10)
               VALUE "AREA TOTAL".
       03   area-total  COLUMN 32   PIC Z(5)9.99
               SUM salesman-total.
  01   TYPE CONTROL FOOTING FINAL
       LINE PLUS 4.
       03   COLUMN 9              PIC X(11)
               VALUE "GRAND TOTAL".
       03   COLUMN 31            PIC Z(6)9.99
               SUM area-total.
```

T Direct Access Files

T1 Disks and disk drives

A disk drive records information on the surfaces of a disk. The basic principle is that a read–write head positioned very close to the disk surface magnetically records the information while the disk is revolving, effectively writing a string of ones and zeros on a circular track on the surface of the disk. It can equally detect the changes in magnetism that denote the difference between a one and a zero, and thus it is able to read the information stored on the disk. By moving the head to different distances from the centre of the disk, many separate concentric tracks can be accessed, or in some high-speed devices a separate head is provided for each track, thus avoiding the need for physical movement of the head.

The number of tracks (and therefore the data capacity) depends upon the size of the disk itself and the quality of the recording surface. Disks range from the $3\frac{1}{2}$ inch diskettes used in personal computers, through the so-called hard disks, up to clusters of disks mounted on a common spindle, usually known as disk packs. Even the humble $3\frac{1}{2}$ inch diskette will normally have data recorded on both its surfaces, and this gives it a capacity of over 1 million characters. Disk packs are typically arranged so that several hundred tracks can be recorded on their surfaces, and with 20 or more surfaces available they are capable of storing hundreds of millions of characters. (There are about half a million characters in this book.)

Figure T.1 illustrates a disk-pack system with a comb of read–write heads attached to a moving access arm. In such a system, the tracks that are accessible to the read–write heads in any one position are known as a cylinder. In the above diagram, there are 10 tracks in a cylinder. A diskette formatted to have 80 tracks on each side will contain 80 cylinders, each of two tracks. It will be appreciated that any record can be accessed directly, provided its position is known, as follows:

1 Move the read–write heads to the appropriate cylinder (this is called a seek).
2 Select the required track (called a head switch).
3 Wait for the disk to rotate until the desired record is under the read–write head (a search).
4 Transfer the data record into the computer.

These operations are undertaken automatically by the operating system, and, as will be explained shortly, they do not concern the programmer from the point of view of the program logic. However, programmers are often expected to be able to estimate how much time will be taken up in accessing records on files, for this has the most direct influence on how quickly the program will run, and for this purpose a knowledge of the characteristics of the backing storage device is needed.

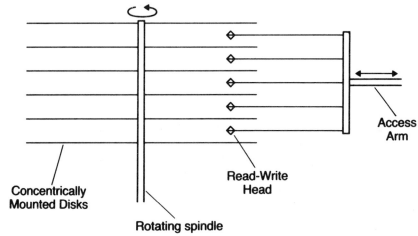

Fig. T.1 The disk pack

Exercises

1 How many cylinders would there be on a disk pack that had 20 surfaces and 200 tracks on each surface?
2 About how much data can be held on one cylinder of a disk pack consisting of six disks (i.e. ten surfaces), if each track contains 8000 characters?
3 About how much data can be held in total on a 6-disk pack with 400 cylinders and 8000 characters per track?
4 Is the data on the innermost tracks recorded with greater, less or the same density as data on the outermost tracks?

T2 Sequential file organisation

Sometimes a distinction is made between a sequentially organised file, in which records are stored in the order dictated by data recorded in some key field of the record, and a serially organised file, in which the records are not in any kind of key order. There is no difference between these two in COBOL. Although the difference may affect the logic of the program, both cases are sequential files to COBOL, meaning that the only order in which records can be read back into the machine is the order in which they were written.

A sequential file on disk is usually created by recording the records one after the other along a track. When the end of a track is reached, recording is continued on the next track of the same cylinder. This technique reduces seek activity, which can be time-consuming; a seek to an adjacent cylinder is made only when the first cylinder is full of data. A seek to an adjacent cylinder usually takes a few milliseconds. Some systems record data simultaneously through more than one write head, increasing the rate of data transfer.

Several files may be held on one disk, or on one disk pack (provided, of course, that the files are small enough), and the operating system ensures that one file does not get mixed up with another. For example, it may become necessary to add records at the end of a file (this is allowed in COBOL by declaring OPEN EXTEND file-name before writing to the file). In such a case the file may need more space than was allocated to it when it was created. With most computer systems the operating system will automatically allocate more space, although this may not be contiguous with the area occupied by the original portion of the file. The method of telling the operating system (from within a COBOL program) how much disk space to reserve for a file is not standard, but varies according to the computer system being used. Most systems allow the programmer to stipulate how much space to reserve in the first instance, and how much additional space to reserve each time the previous allocation becomes full. It is usually possible to stipulate the maximum space that may be occupied by the file, and if this space becomes insufficient, an error condition arises.

For a straightforward sequential file on disk, the FILE-CONTROL statement (in the INPUT-OUTPUT section of the ENVIRONMENT DIVISION) is as follows:

```
FILE-CONTROL.
    SELECT example-file ASSIGN TO DISK
        ORGANIZATION IS SEQUENTIAL.
```

We can omit the words ORGANIZATION IS and just code

```
SELECT example-file ASSIGN TO DISK SEQUENTIAL.
```

or, for that matter, we can omit any mention of its organisation, since COBOL assumes sequential by default. However, if you do include it, notice that COBOL insists that ORGANIZATION is spelt with a Z.

The keyword DISK varies according to the type of computer, and in its place we can use a non-numeric literal, such as the name by which the file is known to the operating system. For example, under MS-DOS we might code:

```
SELECT example-file ASSIGN TO "A:EXFILE.DAT".
```

A disk file described in this way is processed in exactly the same way as a magnetic tape file, except that, being a disk file, it can be updated by over-writing particular occurrences of existing records, a process that is called 'update-in-place'. This can be advantageous in terms of processing time and programming convenience, but it is disadvantageous in terms of security since the previous version of the record is destroyed. This has to be overcome in practice by making copies of the records before updating, as a back-up.

To perform an update-in-place it is necessary to issue a REWRITE command following a READ of the record concerned. When a READ command is issued, the COBOL system remembers the location of the record that was read; when a REWRITE command is executed for a sequential file, the record is written back to that same location. The programmer, of course, has arranged for it to be amended in memory between these two operations. The fact that the sequential file is to be updated 'in place' is signified by opening the file for I-O (meaning that it is to be treated as both an input and an output file).

An example will clarify. Suppose a sequential file exists, containing 80-character records. If a record contains nothing but zeros, it is to be replaced by a record containing the characters **ALL ZEROS** (followed by 67 spaces).

```
FILE CONTROL.
    SELECT diskfile ASSIGN TO DISK SEQUENTIAL.
    :
FD   diskfile.
01   diskrec     PIC X(80).
    :
PROCEDURE DIVISION.
A1-Process-diskfile.
    OPEN I-O diskfile
    PERFORM UNTIL eof-diskfile
        READ diskfile RECORD
        AT END
            MOVE "end" TO eof-flag
        NOT AT END
            IF diskrec = ALL "0"
            THEN
                MOVE "**ALL ZEROS**" TO diskrec
                REWRITE diskrec
            END-IF
        END-READ
    END-PERFORM.
```

To summarise the processing of sequential files on disk:

OPEN OUTPUT – a WRITE statement places the record in the next sequential location.

OPEN INPUT – a READ gets the record from the next sequential location.

OPEN I-O – a READ gets the record from the next sequential location; a REWRITE replaces the record at the location of the last record read

OPEN EXTEND – a WRITE statement places the record at the next sequential location beyond the previous end of the file.

There are no exercises for this frame.

T3   Direct access by RELATIVE KEY

This permits access to a record by nominating the number of the record, counting from ('relative' to) the beginning of the file. This 'relative record number' is put in a RELATIVE KEY data item in working storage. Knowing where the file starts, and the size of the records, the operating system automatically calculates the physical address for the retrieval or storage of the record.

It is usual for the relative record number to have some relationship to the data in the record to which it points. Occasionally it may be possible to use the logical record key directly as a relative record number, for example, a customer orders file might have customer order numbers running upwards from 1, but more often the value has to be calculated from the data by an algorithm known as a key transformation (or 'hashing') function.

The File-control paragraph would appear as

```
FILE-CONTROL.
    SELECT personnel-file ASSIGN TO DISK
        ORGANIZATION IS RELATIVE
        ACCESS MODE IS RANDOM
        RELATIVE KEY IS record-number.
```

If ACCESS MODE IS RANDOM is not declared, the compiler will assume that the file is to be read sequentially in relative record number order (in other words, it will assume ACCESS MODE IS SEQUENTIAL, which is the default). In fact, if you are going to read the file sequentially, there is no need to specify the RELATIVE KEY, since it is not used – unless, that is, you intend to use the START verb, which is explained in frame T4.

It may be appropriate here to underline the difference between the organisation of a file and the access mode in which it is processed. The ORGANIZATION of a file is a fixed physical attribute that cannot be changed, after the file is created, by any declaration in the program. The

ACCESS MODE can vary from program to program, provided that it is compatible with the file's organisation (you could not, for example, declare a sequentially organised file for random access). It might be thought that ACCESS MODE, being something local to the program, would be better declared in the File Definition than in File-control, where the ORGANIZATION clause ascribes the attribute 'global' to all programs; this view has some support from CODASYL, but it is not yet incorporated in the COBOL standard.

An outline of the Data Division for this file could be

```
FILE SECTION.
FD   personnel-file.
01   pers-record.
     03   payroll-no     PIC 9(5).
     ⋮
WORKING-STORAGE SECTION.
⋮
     03   record-number PIC 9(5) USAGE COMPUTATIONAL.
```

A relative file in random access mode can be opened for input (READ statements allowed); output (WRITE statements allowed); input–output (READ, REWRITE and DELETE statements allowed, the last logically removing the record from the file so that it cannot be retrieved by later READ statements). The INVALID KEY clause is available with all these verbs, to detect various error conditions that may arise (e.g. an attempt to READ or DELETE records that are not there).

Suppose that there are 1000 records in the file called 'personnel-file', corresponding to payroll numbers 10,001 to 11,000. A program is to accept from the user a payroll number (storing this in the data-item 'w-pay-no'), retrieve the corresponding personnel record and display this. In this example a very simple key transformation function is used, which subtracts 10,000 from the payroll number. The Procedure Division entries (in outline) could be

```
OPEN INPUT personnel-file
⋮
ACCEPT w-pay-no
SUBTRACT 10000 FROM w-pay-no GIVING record-number
READ personnel-file
INVALID KEY
    DISPLAY "Payroll Number not on file"
    (take other error actions)
NOT INVALID KEY
    (prepare output from pers-record)
    (display output to user)
END-READ
```

The possibility of processing a relative file sequentially has already been mentioned. It is also possible to process such a file **dynamically** (a mixture of random and sequential access). This facility is the same as that described in the next frame, for indexed files.

There are no exercises for this frame.

T4   Indexed files

Probably the most popular form of organisation for direct access is the indexed file (often called indexed-sequential). This is popular because the file can be accessed either sequentially (in the order dictated by a key field data item in the record, which may be a different order from that in which the records were created) or directly (by specifying the key of the desired record), or in a combination of these two modes.

Briefly, the physical address of a record of known key is traced by the computer through a hierarchy of indexes. The mechanics of this vary slightly from one system to another; the important thing for the programmer is that he or she can process the file in record key order, as if it were a straightforward sequential file, or process individual records directly, in any order. The problem of how the data is stored is handled automatically.

To process an indexed file sequentially in record key order, the File-control statements would be

```
SELECT personnel-file ASSIGN TO DISK
    ORGANIZATION IS INDEXED
    ACCESS MODE IS SEQUENTIAL
    RECORD KEY IS employee-number.
```

'Employee-number' is the name of a field in the record description entry of 'personnel-file'; it should be of alphanumeric data-type. (Contrast this with the RELATIVE KEY of a relative file, which must **not** be a part of the file record, and must be of numeric data-type.) In sequential access mode, the indexed file can be opened for OUTPUT, and the WRITE verb used to create the file by writing records in record key order; it can be opened EXTEND, in which case the WRITE verb adds records, still in key order, at the end of an existing file; it can be opened for INPUT, and the READ verb used in the same way as for a sequential file; or it can be opened for I-O, and updated-in-place by REWRITE or DELETE statements. READ takes the AT END clause under these circumstances; the other verbs take the INVALID KEY clause.

It is also possible to arrange for sequential processing to begin at some place other than at the first record of the file, by using the START verb. For example, if in the above case we wanted to start processing at employee-number 10,000, we could code

```
OPEN INPUT personnel-file
MOVE "10000" to employee-number
START personnel-file
INVALID KEY
    DISPLAY "Employee number 10,000 not found"
NOT INVALID KEY
    PERFORM UNTIL end-of-pers-file
        READ personnel-file
        AT END
            MOVE "end" TO end-of-pers-file-flag
        NOT AT END
            (process the personnel record)
        END-READ
    END-PERFORM
END-START
```

In the above case, no file processing could be done at all if employee number 10,000 did not exist. However, we could code

```
MOVE "10000" TO employee-number
START personnel-file
    KEY NOT LESS THAN employee-number
(or:-
    KEY GREATER THAN OR EQUAL TO employee-number)
```

This would enable us to start on number 10,000 if it were there, or otherwise on the first record with a key greater than 10,000. (The other variant that is allowed is KEY GREATER THAN – this would not get us number 10,000, but would start at the next higher key.) If the first two characters of the employee number were in fact a department code, thus:

```
03   employee-number.
    05   department    PIC XX.
    05   emp-serial    PIC XXX.
```

then the above example would still work, except if there were no records for department 10, then it would start processing at department 11, and we might not want this. We can specify a sub-field of the key, provided that it starts at the beginning of the whole key, so we could code

```
MOVE "10" TO department
START personnel-file
    KEY = department
INVALID KEY
    DISPLAY "No records for department 10"
etc.
```

The START verb always looks for the first record in the file that satisfies the key criterion, and if no such record exists then the INVALID KEY statement is executed. It is important to understand that the START verb does not read a record, but gives a value to a record pointer, so that a sequential READ statement can then retrieve the record.

The START verb can give us a form of random processing even while the access mode is sequential, since we can use START to put the appropriate value into the record pointer, followed by READ to retrieve the record at that position in the file. This would be appropriate in a program where the majority of the processing was sequential, but a small amount of random processing was required.

To use the START verb, the file must be opened for INPUT or I-O. The use of the START verb is exactly the same for relative files as it is for indexed files, except that you cannot have a sub-field of a RELATIVE KEY.

To process an indexed file randomly, e.g. to read a record from 'personnel-file' by specifying the desired record key in employee-number, the File-control paragraph would contain:

```
SELECT personnel-file ASSIGN TO DISK
    ORGANIZATION IS INDEXED
    ACCESS MODE IS RANDOM
    RECORD KEY IS employee-number.
```

'personnel-file' may now be opened for INPUT (for reading an existing record of stated employee-number), OUTPUT (for writing a new record of stated employee-number) or I-O (for reading or writing as before, or for rewriting or deleting an existing record of stated employee-number). All these verbs take an INVALID KEY clause; in the case of READ, REWRITE and DELETE this clause is executed if there is no record with the stated key, whereas in the case of the WRITE verb the clause is executed if there is already a record on the file with the stated key. The START verb cannot be used if the access mode is RANDOM. The following example shows how a record on an indexed file is updated during random processing:

```
OPEN I-O indexed-file
⋮
MOVE "1234" TO indexed-file-key
READ indexed-file
INVALID KEY
    DISPLAY "Record " indexed-file-key " not found"
NOT INVALID KEY
    ⋮
    (processing to change record contents)
    ⋮
```

```
REWRITE indexed-file-record
INVALID KEY
    ⋮
    (error procedure)
    ⋮
END-REWRITE
END-READ
```

An INVALID KEY on a REWRITE will occur only if there is no record on the file with the stated key; since we do not intend to change the value of the record key between READ and REWRITE, this should not happen.

An indexed file may be processed partly sequentially and partly randomly, by specifying ACCESS MODE IS DYNAMIC. In this case, all the facilities of random access mode apply, but in addition the file may be read sequentially from the point of the last record accessed directly, or from a point specified in a START statement, by a special form of the READ command:

```
READ personnel-file NEXT [RECORD]
AT END . . .
[NOT AT END . . .]
END-READ
```

It should be appreciated that before any of the random access facilities of indexed organisation can be used, the file must first have been created by writing sorted records to it while open for OUTPUT. (Frame V6 explains how the SORT verb can be used for this purpose.) This initial creation allows the operating system to create the necessary indexes; after creation, the indexes are maintained automatically. Some versions of COBOL allow new files to be opened for I-O, with RANDOM or DYNAMIC access mode, in which case records can be written to the new file in any order, but this is not always to be recommended, since in some cases it will result in an untidy file, on which access times will be high.

Exercise

1 An 'assemblies' file containing 100-character records has been created with indexed organisation, the record key being 'assembly-no' which is located in the first 10 characters of the record. 'Assembly-no' is in two parts: a five-digit 'assembly-group' followed by a five-digit 'sub-assembly'. The records in the file make logical groups, each group comprising one header record for the whole assembly (zeros appear in the sub-assembly field), followed by a variable number of sub-assembly records. The sub-assembly records have the same number for 'assembly-group' as appeared in the header record, but each sub-assembly record has a unique and non-zero number in the sub-assembly field.

A program is to be written to list out the details of all the records for a given assembly. The number of the desired assembly is input from the keyboard; there may be many enquiries to process in a given run. The enquiries may be made in any order.

Sketch out the File-control, Record Description and Procedure Division entries necessary for this program.

T5 ALTERNATE indexes

A very powerful feature available on larger compilers is the ALTER-NATE RECORD KEY facility. This allows the programmer to specify that some other field in the record, in addition to the unique record key primarily chosen to govern the logical sequence of the file, is to be the subject of an index that will allow access to the records. A record of nominated alternate key may then be accessed directly, or the records may be accessed in alternate key sequence. The alternate record key need not have unique values within the file, i.e. the same key value may appear in more than one record.

The following example shows how a 'sale' record may be accessed by 'sale-no', 'customer-no' and 'salesman-no'.

```
FILE-CONTROL.
    SELECT sales ASSIGN DISK INDEXED
        ACCESS SEQUENTIAL
        RECORD KEY sale-no
        ALTERNATE RECORD KEY customer-no WITH DUPLICATES
        ALTERNATE RECORD KEY salesman-no WITH DUPLICATES
    ⋮
FD  sales.
01  sale-record.
    03  sale-no        PIC X(5).
    03  customer-no    PIC X(4).
    03  salesman-no    PIC XXX.
    03  sale-details etc. . . .
```

The file is created initially by writing records to it sorted on 'sale-no':

```
OPEN OUTPUT sales
[repeat until end of input file]
    READ input-file
    AT END
        [set end-of-input-file true]
    NOT AT END
        WRITE sale-record FROM input-record
        INVALID KEY
            [handle error]
        END-WRITE
    END-READ
```

Provided that the records on the input file are sorted in 'sale-no' order, the only thing that would cause invalid key on the WRITE statement is if writing the record would cause the file to be extended beyond any maximum file allocation declared by the programmer.

With the file created, subsequent programs may SELECT it in SEQUENTIAL, RANDOM or DYNAMIC access mode as needed. Additions to the file, e.g. as a result of a WRITE of a new record while the file is open for I-O, will result in all three indexes being updated. The only other change from regular indexed file processing is that programs that read the file must specify, in the READ statement, which index is to be used. For example, to retrieve the first sale record for customer number 27:

```
MOVE "0027" TO customer-no
READ sales
     KEY IS customer-no
INVALID KEY
     PERFORM No-such-customer
NOT INVALID KEY
etc.
```

The system will continue to consider that 'customer-no' is the key of the record, e.g. in a READ NEXT statement, until a further KEY IS clause is executed. So, to read all the records for customer number 27, continuing from the last example,

```
PERFORM UNTIL customer-no NOT = "0027"
        OR end-of-file-flag = "true"
    READ sales NEXT
    AT END
        MOVE "true" TO end-of-file-flag
    NOT AT END
        [process sale record]
    END-READ
END-PERFORM
etc.
```

There are no exercises for this frame.

T6   FILE STATUS

The AT END clause (for sequential operations) and the INVALID KEY clause (for direct access operations) provide paths for the program to take when an input/output operation is not successful. There are times when it is useful to have more information about the result of a file operation than is conveyed by these clauses, and that is where the FILE STATUS word comes in. A two-digit area is declared in working-storage, for preference arranged so that each digit can be examined separately, such as:

```
01   file-status-word.
     03    status-one    PIC 9.
     03    status-two    PIC 9.
```

This data item is then referenced in the SELECT statement, as shown (a relative file is used here for illustration):

```
SELECT rel-file ASSIGN TO DISK
     ORGANIZATION RELATIVE
     ACCESS DYNAMIC
     RELATIVE KEY rel-key
     FILE STATUS IS file-status-word.
```

The principle is that the system reports back after every input/output operation, placing values in the two digits of the status word. In general, a zero in the first digit indicates a successful operation, and a zero in both digits means 'nothing abnormal to report'. As an example, a value of '02' means 'duplicate key detected' on an indexed file; this is a good illustration of how the file status is more informative than the invalid key clause. Another point in its favour is that it reports back on OPEN and CLOSE operations, and even allows the program to 'trap' an error condition which would otherwise have caused the program to crash. For example, an attempt to open for input a file that does not exist will cause an error termination and a return to the operating system, but if a file status item has been declared for the file, this can be interrogated after the open statement has been executed. If it contains the value '35', this means that the file was not present, and appropriate action can therefore be taken.

A FILE STATUS word can be used with any file organisation, but its use is perhaps not so necessary with sequential files, where the processing is generally straightforward. With direct access files, it should be used as a matter of course.

The ANSI COBOL standard defines 28 different file status values – too many to describe in detail here, but they may be looked up in a COBOL manual. In addition, there can be many more (all with a first digit of 9), which are called 'implementor-defined' and which are specific to the particular COBOL system that you are using. Details of these can be obtained from the manual for your COBOL system.

There are no exercises for this frame.

T7   Variable-length records

Records in a single file can have different lengths. Using a personnel system as an example, there may be a mixture of different types of update record – a change of marital status may involve just a couple of small fields but a new employee record could have hundreds of characters. The RECORD CONTAINS clause of a file's FD is used to indicate that a file contains variable-length records.

```
RECORD IS VARYING IN SIZE
    [FROM integer-1] [TO integer-2] CHARACTERS
    DEPENDING ON data-name-1
```

Integer-1 indicates the size of the smallest record and integer-2 indicates the size of the largest record.

Data-name-1 must be an elementary unsigned integer field and is used to hold the actual size of the current record being processed. For reading of records, the operating system puts the actual size of the record read in data-name-1. For writing of records, the programmer must put the size of the current record in data-name-1 before the write statement is executed – only the number of characters specified by the contents of data-name-1 will be written. In this latter case, COBOL 89's LENGTH function can help – see Section W.

There are no exercises for this frame.

Answers – Section T

Frame T1

1 200.
2 10 × 8,000 = 80,000 characters.
3 400 × 80,000 = 32 million characters.
4 With higher density. There is the same amount of data on each track; the tracks nearer to the centre are shorter than the outer tracks, therefore the data must be recorded more densely.

Frame T4

```
1 FILE-CONTROL.
      SELECT assemblies ASSIGN TO DISK
      ORGANIZATION IS INDEXED
      ACCESS MODE IS DYNAMIC
      RECORD KEY IS assembly-no.
   ⋮
   FD   assemblies.
   01   assembly-rec.
        03   assembly-no.
             05   assembly-group      PIC X(5).
             05   sub-assembly         PIC X(5).
        03   other-contents            PIC X(90).
   ⋮
```

```
PROCEDURE DIVISION.
    OPEN INPUT assemblies
    [repeat until no more enquiries]
        [accept enquiry]
        MOVE required-assembly-group TO assembly-group
        MOVE ZEROS TO sub-assembly
        READ assemblies
        INVALID KEY
            [display message 'ASSEMBLY NOT FOUND' etc.]
        NOT INVALID
            [repeat until assembly-group not equal to required-
            assembly-group OR end of assemblies file]
            READ assemblies NEXT RECORD
            AT END
                [set end of assemblies true]
            END-READ
        END-READ
    [end-repeat]
```

U Subprograms and Nested Programs

U1 The object program library

We have already met the concept of a program library with the COPY statement (frame R1). The COPY verb causes the compiler to include code in your program at compilation time by copying statements from the COBOL source statement library.

It is also possible to bring object programs into the machine, at execution time, by copying from the object program library. Just as a utility was used to enter source statements into the source statement library, so a utility, often summoned by the general operating system of the computer, is used to enter object code into the object program library.

This object code may have been produced by COBOL compilations, or it may be the object code resulting from compilation of a program written in some other language.

In practice, the object code that results from any COBOL compilation will usually include calls to many standard subroutines which reside in the object program library. The programmer is not usually made aware of these calls. Typical standard routines would include conversion of a decimal number to an internal binary number; blocking and deblocking records; and locating a record on an indexed file given the record key. The COBOL compiler arranges for this sort of subroutine call to be made automatically.

The logic of compilation and execution may now be described as in Fig. U.1. B/F and C/F stand for Brought Forward and Carried Forward, respectively.

This chart suggests that the object program under development is itself added to the object program library. In practice the library is split up into a production library and development libraries. Programs under test may be stored in one of the development libraries; a program is entered into the production library only when it is fully tested and operational.

During development, the object program produced by the compiler may be loaded straight into the machine at step 4, omitting step 3; but the object program may alternatively be saved and loaded directly into the machine, thereby avoiding recompilation every time the program is to be run.

Exercises

1 In Fig. U.1, the object program library is not used at step 2. Explain why this may not be strictly true.
2 Can you develop a COBOL program without knowing anything about the object library?

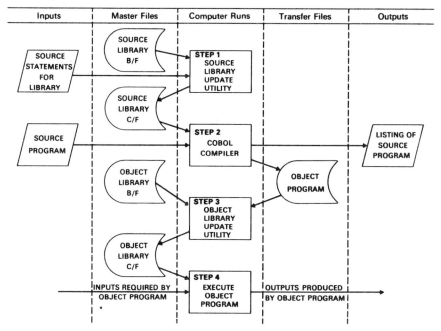

Fig. U.1 Compilation and execution using the source statement and object program libraries

U2   The CALL statement

COBOL includes facilities to allow the programmer to call up a subroutine that resides in the object program library. This usually requires passing information to the subroutine via one or more **parameters**, i.e. variables or constants, which are to be used by the subroutine. A subroutine in the object program library is popularly called a **subprogram** to distinguish it from a subroutine executed by a PERFORM statement within a program.

If we considered the Population Explosion problem (Appendix B) to have two distinct components, one to exercise overall control of reading the input and producing the results, the other to print a page of results, the latter of these two components could have been implemented as a subprogram. It would expect two parameters to be passed, the starting population and the growth factor. With these, it can get on with the job of calculating the new populations and printing the lines to make up a page of results. In the calling program, these parameters are normal data areas in the Data Division – it is their additional use as a link to a subprogram that makes them parameters.

A simplified general form of the CALL statement is:

CALL subprogram-name
    USING   {[BY REFERENCE] {parameter} ...}
            {BY CONTENT {parameter} ...   }   ...

Notice that several parameters may be specified and that each parameter is called by **reference** or by **content**. By default, a parameter is called by reference. With **call by reference**, a subprogram has access to the actual data areas in the calling program associated with the parameter, whereas with **call by content**, a copy only of the data within a parameter's area is passed so that the subprogram cannot affect the parameter data areas back in the calling program. Except where a subprogram needs specifically to pass data back to a calling program, it is safest to call by content.

If in the Population Explosion main program, we have placed the starting population in a variable called wa-starting-population and the growth factor in a variable called wa-growth-factor, we could code in the main program:

```
CALL "PRINTPAGE"
     USING BY CONTENT wa-starting-population
                      wa-growth-factor
```

PRINTPAGE must be the name of the subprogram in the object library. You will need to check in your technical manual for the exact syntax of an object library name as it varies between different manufacturers. The parameters must be listed in the order expected by the subprogram and must have pictures expected by the subprogram; after the subprogram has been executed, control passes to the COBOL statement following the CALL statement. Thus, CALL has a similar logic to PERFORM except that the latter refers to procedures in the same program and so has no need to pass parameters.

Exercise

1 In a set of COBOL programs to process the loan and return of library books, one subprogram is used to check whether a book is overdue and to calculate the appropriate fine. Three parameters are passed to it:

(i) today's date
(ii) the date a book was issued
(iii) an area for the fine (zero if book not overdue)

Provide a CALL statement for such a subprogram, making up appropriate names.

U3   The called subprogram

The called subprogram may be written in any language the computer manufacturer allows for this purpose because being in the object library, and therefore in machine code, it is independent of the original source language. Your technical manual will tell you how to call subprograms that were not written in COBOL. If both calling and called programs are written in COBOL, apart from the name of the object program, the calling conventions are defined by the standard.

A COBOL subprogram is a normal complete COBOL program except that it has to cater for parameters passed from the calling program and be able to return control to the calling program when the logical end of the Procedure Division is reached.

Accepting the parameters

When a **call by reference** is specified in the calling program, the subprogram actually works on the calling program parameter's data area back in that program. COBOL's calling mechanism creates the link between a subprogram's reference to its parameter name and the data area of the calling program's parameter name.

With **call by content**, the data in the calling program's parameter data area is transferred to the subprogram's parameter data area at the time of calling, so that even though the subprogram can alter this local data, it cannot affect the data back in the calling program.

We have already seen in frame U2 that parameters in a calling program are declared as normal in its Data Division. With called programs, however, a special declarative LINKAGE SECTION within the Data Division is used to specify parameters, and a special form of the Procedure Division heading is used to indicate the order of parameters:

PROCEDURE DIVISION [USING parameter-1
                          [parameter-2] . . .]

The parameter names need not be the same as those in the calling program (though they can be) but they must appear in the same order and should have the same picture as those specified in the CALL statement.

Return to the calling program

This is the logical equivalent to STOP RUN in a main program, but instead of actually stopping, control is returned to the statement following the CALL in the calling program. It is achieved by the statement EXIT PROGRAM.

Continuing the example of frame U2, if the subprogram were written in COBOL it might appear as follows (a mixture of COBOL and pseudo-code is used in the Procedure Division):

```
IDENTIFICATION DIVISION.
  ⋮
DATA DIVISION.
  ⋮
LINKAGE SECTION.
01  parameters.
      03  starting-population     PIC 9(10).
      03  growth-factor           PIC 9(6)V9(9).
PROCEDURE DIVISION USING starting-population
                        growth-factor.
  ⋮
      MOVE starting-population TO next-population
      repeat for each decade
          COMPUTE next-population ROUNDED =
              next-population * growth-factor
          ON SIZE ERROR
              print size error line
              EXIT PROGRAM
          NOT ON SIZE ERROR
              compute the density
              ON SIZE ERROR
                  print size error line
                  EXIT PROGRAM
              NOT ON SIZE ERROR
                  print line of results
              END-COMPUTE
          END-COMPUTE
      EXIT PROGRAM.
```

Note how EXIT PROGRAM is used in several places. Strictly, one entry point and one exit point is the best guide for subprograms but a practical variation, as above, is to have error exit points rather than introducing forward GO TOs or complex error flag mechanisms. On exiting, to prevent any unusual happenings the next time the subprogram is executed, COBOL will ensure that any PERFORM loops left 'open' will be 'closed'.

Actually, the last EXIT PROGRAM is not strictly necessary because an implicit EXIT PROGRAM will be assumed if the machine 'runs out of code', i.e. if the physical end of the Procedure Division is reached. However, it is always better to use an explicit EXIT PROGRAM.

INITIAL and CANCEL – initialising a subprogram

Normally, when a subprogram is exited, the state of all the local variables will remain as they are so that when the next call of that subprogram takes place, execution can continue with the same data values. This is the usual requirement and also would be the case if local PERFORMs were used instead of subprograms. Sometimes, however, you want to start with a new copy of the subprogram every time. You achieve this in one of two ways:

(i) By adding to the Program-Id entry in the Identification Division of the subprogram:

   PROGRAM-ID. program-name IS INITIAL PROGRAM.

   This will cause all data areas that had VALUE clauses to be reset to their original values **every time** the subprogram is called. This is usually when a subprogram is solving a sub-problem that is relatively independent of the total problem and requires, say, all its totals to be set to zero each time.

(ii) By using the CANCEL statement in the Procedure Division of the calling program.

   CANCEL program-name

   Usually, this is used when you do not need a subprogram in the immediate future and it has the effect of clearing the subprogram from memory, thereby leaving space for other routines. If that subprogram is wanted again during the same execution period of the main program, a new copy will have to be brought in from the object library and it will be in its initial state.

EXTERNAL – sharing files and data areas

Files are not allowed as parameters. Therefore, if you want to refer to the same file in different programs, you need to add the EXTERNAL attribute to the file declaration in all such programs, e.g.

```
IDENTIFICATION DIVISION.
PROGRAM-ID. first-program.
   :
DATA DIVISION.
FILE SECTION.
FD   main-file IS EXTERNAL
     RECORD CONTAINS 60 CHARACTERS.
01   main-record.
     03   first-field          PIC X(10).
   :
```

```
IDENTIFICATION DIVISION.
PROGRAM-ID. second-program.
   ⋮
DATA DIVISION.
FILE SECTION.
FD   main-file IS EXTERNAL
     RECORD CONTAINS 60 CHARACTERS.
01   main-record.
     03  first-field        PIC X(10).
   ⋮
```

The items declared as EXTERNAL must have exactly the same name in all programs. At execution time, as long as these programs are linked together so that they are in the same 'run unit', they will share access to the single file main-file with its single record area main-record. In the same way, any data items can be declared EXTERNAL so that several programs may share a common data area. However, unless such data items are being shared amongst many programs, it is often better to use the more controlled approach of separate programs having their own data areas and communicating via parameters.

Exercises

1 With reference to Exercise 1 in frame U2, provide a Linkage Section and Procedure Division heading for the subprogram called in that exercise.
2 It was stated in the text that parameters in calling and called programs should have the same picture. This is not strictly true as it is sufficient that they are compatible. Can you suggest in what important respects the pictures should be similar?
3 You are designing a subprogram which is to operate on several fields in the calling program. How can you avoid passing all the names as parameters?

U4   Nested programs

With the subprograms considered above, a main program and a subprogram are independent modules in the object library. In larger software development systems where you may have many different people developing related programs, it can be useful to have some data areas in the main program also available to several other programs without them being subprograms or without using parameters. Such areas are termed **global** and are made available through having programs physically contained (**nested**) within other programs. The concept of nesting has been introduced to COBOL in the 1985 standard.

Consider the example below.

```
IDENTIFICATION DIVISION.
PROGRAM-ID. level-1.
    ⋮
IDENTIFICATION DIVISION.
PROGRAM-ID. level-2A.
    ⋮
END PROGRAM level-2A.
IDENTIFICATION DIVISION.
PROGRAM-ID. level-2B.
    ⋮
END PROGRAM level-2B.
END PROGRAM level-1.
```

This is a main program containing two other programs. END PRO-GRAM is an end-of-program marker that we could have used with single programs but it was not needed because the physical end of a single pro-gram occurs when it runs out of statements! However, with nested pro-grams, the marker is needed to indicate the physical end of one program and the beginning of another. The name that is used with END PRO-GRAM must be the same as the program name in the PROGRAM-ID clause.

GLOBAL – making items available to contained programs

To allow any files and data items in the level-1 program to be referred to in not only its own Procedure Division but also by either of the lower level programs, they need to be declared GLOBAL, e.g. if the level-1 program contained:

```
FILE SECTION.
FD   transaction-file IS GLOBAL
     RECORD CONTAINS 36 CHARACTERS.
01   transaction-record.
        ⋮
```

the inner programs could then refer to the file and any data items in the record description without any definition in their own Data Division. Individual data items in Working-Storage can also be made global, although restricted use of this facility is recommended because there is less scope for errors filtering through program systems if data areas are kept as local as possible. However, in large software systems developed in a team environment, it can be useful during testing for a main program to provide just global file declarations and data areas to allow full checking of the lower-level routines.

If there is a clash of names, e.g. the same name appearing as a global declaration in the Data Division of the level-1 program and also as a separate declaration in the Data Division of the level-2A subprogram, then COBOL will always assume that you are referring to the most local data area, i.e. a reference to the name in the Procedure Division of level-1 would refer to the declaration in level-1 but a reference to that same name in the Procedure Division of level-2A would refer to the completely different data area within the local level-2A program.

Notice that the main difference between GLOBAL and EXTERNAL is that contained programs can refer to global items without any further declaration, but externally declared items must appear as complete declarations in all programs that are sharing such items. Files and data items cannot be declared both GLOBAL and EXTERNAL.

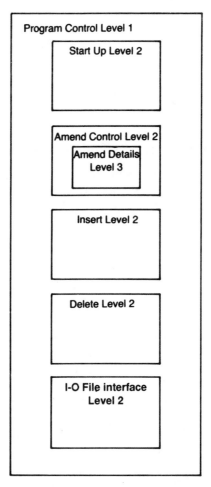

Fig. U.2 A possible nesting of programs for an on-line file update system

COMMON – calling outside the nesting hierarchy

For separately compiled subprograms, there are no restrictions on which programs can call other programs as they are completely independent. With nesting, however, a hierarchy for the calling of subprograms is automatically assumed. Unless subprograms indicate otherwise, a main or nested program at any level can only call a subprogram that it contains at the next level down. Many large programs do not fit into this neat hierarchy, therefore COBOL provides extra constructs to cope with more complex situations. Consider Fig. U.2, which illustrates a possible hierarchy of a set of nested programs for an on-line update problem. All the level-2 subprograms are nested within the level-1 program and there is a single level-3 subprogram which can refer to global data areas both in Amend Control and Program Control.

In Fig. U.2, Program Control can call any of the level-2 programs but it cannot make a direct call of Amend Details; it has to go through Amend Control. However, now look at Fig. U.3 which illustrates the logical interrelationship between the modules.

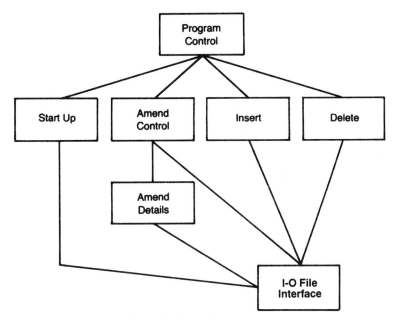

Fig. U.3 A structure chart for the on-line file update system

All the subprograms except Program Control want to call the I-O File Interface module, yet this cannot be possible with the current nesting because it is contained only by Program Control. One solution would be to make I-O File Interface a separately compiled subprogram as considered in frame U3, but if you wished to preserve the nesting, another solution is to override the normal calling hierarchy for such modules by making them **common**. This is indicated in the Program-Id statement, e.g.

```
PROGRAM-ID. io-file-interface IS COMMON.
```

The subprogram would then be able to be called by any other program within that single set of nested programs. A program that is COMMON can also be INITIAL (described in frame U3).

It may seem very complicated to set up a structure of subprograms when internal paragraphs can be performed more simply within one program. This may be true for small software systems but when you have a large number of programs that are dependent upon one another and you have programming teams, it is good to develop fully tested subprograms either as separately compiled object library modules or within a nested environment.

Exercise

1 Consider Fig. U.4 where there is a lot of inter-communication between modules. If the whole set of modules were to be developed in a single COBOL nested environment, draw a diagram similar to Fig. U.2 to show the nesting structure and indicate which subprograms, if any, would need to be COMMON.

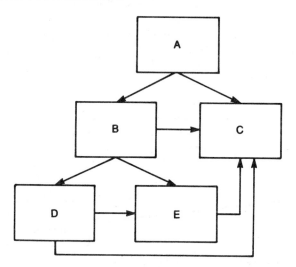

Fig. U.4 Example structure chart for a real-time problem

Answers – Section U

Frame U1

1 All programs of any complexity are likely to include calls to subroutines which reside on the object program library and a COBOL compiler is a complex program.
2 Yes. Introductory programming does not need knowledge of the object library and you may have already developed several programs without being aware of this library. In fact, especially if you are working in a microenvironment, source and object programs are often grouped together without thinking of their being grouped into libraries.

Frame U2

```
1 CALL "OBJECT/PRG46"
       USING
            BY CONTENT todays-date
            BY CONTENT issue-date
            BY REFERENCE fine-due
```

You may have used any appropriate name for the object library sub-program. The first two parameters should be called by content because they contain data to be used by the subprogram, but the fine due must be called by reference, as this value is calculated in the sub-program and needs to be available to the calling program once control is returned.

Frame U3

1 One possible solution for dates in the form YYDDD.

```
LINKAGE SECTION.
01   parameters.
     03   todays-date          PIC 9(5).
     03   issue-date           PIC 9(5).
     03   fine-due             PIC 9999V99.
PROCEDURE DIVISION USING todays-date
                         issue-date
                         fine due.
```

2 They must have the same length.
   Numeric items used in arithmetic should have the same USAGE and decimal points should be in the same position.
3 Group together all the fields in the calling program and pass the single group field as the parameter. Parameters may be either 01, 77 or elementary fields.

Frame U4

1

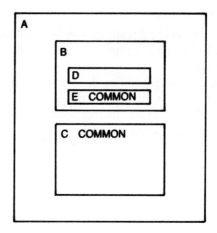

Fig. U.5 Nesting structure for the real-time problem

E needs to be common as it is called by D. C needs to be common as it is called by B, D and E.

V Sorting

V1 Sorting concepts

The purpose of a sort is to place the records of a file into a certain order. Suppose that in a payroll system you have a file that recorded the hours worked by weekly-paid employees, as follows.

Payroll No	Name	Hours worked
0027	Abel D.	27
2146	Baker J.	40
1270	Cooke S.	40
2000	Digby M.	38
0199	Edwards C.	30
1100	Francis H.	42
	etc.	

and you wished to match these against a master payroll file which contained employee records in payroll number order (one record per employee). Clearly the time records file shown above must be resequenced (sorted) into the same order as the master file.

Sorting is a ubiquitous activity in computer systems and the way in which the computer achieves it is quite complex and beyond the scope of this text – it is sufficient to understand that there is a program provided with the computer that will read in a file and produce a new version of it sorted according to your instructions. Sorting is often done by stand-alone utilities – that is to say, programs that are called up from the operating system – but COBOL provides a SORT verb which enables you to perform the sorting from within your COBOL program.

In this example, the payroll number is called the **key field** of the sort, i.e. it is the field that contains the data that determines whereabouts in the file the record should be located. The file could be sorted either into ascending order (lowest numbered record at the start of the file) or descending order (highest number at the start of the file).

Sorting the time records file on a computer (whether in a COBOL program or not) would work broadly like this: the records are read in (the first pass) and transferred to a work-file on backing storage; the records in the work-file are then shuffled about until they are in sequence, finally being output (the last pass) either to the same file in which they were to start with, or to a new file.

During the first pass the records are read into the computer in their original order. During the last pass they are output in key sequence, making the sorted file.

Exercise

1 If the six records of the file above were sorted in descending order, using hours-worked as the key field, which record would appear first on the sorted file?

V2   Major and minor keys

Sometimes it is desired to sort a file on more than one key field. Suppose the management wanted a report of hours worked in descending value of hours. There may be many employees who have worked the same number of hours, and the report is to list these employees in ascending payroll number order. Hours-worked is the **major** key field and payroll-number is the **minor** key field for this sorting operation, and you need to sort 'time-records' on ascending payroll-number within descending hours-worked. This will mean that the first record on the file after it is sorted will be that of the employee who has worked the most hours; if more than one employee has worked this number of hours, the one with the highest payroll number will appear last within this group.

Key fields with numeric pictures are compared algebraically, i.e. negative numbers are lower than positive numbers. All other fields are compared character by character according to the 'collating sequence' of the computer. The two most common collating sequences are known as EBCDIC and ASCII, and their most important differences are in the relative position of upper- and lower-case letters, and numbers. EBCDIC places the upper-case letters after the lower-case and before the numbers, whereas ASCII puts the numbers first, followed by upper-case, then lower-case letters. In the Environment Division of a COBOL program you can specify that a particular collating sequence is to be used; COBOL uses the names STANDARD-1 and STANDARD-2, usually standing for ASCII and EBCDIC, respectively, although you are advised to consult the reference manual for your particular COBOL compiler on this point. To

invoke the ASCII sequence you would code PROGRAM COLLATING
SEQUENCE IS STANDARD-1 in the Object-Computer paragraph of
the Configuration Section, otherwise the collating sequence native to the
machine will be used. Facilities exist to invoke non-standard collating
sequences – again, consult the reference manual.

There are no exercises for this frame.

V3   The SORT verb

In its simplest form, the SORT verb is used to sort an input file to create a
sorted output file. Both files are defined with conventional FD entries.

An extra working file must also be defined, with an SD entry (Sort-file
Description). This file is simply an intermediate file which is used to
achieve the sort. The SD entry is followed by the record description (01)
entries. The file name specified in an SD entry must be SELECTed and
ASSIGNed in the Input-Output Section (FILE-CONTROL paragraph) of
the Environment Division just as any other file, but some manufacturers
make special provision for the name of the device to which a sort-file is
assigned. The ORGANIZATION clause is not used as this is decided by
the particular compiler you are using. In use, the verb might appear as follows:

```
FILE SECTION.
SD   work-file.
01   time-work.
        03   payroll-no   PIC X(4).
        03                PIC X(44).
        03   hours-worked PIC 99.
FD   time-records.
01   time-record-in   PIC X(50).
FD   sorted-time-records.
01   time-record-out  PIC X(50).
PROCEDURE DIVISION.
P1-sorting.
     SORT work-file ON
          DESCENDING KEY hours-worked
          ASCENDING KEY payroll-no
          USING time-records
          GIVING sorted-time-records
     STOP RUN.
```

This program simply prepares the sorted output file 'sorted-time-records'
for use by a subsequent program, e.g. a program to produce the management report. The keys are specified major first, minor last, i.e. in decreasing
significance (this does not have to be the order in which they appear in the
record). The keys are all fields in the record belonging to the sort-file, and

since none of the rest of the data (such as the name) is relevant, no data name has been provided. The sort works as though 'time-record-in' is moved to 'time-work' to be sorted and then moved to 'time-record-out' after sorting. The keywords USING and GIVING specify the names of the unsorted input file and the sorted output file, respectively.

Note that there is neither an OPEN nor a CLOSE statement for the three files; these functions are performed automatically when the SORT verb is used (though you may occasionally find compilers in which this automatic opening and closing applies only to the sort-file).

Had management required the report with ascending hours worked, as well as ascending payroll number, we could have prepared the sorted file with:

```
SORT work-file
    ON ASCENDING KEY hours-worked payroll-no
    USING time-records
    GIVING sorted-time-records
```

If we simply sorted the file on the single sort key of hours-worked, what do you think would happen to all the duplicate values? There is no problem, because all the records with identical keys would appear next to each other in the sorted output file, but we could not predict anything about their order within the block of identical keys. If we wish, we can make sure that records with identical keys are output to the sorted file in the same order in which they appeared on the input file. To do this we simply code:

```
SORT work-file
    ON ASCENDING KEY hours-worked
    WITH DUPLICATES IN ORDER
    USING etc.
```

Exercise

1 A file contains unsequenced 100-character records for books in a library. The author's name is in the first 20 characters, classification in the next 10 characters and title in the remaining characters. Sketch out Data Division and Procedure Division entries to sort this file into title within author within classification (ascending).

2 Will the resulting file be in the sequence the librarian expects?

V4   Own coding – first pass

In the preceding frame, the output file contained exactly the same data as the input file. Only the sequence differed. Suppose you wished to modify, delete or add to the records input to the sort?

To do this, you need to introduce your own coding into the logic of the first pass of the sort. This will save writing and running a separate program to create a modified input file for the sort. To achieve this, replace the USING option in the SORT statement by:

```
INPUT PROCEDURE IS procedure-name-1
                [THRU procedure-name-2]
```

This defines a paragraph or section (or group of paragraphs or sections) in which you read the input file in the usual non-sort way, then prepare the modified or amended record in the data record of the sort-file, and when the record is ready you code 'RELEASE record-name', where 'record-name' is the name of the sort-file record. If you wish to delete a record, you simply do not RELEASE it to the sort. It is helpful to think of RELEASE as a WRITE statement, which writes the record onto the sort-file.

Imagine, for the example in frame V3, that you wanted to prepare a sorted output file only for employees who had worked more than 40 hours. The records for all other employees are to be omitted. With the same Data Division entries, this could be achieved by writing:

```
PROCEDURE DIVISION.
A1-Main.
    OPEN INPUT time-records
    SORT work-file ON
        ASCENDING KEY hours-worked payroll-no
        INPUT PROCEDURE IS B1-First-pass-coding
        GIVING sorted-time-records
    CLOSE time-records
    STOP RUN.
B1-First-pass-coding.
    PERFORM UNTIL eof-time-records
        READ time-records
        AT END
            MOVE "end" TO eof-time-records-flag
        NOT AT END
            MOVE time-record-in TO time-work
            If hours-worked > 40
            THEN
                RELEASE time-work
            END-IF
        END-READ
    END-PERFORM.
```

A better method would have been to define the hours worked field in the input record and inspect its value there, without moving it to the sort record. This would also allow you to use the option

```
"RELEASE time-work FROM time-record-in"
```

thereby eliminating the MOVE instruction.

Exercise

1 Modify your answer to Question 1, frame V3, so that records with all blanks in the classification field do not appear in the output file.

V5   Own coding – last pass

Just as you can control records on the first pass with RELEASE, so you can get hold of records on the last pass with the RETURN statement. In this case you specify 'OUTPUT PROCEDURE IS procedure-name', instead of the GIVING clause in the SORT statement. RETURN is a type of READ statement which reads the sort file and makes the record available to the output file, and therefore it has an AT END option.

Suppose in the example of frame V3, you wanted to prepare not only the report of employees who had worked more than 40 hours, but also a complete sorted file of all employees (both outputs sorted on payroll-number within hours-worked). Assuming a suitable print file (with a record called 'print-line') had been described, we could code

```
OPEN OUTPUT sorted-time-records print-file
SORT work-file ON
    ASCENDING KEY hours-worked payroll-no
    USING time-records
    OUTPUT PROCEDURE IS B1-Last-pass-coding
CLOSE sorted-time-records print-file
STOP RUN.
B1-Last-pass-coding.
    PERFORM UNTIL eof-work-file
        RETURN work-file
        AT END
            MOVE "end" TO eof-work-file-flag
        NOT AT END
            WRITE time-record-out FROM time-work
            If hours-worked > 40
            THEN
                WRITE print-line from time-work
            END-IF
        END-RETURN
    END-PERFORM.
```

Exercise

1 RELEASE is followed by the name of the sort-file record, whereas RETURN is followed by the file name. Why?

V6   Other file organisations

Although the sort-file must be sequentially organised, there is no such restriction on either the input ('USING') file or the output ('GIVING') file, which can just as well be of RELATIVE or INDEXED organisation. This is useful, for example, when creating an indexed file, since you can take an unsorted set of data (on a sequential input file), sort it into the required order and output it to an indexed file, all in one operation. Furthermore, you are not restricted to one output ('GIVING') file; you can specify multiple output files. In the creation of an indexed file, you may wish to produce a listing on the printer at the same time. This can easily be done by selecting a (sequential) print file as well as the indexed file, and coding the SORT statement as follows:

```
SORT sort-work-file
    ON ASCENDING KEY key-field
    USING    input-file
    GIVING   indexed-file
             print-file
```

Exercise

1 Write the Data Division statements for a sequential input file, a sort work file and an indexed output file which is to be created from the sorted input file. The records are to be 100 characters long, and the first eight characters contain an item-number which is to be used as the record key. Then write a SORT statement that will sort the input file in ascending item-number order and output it to the indexed file.

V7   The MERGE verb

This allows two or more input files, which are already in the same sequence, to be merged together to form a single output file.

The MERGE verb works on a sort-file in the same way as SORT, and the syntax of the two verbs is practically identical, except that MERGE cannot have own-coding on the first pass. As with the SORT verb, there can be multiple output files, and their organisations can be sequential, relative or indexed. The complete format is given in Appendix D.

There are no exercises for this frame.

Answers – Section V

Frame VI

1 The record for payroll number 1100.

Frame V3

```
1 FILE SECTION.
  SD sort-work.
  01  sort-work-rec.
      03  author-name      PIC X(20).
      03  classification   PIC X(10).
      03  book-title       PIC X(70).
  FD  books-in.
  01  books-in-rec         PIC X(100).
  FD  books-out.
  01  books-out-rec        PIC X(100).
  PROCEDURE DIVISION.
  A1.
      SORT sort-work
          ON ASCENDING KEY
              classification author-name book-title
          USING books-in
          GIVING books-out
      STOP RUN.
```

2 Probably not. The file will be in the order dictated by the collating
sequence of the computer. The librarian would probably want the file
sequenced according to the indexing rules of the library. The latter do
all sort of things the computer does not, e.g. 'ignoring' spaces, expand-
ing abbreviations to full words (Dr to be filed under 'doctor'), translat-
ing numbers into words ('2001 – a Space Odyssey' to be filed under
'twothousandandone').

Frame V4

```
1     SORT sort-work
          ASCENDING KEY etc.
          INPUT PROCEDURE IS B1-Drop-blanks
          GIVING books-out.
      ⋮
  B1-Drop-blanks.
      PERFORM UNTIL eof-books-in
          READ books-in
          AT END
              MOVE "true" TO eof-books-in-flag
          NOT AT END
              EVALUATE classification = SPACES
                  WHEN FALSE
                      RELEASE sort-work-rec
                          FROM books-in-rec
              END-EVALUATE
          END-READ
      END-PERFORM.
```

Frame V5

1 RELEASE is akin to the WRITE verb, whereas RETURN is akin to the READ verb. Turn back to frame G2, Exercise 3, if you are not sure why WRITE operations need the record name rather than the file name.

Frame V6

```
1 FD   seq-file.
  01   seq-file-rec    PIC X(100).
  FD   ind-file.
  01   ind-file-rec.
       03   item-no    PIC X(8).
       03              PIC X(92).
  SD   sort-work-file.
  01   sort-rec.
       03   key-area   PIC X(8).
       03              PIC X(92).
  ⋮
  SORT sort-work-file
       ON ASCENDING KEY key-area
       USING seq-file
       GIVING ind-file
```

Notice that the item-number field is defined within the indexed file record even though it is not needed for the SORT. It will, however, be needed for the creation of the indexed file, and will have been referenced (as the RECORD KEY) in the File-Control paragraph.

W Intrinsic Functions

W1 COBOL 89

In 1989, an addition to the 1985 ANSI (American National Standards Institute) and ISO (International Standards Organisation) COBOL standards was made. This was announced as Addendum 1 of the 1985 standard, but some people have adopted the term COBOL 89. This Addendum defines a set of intrinsic functions to satisfy a variety of common computing needs. Such functions are not new to programming languages in general but it has been seen as an area in which COBOL was lacking.

'Intrinsic' means 'belonging to' or 'inherent to' the language, emphasising that these are predefined functions rather than ones that a programmer has to create. COBOL has already provided something like these predefined functions, e.g. the reserved word DATE. When used with the ACCEPT statement, DATE provides the current date in the format YYMMDD. However, if the full 4-character version of the year were required so that a comparison, say, could be made between dates in the 20th and 21st centuries, this was not provided by standard COBOL. COBOL 89 introduces a CURRENT-DATE function which, amongst other information, provides the date in the form YYYYMMDD.

These intrinsic functions can be used in other contexts in the Procedure Division rather than just with the ACCEPT statement. Functions are classified as integer, numeric or alphanumeric. Integer and numeric functions can only be used as part of an arithmetic expression, normally on the right-hand side of a COMPUTE statement. Alphanumeric functions would normally be used with MOVE. For example, the above CURRENT-DATE is classified as alphanumeric and could be part of a MOVE statement so that the full date is retrieved and moved to another field within the program:

```
MOVE FUNCTION CURRENT-DATE TO ws-full-date-field
```

Each use of an intrinsic function is prefixed by the reserved word FUNC-TION and some of the functions, like the example above, have no arguments (or parameters) but others do. The arguments may be identifiers, literals or arithmetic expressions, depending upon the type of function. The ANSI standard does not define specific error procedures for invalid arguments but, in most cases, these are likely to cause runtime errors.

The various functions are discussed in detail in the rest of this section, each frame containing related functions. There are 42 intrinsic functions in total.

There are no exercises for this frame.

W2   Date functions

The complete set of date-oriented intrinsic functions is

- CURRENT-DATE – returns 21 positions of date/time information
- DATE-OF-INTEGER – converts an integer to calendar date format
- DAY-OF-INTEGER – converts an integer to Gregorian date format
- INTEGER-OF-DATE – converts calendar date to an integer
- INTEGER-OF-DAY – converts Gregorian date to an integer
- WHEN-COMPILED – returns compile date/time information

N.B. The Gregorian date format is also known as the Julian date format.

CURRENT-DATE and WHEN-COMPILED are alphanumeric. The other four functions are integer.

Here is a typical Data Division entry to hold the information returned by calling CURRENT-DATE. It provides the full YYYYMMDD date, detailed local time information and an indication of how local time relates to Greenwich Mean Time (GMT).

```
WORKING-STORAGE SECTION.
01  wa-current-date-and-time.
    03  wa-todays-date.
            05  wa-current-year              PIC 9999.
            05  wa-current-month             PIC 99.
            05  wa-current-day               PIC 99.
    03  wa-todays-time.
            05  wa-current-hour              PIC 99.
            05  wa-current-minute            PIC 99.
            05  wa-current-second            PIC 99.
            05  wa-current-hundredth         PIC 99.
    03  wa-time-offset.
            05  wa-current-offset            PIC X.
            05  wa-current-offset-hours      PIC 99.
            05  wa-current-offset-minutes    PIC 99.
```

'+' for local time ahead of or same as GMT, '−' for local time behind GMT and 0 if an offset is not provided by your system

Current hours and minutes offset from GMT

It is likely that such an entry would be part of a source library so that all programs in the same department or team could use the one standard date definition.

A Procedure Division statement to retrieve the date is:

```
MOVE FUNCTION CURRENT-DATE TO
                    wa-current-date-and-time
```

and usually, for dates, this would be executed once in an initialisation module. However, for time-dependent operations related to interactive I-O, the CURRENT-DATE would have to be accessed several times in a program.

Determining the number of days between two dates has always been a problem that has had to be solved carefully. Some of the factors that need to be considered are:

the varying number of days per month
whether the two dates are in the same or different years
whether either of the years are leap years.

The DATE-OF-INTEGER, DAY-OF-INTEGER, INTEGER-OF-DATE and INTEGER-OF-DAY functions are provided to make this operation simpler. An arbitrary date of Sunday 31 December 1600 has been fixed as a base date and either INTEGER-OF-DATE or INTEGER-OF-DAY applied to a date, returns an integer value which is the number of days since the base date, e.g. 1st January 1601 returns 1 as it is 1 day later than the base date. This early base date was chosen to allow for applications that hold a lot of historical data but to have gone much earlier would be more controversial because a correction was made to the calendar in 1582. The integer result can be used to derive the day of the week (see Question 3 of frame W4). Also, the subtraction of two such integers derived from different dates gives the number of days between the two dates.

The INTEGER-OF-DATE function has an argument that represents a date in the form YYYYMMDD and INTEGER-OF-DAY's argument represents a date in the Gregorian form YYYYDDD. However, not only do these two functions produce an integer as a result but they also require the date argument to be provided as an integer, i.e. a PIC 9s field. Normally, a date is in a group field and therefore alphanumeric, so such a group field can be redefined as an integer. For example, the Working-Storage entry for CURRENT-DATE could be redefined as follows:

```
WORKING-STORAGE SECTION.
01  wa-current-date-and-time.
        03  wa-todays-date.
                05  wa-current-year          PIC 9999.
                05  wa-current-month         PIC 99.
                05  wa-current-day           PIC 99.
```

```
      03   wa-todays-time.
             05   wa-current-hour              PIC 99.
             05   wa-current-minute            PIC 99.
             05   wa-current-second            PIC 99.
             05   wa-current-hundredth         PIC 99.
      03   wa-time-offset.
             05   wa-current-offset            PIC X.
             05   wa-current-offset-hours      PIC 99.
             05   wa-current-offset-minutes    PIC 99.
01   wa-current-date-integer REDEFINES
                                  wa-current-date-and-time.
      03   wa-todays-date-integer              PIC 9(8).
      03                                       PIC X(13).
```

After the function CURRENT-DATE has been called, the date part in YYYYMMDD format is available as an integer in wa-todays-date-integer and it is this latter data-name that is used as an argument to INTEGER-OF-DATE.

As an example of the use of these date/integer functions, assume a program needs to calculate the age, in days, of debts, i.e. customers have bought goods on a certain purchase date and a program is trying to determine if the age of any debt exceeds a certain figure, say, 30 days. Assuming that fa-purchase-date-integer contains the date of purchase in a redefined form of a YYYYMMDD date as above, then calculation of the age of debt could be :

```
COMPUTE wa-age-of-debt =
    FUNCTION INTEGER-OF-DATE (wa-todays-date-integer) -
        FUNCTION INTEGER-OF-DATE (fa-purchase-date-integer)
```

The purchase date has a lower integer result as it should be earlier than today's date and is, therefore, subtracted from today's date.

Integer results can be converted back to normal date forms by applying the functions DATE-OF-INTEGER or DAY-OF-INTEGER, e.g. applying the function DAY-OF-INTEGER to the value 1 returns 1601001, the 1st January 1601 in Gregorian format.

Here is an example of converting a 'standard' YYYYMMDD date to its equivalent YYYYDDD Gregorian date by applying INTEGER-OF-DATE to generate an integer value representing the number of days since 31st December 1600, then applying DAY-OF-INTEGER to convert this figure to a Gregorian format. It also illustrates the use of a function call within a function call.

```
COMPUTE wa-gregorian-date-integer =
    FUNCTION DAY-OF-INTEGER
        (FUNCTION INTEGER-OF-DATE (wa-standard-date-integer))
```

Here, wa-gregorian-date-integer is a PIC 9(7) redefining a YYYYDDD format and wa-standard-date-integer a PIC 9(8) redefining a YYYYMMDD format.

These functions are also very useful for adding a figure to a date, e.g. a library book can be on loan for 2 weeks from the current date:

```
COMPUTE wb-return-date =
    FUNCTION DAY-OF-INTEGER (FUNCTION
        INTEGER-OF-DAY (wb-todays-date) + 14)
```

The function WHEN-COMPILED is a useful 'version control' facility. There are usually several different versions of a program available in a system at any one time and most programmers have experienced the confusion of relating the execution of a program to the wrong source program. This is true both during initial development of software and when a program is undergoing maintenance. This function allows an executing program to be linked to its equivalent source version by providing the date and time of compilation of the source program, from which, the object program was created. If WHEN-COMPILED is used, the compiler passes relevant information on to the object program.

Here is an illustration using Working-Storage entries very similar to those for the CURRENT-DATE function because the date and time information returned from WHEN-COMPILED is in the same format as that function.

```
WORKING-STORAGE SECTION.
    01   wa-compile-date-and-time.
        03   wa-compile-date.
            05   wa-compile-year            PIC 9999.
            05   wa-compile-month           PIC 99.
            05   wa-compile-day             PIC 99.
        03   wa-compile-time.
            05   wa-compile-hour            PIC 99.
            05   wa-compile-minute          PIC 99.
            05   wa-compile-second          PIC 99.
            05   wa-compile-hundredth       PIC 99.
            05   wa-compile-offset          PIC X.
            05   wa-compile-offset-hours    PIC 99.
            05   wa-compile-offset-minutes  PIC 99.
            ⋮
PROCEDURE DIVISION
⋮
        MOVE FUNCTION WHEN-COMPILED TO wa-compile-date-and-time
        DISPLAY "The compile date is   " wa-compile-day "/"
                                         wa-compile-month "/"
                                         wa-compile-year
```

Exercises

1 Delay loops may be used for displaying messages on a screen for a period of time. Here is example pseudo-code which assumes that no delay greater than 1 minute is required.

get start system seconds
get new system seconds
DO UNTIL new system seconds > start system seconds + delay
   get new system seconds
   IF new system seconds < start system seconds
      add 60 to new system seconds
  ENDIF
ENDDO

The IF statement is required within the loop because a new time in the next minute would cause the number of seconds to start from zero again. Using the Working-Storage date description at the beginning of this frame and adding any other declarations, provide suitable code to implement this delay loop.

2 Remote transactions from Eastern North America and the United Kingdom are collected and logged at a central site in the United Kingdom. The transactions are sent with their local date and time in the format of the CURRENT-DATE function but the logged time has to be GMT (Greenwich Mean Time). Using the declarations:

```
03   wa-gmt-hour          PIC 99.
03   wa-gmt-minute        PIC 99.
```

and the Working-Storage date description at the beginning of this frame, provide Procedure Division code that converts all local times to GMT time, assuming that all local times are full hours behind or the same as GMT and that a local time is always provided. British Summer Time can be ignored for UK transactions. For this example, also assume that transactions are sent during normal working hours only so that the GMT time will always be on the same day as the local time.

3 A report is required of debtors who have not paid invoices within a 30-day period. Assuming that the invoice date is available as an integer version of YYYYMMDD in fb-invoice-date-integer and the system date is available as an integer version of YYYYMMDD in wa-todays-date-integer, provide an IF statement as part of the report program, that executes the paragraph c2-process-old-debt if the invoice is older than 30 days.

W3   MAX/MIN functions

- MAX – returns the maximum of the supplied arguments
- MIN – returns the minimum of the supplied arguments
- ORD-MAX – returns the position of the maximum in the argument list
- ORD-MIN – returns the position of the minimum in the argument list

ORD-MAX and ORD-MIN are of type integer. The type of MAX and MIN depends upon the type of their arguments.

The MAX, MIN, ORD-MAX and ORD-MIN functions are separated from the statistical functions of frame W4 because, though normally applied to numerical arguments, they can also be used with non-numerical data. Comparison of non-numerical data follows the same rules as for alphanumeric comparison, e.g. 'B' is greater than 'A' and characters are compared from left to right. If the arguments can be of mixed case, it may be wise to convert to the same case first – see frame W6.

Here are some examples of all four functions using constant arguments to illustrate their operation.

FUNCTION MAX (1,6,3,-5) = 6
FUNCTION ORD-MAX (1,6,3,-5) = 2 as the largest is in the 2nd position
FUNCTION MIN (1,6,3,-5) = -5
FUNCTION ORD-MIN (1,6,3,-5) = 4 as the smallest is in the 4th position
FUNCTION MAX ("LONDON", "CARDIFF","EDINBURGH") = "LONDON" as the 'L' in 'LONDON' is greater than the 'C' of 'CARDIFF' and the 'E' of 'EDINBURGH'
FUNCTION ORD-MIN ("LONDON", "CARDIFF", "EDINBURGH") = 2 as 'CARDIFF' is the 2nd entry and 'C' is lower than 'E' or 'L'

For all these functions, if there is more than one maximum/minimum value, it is the leftmost maximum/minimum value that is returned, e.g.

FUNCTION ORD-MAX (1,2,6,6) = 3 as the leftmost largest value is in the 3rd position.

The following examples illustrate these functions in various program contexts, the first within an IF statement.

```
IF FUNCTION MAX (wg-main-stock-group,
                 wg-subsid-stock-group,
                 wg-internal-stock-group) > wa-stock-limit
   DISPLAY "warning - largest stock group is exceeding limit"
END-IF
```

MAX can have any number of arguments but returns just the largest as the function value. Here, the largest of the three wg variables is compared against the contents of wa-stock-limit and a message displayed if it is greater than this limit.

An alphanumeric example for MIN is provided below. All the variables contain the name of a country within a continent and each has a PIC X(20).

```
COMPUTE wb-first-country =
    FUNCTION MIN (wb-african-country,
                  wb-european-country,
                  wb-american-country,
                  wb-asian-country)
```

If the four arguments contained Kenya, France, Canada and China, left-justified within their 20 characters, after execution of this statement, wb-first-country would contain Canada as this is the lowest in the alphabet working from left to right, i.e. the same rules for comparison as in a simple condition.

If the continent of the country lowest in the alphabet were also required, ORD-MIN could be used as follows:

```
DISPLAY wb-first-country " is in "
EVALUATE FUNCTION ORD-MIN (wb-african-country,
                           wb-european-country,
                           wb-american-country,
                           wb-asian-country)
    WHEN 1 DISPLAY "Africa"
    WHEN 2 DISPLAY "Europe"
    WHEN 3 DISPLAY "America"
    WHEN 4 DISPLAY "Asia"
END-EVALUATE
```

The above two examples for MAX and MIN are fairly limiting because the functions are being applied to a small number of arguments, whereas many applications might require the maximum or minimum value from a table/array of values. It would be tedious for a programmer to have to specify all the elements of a table separately, so the reserved word ALL is used to specify every element.

As an example, a company has a maximum of 120 salespeople and the amount each one of them has sold over a certain period is held in the one-dimensional table:

```
01  wb-salesperson-earnings-table.
    03  wb-one-salesperson-earnings    PIC 9(6)V99
                                       OCCURS 120 TIMES.
```

Assume that any unused elements of the table are set to zero. The largest amount sold can be derived by the following Procedure Division statement:

```
COMPUTE wd-largest-earnings =
    FUNCTION MAX (wb-one-salesperson-earnings(ALL))
```

If, in addition, the position of the salesperson with the largest earnings were required, ORD-MAX could be used, e.g.

```
COMPUTE wb-max-sales-position =
    FUNCTION ORD-MAX (wb-one-salesperson-earnings(ALL))
CALL pr4-display-top-salesperson
    USING BY CONTENT wb-max-sales-position
```

This passes to a subprogram pr4-display-top-salesperson, the current position in the table of the element with the largest value, e.g. if the largest value were in wb-one-salesperson-earnings (48), the function would return 48. In the code above, this integer value is then passed to the subprogram BY CONTENT so that the subprogram has access only to this number rather than to the table itself. The subprogram might use this value to reference a relative file or another table of salesperson names.

With multi-dimensional tables, ALL can be used several times as a subscript or there can be a mixture of ALL and specific subscript references if only a part of a table needs to be examined. ALL can be used with any of the intrinsic functions where a variable number of arguments is allowed.

Exercise

1 A set of monthly rainfall figures is held in the following table:

```
01   wb-monthly-rainfall-table.
     03   wb-one-months-rainfall     PIC 9(4)
                                     OCCURS 12 TIMES.
```

Provide Procedure Division code to return the amounts and month numbers (in the range 1–12) with the maximum and minimum rainfall amounts. The results are to be put into wa-max-monthly-rainfall, wa-min-monthly-rainfall, wa-max-month, wa-min-month, respectively. Assume, for this example, that no two rainfall figures are the same.

W4   Statistical functions

As these are well-established functions that have been present in scientific languages for many years, discussion and examples are provided for just a selection of them. However, a complete list is provided first, related functions being grouped together. They are all of integer or numeric type.

- SUM – returns the sum of the arguments
- MEAN – returns the arithmetic mean of the arguments
- MEDIAN – returns the middle entry of the arguments, once they are sorted into order
- MIDRANGE – returns the mean of the minimum and maximum arguments
- RANGE – returns the maximum minus the minimum of the arguments
- FACTORIAL – returns the factorial of the integer argument

- SQRT – returns the square root
- INTEGER – converts a decimal number to the lowest integer, taking account of signs

- INTEGER-PART – truncates a decimal number to just its integer part
- REM – returns the remainder of argument-1 divided by argument-2
- MOD – returns argument-1 modulo argument-2

- RANDOM – returns a pseudo-random number
- STANDARD-DEVIATION – returns the standard deviation of the arguments
- VARIANCE – returns the variance of its arguments

All arguments must be class numeric.

Assume that in a traffic survey, a total of vehicles passing a certain point for different parts of the day was held in the following variables and for a particular execution of a program, these variables contained the values listed with them.

wa-morning-count	2356
wa-afternoon-count	1860
wa-evening-count	1288
wa-night-count	427

The mean of these values could be deduced as follows:

```
COMPUTE pa-mean-traffic-out =
    FUNCTION MEAN (wa-morning-count,
                   wa-afternoon-count,
                   wa-evening-count,
                   wa-night-count)
```

The actual mean value is 1482.75 but if pa-mean-traffic-out were an integer, its contents would be 1482 after execution of the COMPUTE because the .75 would be truncated. In a similar way, the other functions in this same group above would generate the following values if applied to these four arguments.

SUM	5931
MEDIAN	1574 (the mean of the two middle values when there are an even number of arguments)
MIDRANGE	1391.5
RANGE	1929

SUM, MEAN, MEDIAN, MIDRANGE and RANGE can all be used with tables and with the reserved word ALL as the subscript in the function reference.

FACTORIAL has a single argument which must be an integer variable or constant, greater than or equal to zero. For a non-zero argument, the factorial of the integer value is returned, e.g. FUNCTION FACTORIAL $(4) = 4 \times 3 \times 2 \times 1 = 24$. For a zero argument, 1 is returned.

SQRT returns the square root of its zero or positive numeric argument. The value returned is an approximation to the square root and the accuracy depends upon the word-size of your computer. However, this will normally be sufficient for most calculations. If the result is to be stored, the programmer can decide on the number of digits to be held before and after the decimal point by providing a suitable definition, e.g. PIC 9999V999.

INTEGER and INTEGER-PART are functions with a similar aim, i.e. to produce the nearest integer from a real number, but they operate slightly differently. INTEGER-PART is a straight truncation of the decimal part of a number, whereas INTEGER returns the greatest integer that is less than or equal to the argument. For positive arguments, the result of both functions is the same but for negative arguments the results are different, e.g. INTEGER-PART $(-1.5) = -1$ but INTEGER$(-1.5) = -2$.

REM works in a similar way to the REMAINDER part of the DIVIDE statement but it allows the remainder only to be returned. Its general format is:

FUNCTION REM (argument-1,argument-2)

and the remainder is defined as

argument-1 - (argument-2 * FUNCTION INTEGER-PART
            (argument-1 / argument-2))

As an example, for a particular year being a leap year, it must be exactly divisible by 4, e.g. 1996. However, at the turn of a century, this is only true every 400 years so that 1900 is not a leap year but 2000 is a leap year. A check for whether the current date is within a leap year could be coded as:

```
IF (wa-is-turn-of-century
        AND
    FUNCTION REM (wa-current-year,400) = ZERO)
    OR
    (NOT wa-is-turn-of-century
        AND
    FUNCTION REM (wa-current-year,4) = ZERO)
        SET wa-is-leap-year TO TRUE
END-IF
```

where wa-is-turn-of-century is an 88-level name associated with the last two digits of the 4-digit year being 00. The MOD function could also have been used for this check. For positive numbers, REM and MOD give the same result but as with INTEGER and INTEGER-PART, MOD works differently with negative numbers. The formal definition of MOD is:

FUNCTION MOD (argument-1,argument-2)

with the modulus value defined as

argument-1 - (argument-2 * FUNCTION INTEGER
                                    (argument-1 / argument-2))

The only difference from REM is that INTEGER rather than INTEGER-PART is used.

The RANDOM function for generating pseudo-random numbers has an optional numeric argument. It is optional because the first use of the RANDOM function in a program should be with a zero or positive seed which allows the computer to set up the first random number, e.g. FUNC-TION RANDOM(12345). Subsequent uses, however, should then be without the seed. A pseudo-random number greater than or equal to zero and less than 1 is returned on each use of RANDOM. Pseudo-random means that the same starting seed always generates the same set of random numbers, which is very useful for controlling the testing of programs that require random numbers.

STANDARD-DEVIATION and VARIANCE are the two common statistical functions.

Exercises

1 Exercise 1 of the previous frame defined the following table for a set of monthly rainfall figures:

```
01   wb-monthly-rainfall-table.
       03   wb-one-months-rainfall    PIC 9(4)
                                      OCCURS 12 TIMES.
```

Provide Procedure Division code to return:

the average (mean) monthly rainfall in wb-monthly-average
the total annual rainfall in wb-annual-rainfall
the difference between the minimum and maximum months in wb-rainfall-range.

2 As part of a tax calculation, a tax-due amount is produced in wb-tax-total which has a PIC 99999V99 declaration. However, some further calculations require just the integer £ part to be extracted from wb-tax-total, with any pence figures lost. Provide a function call that returns just this integer amount. Would it make any difference if wb-tax-total were a signed field?

3 The reserved word DAY-OF-WEEK used with ACCEPT returns an integer representing the day of the week, e.g. 1 is Monday and 7 is Sunday (see frame R3). Using one of the date functions and REM, produce an expression that returns the same integer value as DAY-OF-WEEK, given that the date in YYYYMMDD form is available in the

PIC 9(8) field wa-purchase-date. Hint – the standard start date of 1st January 1601 was a Monday.

4 A marketing department often wants to select at random one of 87 geographical regions for testing of new products. Using the RANDOM function, provide a Procedure Division expression that returns an integer value between 1 and 87 where each number has an equal chance of being selected.

W5   Trigonometric and log functions

The list below is of the trigonometric and log intrinsic functions and they are all of numeric type. The inclusion of mathematical functions not only widens the scope of COBOL as a language suitable for scientific applications, but also, there are sometimes applications in the business mainstream which require the limited use of mathematical formulae. Often in such situations, a special CALL has to be made to a more suitable language like FORTRAN.

- SIN – returns the sine of an angle specified in radians; the value returned is in the range −1 to +1
- COS – returns the cosine of an angle specified in radians; the value returned is in the range −1 to +1
- TAN – returns the tangent of an angle specified in radians
- ASIN – returns a value, in radians, representing the arcsine of a numeric argument which must be in the range −1 to +1
- ACOS – returns a value, in radians, representing the arccosine of a numeric argument which must be in the range −1 to +1
- ATAN – returns a value in radians representing the arctangent of a numeric argument
- LOG – returns the log to the base e of the argument which must be greater than zero
- LOG10 – returns the log to the base 10 of the argument which must be greater than zero

The trigonometric functions require a single numeric argument and return the appropriate sine, cosine, etc. value. The number of decimal places returned depends upon the word-size of your machine, but as with the SQRT function of frame W4, it is normally sufficient for most mathematical calculations. Like COBOL, in general, the actual number of significant digits used is defined by the size of the field to which the result of the function is moved.

As a reminder, the sine of an angle in a right-angled triangle is Opposite/Hypotenuse, the cosine is Adjacent/Hypotenuse and the tangent is Opposite/Adjacent. The arcsine, arccosine and arctangent functions work the other way, i.e. the arcsine function returns the value of the angle, in radians, whose sine is equal to the argument.

An angle in degrees can be converted to radians by the formula:

angle in radians = $(\pi/180) \times$ angle in degrees

where π is approximately 3.14159. The sine of a 60 degree angle is the same as the sine ($\pi/3$) in radians and the value returned is 0.5. The arcsine of 0.5 is, therefore, $\pi/3$ which is approximately 1.0472.

Here is an example of their use in COBOL:

```
COMPUTE ws-height =
    FUNCTION SIN (ws-angle-radians) * ws-hypotenuse
```

The LOG and LOG10 functions both require a single numeric argument greater than zero. Here is an example of their use in thermodynamics:

```
COMPUTE wd-curve-equation = FUNCTION LOG (x1/(1 - x1))
```

with wd-curve-equation having a PIC 9V9999.

Exercise

1 Provide a Procedure Division extract to verify that sine/cosine = tangent. Display an appropriate message for it being true or being false. Why might the answer be false?

W6   String/character functions

String handling has been a part of COBOL for many years and Section O of this book discusses reference modification, INSPECT, STRING and UNSTRING. The functions below aim to complement these features so that COBOL now provides a more complete set of operations for solving character-oriented problems. However, the language still falls short of having flexible string-handling features where, for example, the length of strings varies at runtime.

- CHAR – returns a specific character from the full character set; alphanumeric type
- ORD – returns the position of a character in the full character set; integer type
- REVERSE – reverses a string; alphanumeric type
- LOWER-CASE – converts to lower-case; alphanumeric type
- UPPER-CASE – converts to upper-case; alphanumeric type
- NUMVAL – returns the numeric value of a simple string; numeric type
- NUMVAL-C – returns the numeric value of a formatted string; numeric type

The collating sequence within a language allows characters to be compared, e.g. 'B' is greater than 'A' in all common character sets. The collating sequence concept is discussed in frame V2. An **ordinal number** is a unique integer that is associated with every character and is a formalisation of the collating sequence idea. The actual integer value depends upon the character set being used. In ASCII (American Standard Code For Information Interchange), the ordinal value of 'A' is 65 and the ordinal value of 'B' is 66 and because 66 > 65, 'B' is greater than 'A'.

CHAR and ORD are intrinsic functions that allow for conversion between characters and ordinal numbers. CHAR has a single integer argument and returns the equivalent alphanumeric character. ORD has a single alphanumeric or alphabetic argument and returns an integer value which is that character's ordinal number, e.g. CHAR(65) = "A" and ORD("A") = 65.

A major use of CHAR is to have easy access to special (often non-printable) characters through their equivalent ordinal numbers, e.g. the ASCII ordinal value to sound a bell or beeper is 7 and the null character has ordinal value 0. The bell can be output as part of a message as follows:

```
DISPLAY "Input error!" FUNCTION CHAR(7)
```

In general, however, care must be taken to highlight those parts of a program that are strongly linked to specific character sets. Ordinal value 7 may not sound the bell in all character sets. Ideally, such characters should be defined in Working-Storage as variables with an initial value so that they act like constants. However, a variable cannot be initialised to the result of a function call, so the best compromise is to establish the variable's value in a program's initialisation routine, e.g.

```
01   wa-special-constants.
     03   wa-sound bell        PIC X.
     :
A1-Initialisation.
     MOVE FUNCTION CHAR(7) TO wa-sound-bell
     :
D3-Error-Check.
     :
     DISPLAY "Input error!" wa-sound-bell
```

Even though collating systems do vary in terms of which characters the ordinal numbers represent, there is usually some consistency within particular groups of characters, e.g. the ordinal value of 'B' is always 1 greater than the ordinal value of 'A'. This does allow for string-oriented problems to be independent of the character set, e.g. if part of a problem required the searching of a piece of text for each of the upper-case letters in the alphabet, this could be achieved by the following language-independent code:

```
PERFORM VARYING wb-current-ordinal-value
    FROM ORD("A") BY 1
    UNTIL wb-current-ordinal-value > ORD("Z")
    :
    IF wb-current-character = CHAR(wb-current-ordinal-value)
        :
        :
    ENDIF
    :
END-PERFORM
```

To make this even more general, ORD("A") and ORD("Z") could also be set up like constants in an initialisation routine as mentioned above.

The REVERSE function reverses all the characters within an alphabetic or alphanumeric item, e.g. FUNCTION REVERSE ("abcd") = "dcba". Its single argument can be a group or elementary field. A direct use of REVERSE could be to check for palindromes in a document but this is unlikely to be a common request!

It could, however, be used as a part of a password encryption algorithm by reversing the password text. Rather than reversing the whole password, a more subtle approach might be to break down the password field into several elementary fields and just reverse some of them. Here is an example for a six-character password:

```
01  ws-password-in.
    03    ws-password-in-part1              PIC XXX.
    03    ws-password-in-part2              PIC X.
    03    ws-password-in-part3              PIC XX.
01  ws-encrypted-password.
    03    ws-encrypted-password-part1       PIC XXX.
    03    ws-encrypted-password-part2       PIC X.
    03    ws-encrypted-password-part3       PIC XX.
    :
    ACCEPT ws-password-in
    MOVE FUNCTION REVERSE (ws-password-in-part1)
        TO ws-encrypted-password-part1
    MOVE ws-password-in-part2 TO ws-encrypted-password-part 2
    MOVE FUNCTION REVERSE (ws-password-in-part3)
        TO ws-encrypted-password-part3
```

For a password of 'peanut', after the above MOVE statements, the contents of ws-encrypted-password would be 'aepntu'.

UPPER-CASE and LOWER-CASE are complementary functions to ensure that letters in a string are either all in upper case or all in lower case. Only letters are changed so that if fields contain other characters, they remain unaltered. Some examples are

```
FUNCTION UPPER-CASE ("Alfred") = "ALFRED"

FUNCTION LOWER-CASE ("Alfred") = "alfred"

FUNCTION UPPER-CASE ("abc123") = "ABC123"

FUNCTION LOWER-CASE ("A1B2C3") = "a1b2c3"
```

These functions are useful editing facilities to ensure that keyed input is converted to all of one case before being stored on disk, e.g., say a name in ws-forename needs to be displayed so that the first letter is in upper case and the rest in lower case; here, the first letter and the remaining string are extracted separately using reference modification:

```
DISPLAY "The name is "
        FUNCTION UPPER-CASE (ws-forename (1:1))
        FUNCTION LOWER-CASE (ws-forename (2:))
```

For ws-forename containing 'katheRinE', the output displayed would be:

The name is Katherine

NUMVAL and NUMVAL-C are used for converting character strings produced by edited PICTUREs to internal numeric form so that arithmetic can be performed upon them. The two functions work in a similar way but NUMVAL-C also extracts the numeric value from a string containing a currency symbol. Some examples are

```
FUNCTION NUMVAL ("123.456") = 123V456

FUNCTION NUMVAL-C ("£123.456" "£") = 123V456

FUNCTION NUMVAL ("123.456-") = -123V456

FUNCTION NUMVAL ("123.456CR") = -123V456
```

The V in the result value is used to indicate a notional decimal point. In the second example above, the '£' argument could be omitted if the Special-Names paragraph has already specified '£' as the currency symbol. The use of these functions is similar to de-editing, discussed in frames F3 and G4. However, with de-editing, a separate numeric field must be defined, whereas these functions can be used directly in arithmetic expressions.

Exercises

1 Some languages, but not COBOL, have an intrinsic function **successor**
   to produce the next character in the character set, e.g. the successor of
   'A' is 'B'. For a variable ws-char that contains a single character, provide Procedure Division code to generate its successor.
2 An on-line edit program allows input to fa-name-in in either upper-case
   or lower-case. Provide Procedure Division code that accepts data into
   fa-name-in and, if valid alphabetic characters, converts the data to
   upper-case before moving it to wa-name-out. If the data is not alphabetic, a message is to be displayed. Assume, for this example, that names
   do not contain hyphens, apostrophes, etc.
3 In the same on-line edit program as Question 2, a monetary amount is
   keyed into an input/output field ws-amount that has a PIC £££,££9.99.
   Often, this would be displayed as '£0.00' to a user and the £ would move
   left as digits were keyed in. However, the exact operation of such a field
   is not defined in the ANSI standard other than to specify that edited
   fields can be used for input as well as output. In this example, accept the
   input field then add 1000.00 to give ws-amount-bonus.

W7   Financial functions

* ANNUITY – regular payment calculation for a given sum invested/
           loaned
* PRESENT-VALUE – calculation of sum to be invested/loaned now for
                 a return in the future

These are both numeric functions. The ANNUITY function allows calculation of regular payments for a given sum being invested or loaned over a
period of time. Consider your receiving a £1000 legacy which, rather than
being wasted in a wild spending spree, is wisely invested for an annual
income over a period of 5 years. Without interest, this would be £200 per
year but, normally, interest would apply to the remaining capital amount
at the end of each year, causing the regular annual payments to be some-
what more than the £200. The regular payments could be calculated in a
program as follows:

```
COMPUTE ws-regular-payment = ws-amount-invested *
   FUNCTION ANNUITY (ws-interest-decimal,ws-no-of-years)
```

The first argument for the function is the interest, expressed as a decimal
and the second argument is the number of payments. The value returned
from the function is based upon an initial investment of 1 currency unit,
say £1, which is why the returned result needs to be multiplied by the
amount invested. For ws-amount-invested = 1000, ws-interest-decimal =
0.08 (8% as a decimal) and ws-no-of-years = 5, after execution of the

above COMPUTE statement, ws-regular-payment would hold approximately 250.46, representing £250.46p per year, a not unremarkable sum to cover your Christmas expenses for the next five years!

The general form of the ANNUITY function is:

<u>FUNCTION ANNUITY</u> (argument-1, argument-2)

and, using operators as in the COMPUTE statement, is formally defined as

argument-1/(1 - (1 + argument-1) ** (-argument-2))

but for zero interest, where argument-1 = 0, the formal definition is

1/argument-2

Interest is applied at the end of each period, before payment.

From a lender's point of view, e.g. a Building Society, the ANNUITY function could be used to calculate the regular mortgage payments for a borrower. As the period for payments is usually monthly, the interest rate supplied to the function would then be monthly, say 1% per month. Consider a loan of £20,000 for 10 years at a monthly interest rate of 1%; this could be coded as:

```
COMPUTE ws-mortgage-payment = ws-amount-loaned *
   FUNCTION ANNUITY (ws-interest-decimal,ws-no-of-months)
```

where ws-amount-loaned = 20000, ws-interest-decimal = 0.01 and ws-no-of-months = 120. This gives an approximate result in ws-mortgage-payment of 286.94, representing £286.94p monthly payments.

The PRESENT-VALUE function is used for calculating an investment amount now which will produce a specified return in the future, e.g. if a sum of £5000 is required in a year's time and the current annual rate of interest is 10%, what amount needs to be provided now? This could be coded as:

```
COMPUTE ws-current-value = FUNCTION PRESENT-VALUE
   (ws-interest-decimal,ws-amount-required)
```

where ws-interest-decimal = 0.1 (10% in decimal format) and ws-amount-required = 5000. After execution of the above COMPUTE statement, ws-current-value would hold approximately 4545.45, representing an initial investment of £4545.45p.

For a single return value in the future, the definition of the PRESENT-VALUE function is

<u>FUNCTION PRESENT-VALUE</u> (argument-1, argument-2)

where the result is

argument-2/(1 + argument-1)

However, the PRESENT-VALUE function can also be used to calculate a current value that will generate a series of returns over a period of time, e.g. if a requirement were to find out how much would need to be invested now to generate £1000 at the end of each year for the next 3 years at a prevailing annual interest rate of 10%, using constant values for illustration purposes, this could be coded as

```
COMPUTE ws-current-value = FUNCTION PRESENT-VALUE
   (0.1,1000,1000,1000)
```

which gives a value of 2547.22 in ws-current-value. The more general form of the function, therefore, is

<u>FUNCTION PRESENT-VALUE</u> (argument-1, {argument-2}...)

where the result is the summation of a series of terms, each term being defined as

argument-2/(1 + argument-1)**n

There is one term for each occurrence of argument-2 and the exponent, n, is incremented from 1 by 1 for each term in the series, e.g.

```
FUNCTION PRESENT-VALUE(0.1,1000,2000,4000)
```

gives the current amount needed to generate a return of 1000, 2000 and 4000 at the end of each of the next three periods, say years, where the rate of interest throughout the whole 3 periods is 10% per year At execution time, this would give a value of approximately £5567.24p.

Exercises

1 Produce a COBOL statement to generate the regular monthly payments that would be required to repay a loan of £5000 over a 3-year period, the annual interest rate of 8% to be applied monthly in equal instalments of 8/12. Constant values can be used as arguments.
2 A PRESENT-VALUE routine is being written to allow for 3 variable returns in the future of wa-return-1, wa-return-2 and wa-return-3. Provide a single statement that will generate wa-required-investment, where the interest rate for the whole period is wa-interest %.

W8   The LENGTH function

- LENGTH – returns the length of its argument and is of integer type

The function LENGTH is mainly of use with variable-length tables so that during execution of a program, the part of the table being used for storing data can be determined. It is stressed that this is not a string-handling function to find the length of a string. As yet, COBOL does not support strings where the physical length alters during execution of the program.

An example is

```
01  ws-table-size-parameters.
    03  ws-table-size                    PIC 9(4).
    03  ws-number of elements            PIC 99.
01  ws-creditors.
    03  ws-max-creditors-table.
        05  ws-one-creditor     OCCURS 1 TO 100 TIMES
                                DEPENDING ON
                                    ws-number-of-elements.
            07  ws-creditor-code         PIC X(5).
            07  ws-amount-owed           PIC 9(6)V99.
    :
    COMPUTE ws-table-size =
        FUNCTION LENGTH (ws-max-creditors-table)
```

ws-max-creditors-table is a variable-length table in the sense that the number of table *elements* in use at execution time is determined by the contents of ws-number-of-elements. However, the size in *characters* can be found by use of the LENGTH function. If the contents of ws-number-of-elements were 4, ws-table-size would hold 52, the actual number of characters in the first four elements of the table.

The table size in characters is useful when handling variable-length records as the programmer must provide/receive the actual length of a record in characters. Prior to COBOL 85, variable-length records were determined only by the DEPENDING ON phrase within a variable-length table declaration, so that the actual record size was not needed. The LENGTH function can be applied at a group level and it will return the total size from fixed and variable-length items within the group, including any FILLERs.

Exercise

1 The following variable-length record description is used for output.

```
FD  fc-customer-orders-file
    RECORD IS VARYING IN SIZE
        FROM 129 TO 2409 CHARACTERS
        DEPENDING ON ws-order-record-size.
```

```
01  fc-customer orders-record.
    03      fc-customer-id                      PIC X(9).
    03      fc-customer-orders-table.
        05      fc-one-customer-order   OCCURS 1 TO 20 TIMES
                DEPENDING ON            ws-number-of-orders.
            07  fc-order-no                     PIC X(8).
            07  fc-order-date                   PIC 9(5).
                    ⋮
```

Also, the following Working-Storage entries are used by this record description:

```
01  ws-order-parameters.
    03      ws-order-record-size                PIC 9(4).
    03      ws-number-of-orders                 PIC 99.
```

Provide Procedure Division code to WRITE one record given that the number of customer orders is in ws-number-of-orders.

Answers – Section W

Frame W2

1 With the additional Working-Storage entry

```
01  wa-start-date-and-time.
    03                                          PIC X(12).
    03  wa-start-second                         PIC 99.
    03                                          PIC X(12).
```

Procedure Division code for the delay loop is:

```
MOVE FUNCTION CURRENT-DATE TO wa-start-date-and-time
MOVE FUNCTION CURRENT-DATE TO wa-current-date-and-time
PERFORM UNTIL wa-current-second > wa-start-second + wa-delay
    MOVE FUNCTION CURRENT-DATE TO wa-current-date-and-time
    IF wa-current-second < wa-start-second
        ADD 60 TO wa-current-second
    END-IF
END-PERFORM
```

2 The current offset is either '-hh' for local times behind GMT or '+00' for the UK. The offset must be *added* to the local time to give the GMT time.

```
MOVE wa-current-minute TO wa-gmt-minute
EVALUATE    wa-current-offset
    WHEN        "-"
```

```
               ADD wa-current-hour wa-current-offset-hours
                 GIVING wa-gmt-hour
         WHEN      "+"
             MOVE wa-current-hour TO wa-gmt-hour
         WHEN     OTHER
             DISPLAY "Error in local time"
      END-EVALUATE
```

```
3  IF FUNCTION INTEGER-OF-DATE (fb-invoice-date-integer) + 30
          > FUNCTION INTEGER-OF-DATE (wa-todays-date-integer)
         PERFORM c2-process-old-debt
    END-IF
```

Frame W3

```
1  COMPUTE wa-max-monthly-rainfall =
        FUNCTION MAX (wb-one-months-rainfall(ALL))
    COMPUTE wa-min-monthly-rainfall =
        FUNCTION MIN (wb-one-months-rainfall(ALL))
    COMPUTE wa-max-month =
        FUNCTION ORD-MAX (wb-one-months-rainfall(ALL))
    COMPUTE wa-min-month =
        FUNCTION ORD-MIN (wb-one-months-rainfall(ALL))
```

Frame W4

```
1  COMPUTE wb-monthly-average =
        FUNCTION MEAN (wb-one-months-rainfall(ALL))
    COMPUTE wb-annual-rainfall =
        FUNCTION SUM (wb-one-months-rainfall(ALL))
    COMPUTE wb-rainfall-range =
        FUNCTION RANGE (wb-one-months-rainfall(ALL))
```

```
2  FUNCTION INTEGER (wb-tax-total)
```

or

```
FUNCTION INTEGER-PART (wb-tax-total)
```

These would give the same integer result for unsigned numbers. If wb-tax-total were signed and contained a negative amount, this would represent a tax rebate. If the pence field were still to be lost for the whole £ calculation then INTEGER-PART is the correct function as INTEGER would round to the next integer value, e.g. −£126.02p would become £127.

3 ```
COMPUTE wa-day-of-week = FUNCTION REM
     (FUNCTION INTEGER-OF-DATE (wa-purchase-date) , 7)
IF wa-day-of-week = ZERO
   MOVE 7 TO wa-day-of-week
END-IF
```

The extra IF is required because the REM function returns a correct value for all days except Sunday.

4 Each value returned from the random number generator is greater than or equal to 0 and less than 1. This figure can then be multiplied by 87 and the result truncated to just the integer part. This gives a random number in the range 0 to 86 so that 1 is added to this result. The code is:

```
FUNCTION INTEGER-PART (FUNCTION RANDOM (92641) * 87) + 1
```

where the seed is an arbitrary value.

Frame W5

1 ```
IF FUNCTION TAN (wa-angle-in radians) =
                  FUNCTION SIN (wa-angle-in radians) /
                  FUNCTION COS (wa-angle-in radians)
   DISPLAY "Sin/Cos = Tan verified"
ELSE
   DISPLAY "Sin/Cos = Tan not verified"
END-IF
```

The result is very likely to be false as each of the separate function calls is only accurate to the word-size of the machine you are using and standard COBOL states nothing about such accuracy. A much safer way to achieve an equality would be to move each of the left-hand-side and right-hand-side results to variables with, say, 4 decimal places each and compare these two variables.

Frame W6

1 ```
FUNCTION CHAR (FUNCTION ORD (ws-char) + 1)
```

Care would have to be taken that there is a valid successor character, e.g. the last character in a character set does not have a successor and trying to generate a value in this situation would probably give a run-time error.

2 ```
ACCEPT fa-name-in
IF fa-name-in IS ALPHABETIC
    MOVE FUNCTION UPPER-CASE (fa-name-in) TO wa-name-out
ELSE
    DISPLAY fa-name-in " is not alphabetic"
END-IF
```

```
3 ACCEPT ws-amount
  COMPUTE ws-amount-bonus =
        FUNCTION NUMVAL-C (ws-amount) + 1000.0
```

Frame W7

```
1 COMPUTE wa-monthly-payment = 5000 *
        FUNCTION ANNUITY (0.0066667,36)
```

The percentage interest of 8/12 expressed as a decimal gives 0.00666 recurring. The approximation above of 0.0066667 would give enough accuracy to the nearest pence on most machines. In general, some test cases may have to be tried before it can be decided how many decimal places are necessary.

```
2 COMPUTE wa-required-investment =
        FUNCTION PRESENT-VALUE
        (wa-interest/100,wa-return-1, wa-return-2, wa-return-3)
```

Frame W8

```
1 COMPUTE ws-order-record-size =
        FUNCTION LENGTH (fc-customer-orders-record)
  WRITE fc-customer-orders-record
```

Part 4
Appendices

Appendix A
Example Program

This example program is an update to an indexed customer master file by a serial validated transaction file. The run chart is given in Fig. AA.1.

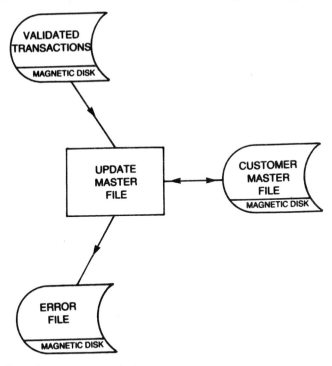

Fig. AA.1 Example program – run chart

Input

A Validated Transaction file has 127-character records in the following formats:

(i)

Character Positions	Field	Type
1	Update Code	One of "A", "D" or "I"
2–6	Customer Number	5 digits
7	Credit Code	An alphabetic character
8–37	Customer Name	30 alphanumeric characters
38–127	Customer Address	90 alphanumeric characters

This format is for all records except the last and contains details of the updates to the customer master file, e.g. a new customer or a customer change of address. An Amendment record may have any of the Credit Code, Customer Name or Customer Address fields blank. A Deletion record will always have those fields all blank. An Insertion record will have non-blank entries for all fields except that the Customer Address field may be blank.

(ii)

Character Positions	Field	Type
1	Transaction Type	"T"
2–7	Control Total	6 digits
8–127	Unused	Spaces

This is a trailer record which contains a count of the number of data records in the file, i.e. a total not including the trailer record itself.

The data has been validated in the previous program (not unlike the Example Program Specification of frame J3) and you can assume that a control record will be present. It is an unsorted serial file.

Input–Output

An Indexed Customer Master file has 134-character records in the following formats:

(i)

Character Positions	Field	Type
1–5	Customer Number	(Key field) any 5 digits except "99999"
6	Credit Code	An alphabetic character
7–14	Debit Balance	An 8-digit monetary field with 2 decimal places and the sign held with the last digit
15–44	Customer Name	30 alphanumeric characters
45–134	Customer Address	90 alphanumeric characters

This is the normal data record, one for each customer.

(ii) Character Positions	Field	Type
1	Control Code	(Key field) "99999"
2–7	Control Total	6 digits
8–134	Unused	Spaces

This is a master control record which must always reflect the total number of master records in the file.

Output

An error file of 148 characters with the same record formats as the transaction file except a message field is added.

(i) Character Positions	Field	Type
1	Update Code	One of "A", "D" or "I"
2–6	Customer Number	5 digits
7	Credit code	An alphabetic character
8–37	Customer Name	30 alphanumeric characters
38–127	Customer Address	90 alphanumeric characters
128–148	Error Message	21 alphanumeric characters

This format is for all records except the last. The message is one of:

"MASTER RECORD PRESENT"
"NO MASTER RECORD"
"BALANCE NOT ZERO"

(ii) Character Positions	Field	Type
1	Transaction Type	"T"
2–7	Control Total	6 digits
8–148	Unused	Spaces

This is a trailer record which contains a count of the number of error records in the file, i.e. a total not including the trailer record itself.

Processing

For each transaction record read, the appropriate update to the master file must take place. This will involve an attempted random read of the matching master record. The updates are to take place as follows:

For Amendments (type "A")

If no matching master record is found, the transaction is to be written to the error file with the message "NO MASTER RECORD". If there is a matching master record the Credit Code, Customer Name and Customer Address master fields are to be overwritten by equivalent fields from the transaction but only where the transaction fields are non-blank. The master record is then to be rewritten to the master file.

For Deletions (type "D")

If no matching master record is found, the transaction is to be written to the error file with the message "NO MASTER RECORD". If there is a matching master record and the debit balance field contains zero, it is to be deleted from the file and the master control record updated. If the debit balance field is non-zero, the transaction is to be written to the error file with the message "BALANCE NOT ZERO" and the master record left on the master file.

For Insertions (type "I")

If a matching master record is found, the transaction is to be written to the error file with the message "MASTER RECORD PRESENT". If there is no matching master record, a new master record is to be created from the transaction. The master debit balance field is to be set to zero. This new record is then to be written to the master file and the master control record updated.

In addition, a program count of the number of transactions processed must be kept and if this does tally with the control total in the final transaction record, a control record, with a count of the number of error records, is to be written to the end of the error file. If it does not tally, a message is to be displayed on the console and no control record written to the error file.

A JSP solution to the example program

Figure AA.2 is a final program structure chart solution. Operations and conditions are listed below.

Operations

1 Open all files
2 Read a transaction record
3 Read a master record randomly

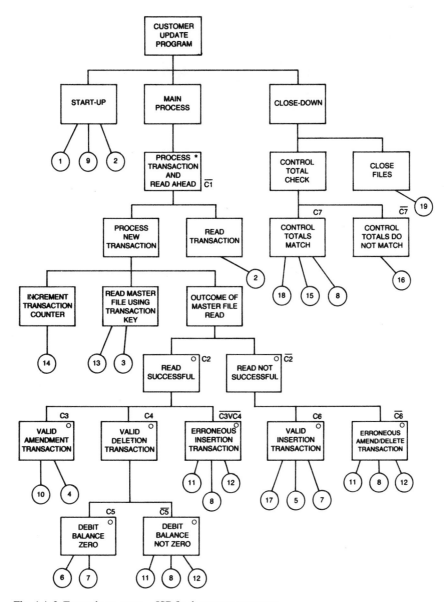

Fig. AA.2 Example program – JSP final program structure

4 Rewrite a master record
5 Write a new master record
6 Delete a master record
7 Update master control record
8 Write an error record
9 Initialise transaction and error record counters
10 Update master record from non-blank transaction fields

11 Create error record from transaction and message
12 Increment error record counter
13 Move transaction key to master key field
14 Increment transaction counter
15 Move error record counter to error record output field
16 Display control total failure message
17 Create master record from transaction
18 Create error control record from transaction record
19 Close all files

Conditions

C1 Transaction trailer record read?
C2 Master record read successfully?
C3 Amendment transaction?
C4 Deletion transaction?
C5 Debit balance zero?
C6 Insertion transaction?
C7 Control totals match?

Implementation into COBOL

The implementation of a JSP final program structure into a target language like COBOL can be done in many ways. The most effective is to have a JSP pre-processor, a piece of software that will generate the Procedure Division for you after you have created the final program structure, operations and conditions on a machine. The Procedure Division produced is very unstructured but this is usually not important because maintenance is performed via the JSP pre-processor software as well.

If you do not have such software available, you can mechanically generate a correct Procedure Division by following a strict set of rules applied to the final program structure. One approach includes having a separate paragraph for every box on the diagram, and for each level down the diagram you pass through one PERFORM statement in the coding. The bottom boxes on our diagram would only be executed after seven levels of PERFORM. This has the benefit of being able to match closely, the Procedure Division and the JSP final structure chart, but it is not easy to follow the logic of the code itself.

A third approach is to produce well-structured, in-line code and the programmer decides when to create a new paragraph level. As COBOL 85 is a particularly good language for this approach, we have adopted it here. There is a paragraph break only at the top level of the JSP diagram to create the traditional initial control paragraph.

```
IDENTIFICATION DIVISION.
PROGRAM-ID. CMFU2.
****************************************************************
* Author R Yorke.                                             *
* Date Written. Mar 1995.                                     *
* Installation. De Montfort University.                       *
*                                                             *
* The purpose of this program is to update customer records   *
* on an indexed master file from a serial file of validated   *
* transactions. Errors are written to a serial disk file.     *
*                                                             *
*                                                             *
* Transactions can be:                                        *
*                                                             *
*     "A" - amendment to certain fields of the master file    *
*     "D" - deletion of a master file record                  *
*     "I" - insertion of a new customer record                *
*                                                             *
* In addition, there is a control total of records at the     *
* end of the transaction file (a type "T" record) which       *
* is to be checked against a program count. A similar         *
* control total is to be created for the error file as        *
* long as the above match succeeds.                           *
*                                                             *
* The master file has a control record to hold the current    *
* number of master records. This must be updated              *
* immediately for deletions and insertions.                   *
****************************************************************
ENVIRONMENT DIVISION.
CONFIGURATION SECTION.
SOURCE-COMPUTER. IBM PC.
OBJECT-COMPUTER. IBM PC.
INPUT-OUTPUT SECTION.
FILE-CONTROL.
    SELECT fa-trans-file
        ASSIGN TO "CB85AP01.DAT"
        ORGANIZATION IS LINE SEQUENTIAL.
    SELECT fb-master-file
        ASSIGN TO "CB85AP02.DAT"
        ORGANIZATION IS INDEXED
        ACCESS MODE IS RANDOM
        RECORD KEY IS fb-customer-no
        FILE STATUS IS wa-master-file-status.
    SELECT fc-error-file
        ASSIGN TO "CB85AP03.DAT"
        ORGANIZATION IS LINE SEQUENTIAL.
DATA DIVISION.
FILE SECTION.
FD fa-trans-file
    RECORD CONTAINS 127 CHARACTERS.
```

```
01  fa-trans-record.
    03  fa-trans-record-type                  PIC X.
        88  fa-amendment                      VALUE "A".
        88  fa-deletion                       VALUE "D".
        88  fa-insertion                      VALUE "I".
        88  fa-trailer-record-found           VALUE "T".
    03  fa-customer-no                        PIC X(5).
    03  fa-credit-code                        PIC X.
    03  fa-customer-name                      PIC X(30).
    03  fa-customer-address                   PIC X(90).
01  fa-trans-trailer-record.
    03                                        PIC X.
    03  fa-no-of-trans-records                PIC 9(6).
    03                                        PIC X(120).
FD  fb-master-file
    RECORD CONTAINS 134 CHARACTERS.
01  fb-master-record.
    03  fb-customer-no                        PIC X(5).
    03  fb-credit-code                        PIC X.
    03  fb-debit-balance                      PIC S9(6)V99.
    03  fb-customer-name                      PIC X(30).
    03  fb-customer-address                   PIC X(90).
01  fb-master-control-record.
    03                                        PIC X(5).
    03  fb-no-of-master-records               PIC 9(6).
    03                                        PIC X(123).
FD  fc-error-file
    RECORD CONTAINS 148 CHARACTERS.
01  fc-error-record.
    03  fc-error-data                         PIC X(127).
    03  fc-error-message                      PIC X(21).
01  fc-error-trailer-record.
    03  fc-error-record-type                  PIC X.
    03  fc-error-customer-no                  PIC X(5).
    03  fc-no-of-error-records                PIC 9(6).
    03                                        PIC X(136).
WORKING-STORAGE SECTION.
01  wa-independent-fields.
    03  wa-trans-record-counter               PIC 9(6).
    03  wa-error-record-counter               PIC 9(6).
    03  wa-master-file-status                 PIC XX.
        88  wa-master-record-found            VALUE "00".
01  wb-error-messages.
    03  wb-invalid-insert-message             PIC X(21).
        VALUE "MASTER RECORD PRESENT".
    03  wb-invalid-update-message             PIC X(21).
        VALUE "NO MASTER RECORD".
    03  wb-non-zero-balance-message           PIC X(21).
        VALUE "BALANCE NOT ZERO".
PROCEDURE DIVISION.
```

```
A1-Main-Control.
    PERFORM B1-Start-Up
    PERFORM B2-Main-Process
    PERFORM B3-Close-Down
    STOP RUN.
B1-Start-Up.
    OPEN INPUT fa-trans-file
         I-O fb-master-file
         OUTPUT fc-error-file
    MOVE ZERO TO wa-trans-record-counter
                 wa-error-record-counter
    READ fa-trans-file.
B2-Main-Process.
    PERFORM UNTIL fa-trailer-record-found
        ADD 1 TO wa-trans-record-counter
        MOVE fa-customer-no TO fb-customer-no
        READ fb-master-file
        IF wa-master-record-found
        THEN
            EVALUATE TRUE
            WHEN fa-amendment
            IF fa-credit-code NOT EQUAL TO SPACES
                THEN
                    MOVE fa-credit-code TO fb-credit-code
                END-IF
                IF fa-customer-name NOT EQUAL TO SPACES
                THEN
                    MOVE fa-customer-name TO fb-customer-name
                END-IF
                IF fa-customer-address NOT EQUAL TO SPACES
                THEN
                    MOVE fa-customer-address
                        TO fb-customer-address
                END-IF
                REWRITE fb-master-record
            WHEN fa-deletion
                IF fb-debit-balance = ZERO
                THEN
                    DELETE fb-master-file RECORD
                    MOVE all "9" TO fb-customer-no
                    READ fb-master-file
                    SUBTRACT 1 FROM fb-no-of-master-records
                    REWRITE fb-master-record
                ELSE
                    MOVE fa-trans-record TO fc-error-data
                    MOVE wb-non-zero-balance-message
                        TO fc-error-message
                    WRITE fc-error-record
                    ADD 1 TO wa-error-record-counter
                END-IF
```

```
            WHEN OTHER
                MOVE fa-trans-record TO fc-error-data
                MOVE wb-invalid-insert-message
                    TO fc-error-message
                WRITE fc-error-record
                ADD 1 TO wa-error-record-counter
            END EVALUATE
        ELSE
            IF fa-insertion
            THEN
                MOVE fa-credit-code TO fb-credit-code
                MOVE ZERO TO fb-debit-balance
                MOVE fa-customer-name TO fb-customer-name
                MOVE fa-customer-address TO fb-customer-address
                WRITE fb-master-record
                MOVE ALL "9" TO fb-customer-no
                READ fb-master-file
                ADD 1 TO fb-no-master-records
                REWRITE fb-master-record
            ELSE
                MOVE fa-trans-record TO fc-error-data
                MOVE wb-invalid-update-message
                    TO fc-error-message
                WRITE fc-error-record
                ADD 1 To wa-error-record-counter
            END-IF
            END-IF
        READ fa-trans-file
    END-PERFORM.
B3-Close-Down.
    IF wa-trans-record-counter = fa-no-of-trans-records
    THEN
        MOVE fa-trans-record TO fc-error-trailer-record
        MOVE wa-error-record-counter TO fc-no-of-error-records
        WRITE fc-error-record
    ELSE
        DISPLAY "Control total failure"
        DISPLAY "No. of file:" fa-no-of-trans-records
        DISPLAY "No. counted:" wa-error-record-counter
    END-IF
    CLOSE fa-trans-file
          fb-master-file
          fc-error-file.
```

Example Test

Starting with the CUSTOMER MASTER FILE as below:

```
00019B0000007648BAKER        FJ  68 GREEN LANE              LEICESTER             LE2 3HZ
00036A0000425pPOLDARK        P   8 GUNDARA STREET           MAYFAIR               LONDON W1
00107D00087235ASHMAN         F   1 VICTORIA ROAD            DOVER                 KENT
01212B00005400RICHARDSON     GG  17 MARLBOROUGH AVENUE      LIVERPOOL             LV8 9AQ
01480A0000000WALSHE          SJ  48 SCULLIN STREET          CRAWLEY               SUSSEX RH10 4XF
01809C0001624OPATEL          D   17 POPLAR DRIVE            REDCAR                CLEVELAND TS12 8AQ
02313E0024620ORICHARDSON     GH  14 YARRALUMLA STREET       PYMBLE, SYDNEY        NSW 2641, AUSTRALIA
02321A0000364rSMITH          F   48 LEAZES PARK ROAD        NEWCASTLE             NE4 3RT
02331E00487250ZINSKY         V   4 MAIN ROAD                GARFORTH              BRISTOL
02676D00088888BARKER         G   6 GLAISDALE ROAD           WANDSWORTH COMMON     LONDON SW18 3RS
09997C00016420JONES          DD  FLAT 2A                    14 HAZEL DRIVE        NEWCASTLE NE8 2DB
99999000011
```

and an input VALIDATED TRANSACTIONS file:

```
I00001ABAKER        CW  25 BROAD STREET         ORPINGTON      KENT BR5 3WQ
I02321BSMITH        F   48 LEAZES PARK ROAD     NEWCASTLE      NE4 3RT
A01212                  23 VICTORY ROAD         BRIGHTON       BN2 2JX
A09997D
A00063B
D01480
D02333
D00019
I99998AMACTAVISH    R   27 ANGEL STREET         NORTHFIELD     BIRMINGHAM
T000009
```

after one run of the program, the CUSTOMER MASTER FILE contained:

```
00001A00000000BAKER       CW  25 BROAD STREET          ORPINGTON           KENT BR5 3WQ
00019B0007648BAKER        FJ  68 GREEN LANE            LEICESTER           LE2 3HZ
00036A0000425pPOLDARK     P   8 GUNDARA STREET         MAYFAIR             LONDON W1
00107D00087235ASHMAN      F   1 VICTORIA ROAD          DOVER               KENT
01212B00005400RICHARDSON  GG  23 VICTORY ROAD          BRIGHTON            BN2 2JX
01809C00016240PATEL       D   17 POPLAR DRIVE          REDCAR              CLEVELAND TS12 8AQ
02313E00246200RICHARDSON  GH  14 YARRALUMLA STREET     PYMBLE, SYDNEY      NSW 2641, AUSTRALIA
02321A0003364rSMITH       F   48 LEAZES PARK ROAD      NEWCASTLE           NE4 3RT
02331E00487250ZINSKY      V   4 MAIN ROAD              GARFORTH            BRISTOL
02676D00088888BARKER      G   6 GLAISDALE ROAD         WANDSWORTH COMMON   LONDON SW18 3RS
09997C00016420JONES       DD  FLAT 2A                  14 HAZEL DRIVE      NEWCASTLE NE8 2DB
99998A00000000MACTAVISH   R   27 ANGEL STREET          NORTHFIELD          BIRMINGHAM
9999900012
```

and the ERROR FILE contained:

```
I02321BSMITH      F   48 LEAZES PARK ROAD      NEWCASTLE NE4 3RT   MASTER RECORD PRESENT
A00063B                                                            NO MASTER RECORD
D02333                                                             NO MASTER RECORD
D00019                                                             BALANCE NOT ZERO
T00000000004
```

Appendix B
A Selection of Practical Exercises

1 The population explosion

The population of the world is currently around 6,000 million people. The earth is a sphere of radius 3,984 miles and two-thirds of its surface is water. The surface area of a sphere is 4 × 3.1416 × the square of the radius.

Write a program that will print out the population of the world and the population density (people/square mile of land) at ten year intervals for the next twenty decades (the first detail line starting with the population ten years from now).

The printout is to appear as follows:

First line	Positions 1–5	Assumed growth rate % p.a. (Z9.99%)
Subsequent lines	Positions 1–4	The year (9999)
	8–17	The population (99,999,999) in millions
	23–29	The density/square mile (999,999)

The lines are to be double spaced and the results are to be zero suppressed.

The rate of growth per cent is stored on a record in columns 1–4, with an assumed decimal point between the second and third digit. There may be several records in the growth rate file, in which case the results for each growth rate are to be printed on a fresh page (one page for each record read in).

If a size error occurs in the calculations for any record, print SIZE ERROR in positions 1–10 and, without printing any further lines on that page, continue to the next record.

2   Student attendance

A student file has been maintained in the following format:

Identification: STUDENTS
Data records

1–6	Student number
7–25	Student name
	7–21 Surname
	22–25 Initials
26–30	Course code
31–33	Possible hours to date
34–36	Actual hours to date
37–39	Possible coursework mark
40–42	Actual coursework mark

A report is to be produced naming those students who have missed 25% or more class hours, and are thus in danger of failing to qualify to sit the final examination. Students not in danger should not appear on the report.

The report should be printed as follows:

1–6	Student number
10–29	Student name
35–39	Course code
45–47	Possible hours to date
53–55	Actual hours to date
61–62	% attendance (two digits, fractions truncated, followed by percent sign)

The report is to be headed up LOW ATTENDANCE LIST. If there are no low attenders, the message NO LOW ATTENDERS is to follow immediately after the heading line.

The report is to be concluded with a count of the total number of students on the file (each student appears in only one record).

3   Population explosion Part 2

Amend the report produced in Exercise 1 as follows:

(a) A heading POPULATION ESTIMATES: ASSUMED GROWTH RATE = Z9.99% is to be printed at the top of each page, followed by a heading YEAR POPULATION DENS./SQ.M. printed TWICE across the page, i.e. starting in position 1 and again in position 60.

(b) The results are to be listed in two halves of the page so produced, the first ten decades in positions 1–29 as before, the next ten decades in positions 60–88. The message SIZE ERROR is to appear, starting in positions 1 or 60 as appropriate. (Store the results in a table before printing them out.)

4 Poem

A series of English words is held on a magnetic tape labelled POEM. The series of words are divided into variable length lines, of not more than 80 characters each, by the single character "/". Each record on the tape is 800 characters long. The last line of a record continues onto the next record, i.e. lines are broken over record boundaries.

Write a program to read the tape and print the words such that each new line begins in print position 30. The character "*" in the input signifies the end of a line **and** that there are no further lines in the record; the next record is to be read in. Any characters beyond the "*" are to be ignored.

The delimiting characters "/" and "*" must not be printed. Empty lines must be printed as blank lines.

At the end of the printout, you must print (with suitable legends) the number of vowels in the file and the number of consonants in the file (special characters, spaces and digits are not to be counted).

5 Purchasing habits

(a) Write a program to create a master file of customers' purchasing habits. Each record has the format:

1–40	Name and address
42–45	Four-digit account number
50–55	Number of orders placed over £1,000
60–65	Number of orders placed £1,000 or less
70–80	Average value of orders placed to date.

The records are in account-number order.

(b) Records are available to update the above file. These records have the format:

1–4	Account number
10–20	Value of order placed this week.

Assume the records are in order of account number and that the two fields are numeric.

Perform the update by copying forward, creating a new master and listing on the printer any transactions for non-existent customers. The value fields have two places of decimals. Not all master records are necessarily updated each week. Design your own report layout.

6   Magic square

A magic square is a two-dimensional table with the property that the sums of the numbers in each row, each column and each diagonal are all equal.

Write a program, using PERFORM ... VARYING, which will establish whether or not a given 4 × 4 table of two-digit numbers is a magic square. Print out the square with a suitable message. Input the squares to be tested from records with a layout of your choice. (Enthusiasts can write the program for tables of any size up to 20 × 20, the table dimension being contained in the record along with the table data.)

7   Student attendance Part 2

Amend Exercise 2 so that the lines of the report are produced in ascending order of student number within actual hours to date within course code.

8   Purchasing habits Part 2

Amend Exercise 5 so that the master file is a relative or indexed file on disk. Update the records in place.

Appendix C
COBOL 85 Reserved Words

ACCEPT	BINARY	CONTENT
ACCESS	BLANK	CONTINUE
ADD	BLOCK	CONTROL
ADVANCING	BOTTOM	CONTROLS
AFTER	BY	CONVERTING
ALL		COPY
ALPHABET	CALL	CORR
ALPHABETIC	CANCEL	CORRESPONDING
ALPHABETIC- LOWER	CD CF	COUNT CURRENCY
ALPHABETIC- UPPER	CH CHARACTER	DATA
ALPHANUMERIC	CHARACTERS	DATE
ALPHANUMERIC- EDITED	CLASS CLOCK-UNITS	DATE-COMPILED DATE-WRITTEN
ALSO	CLOSE	DAY
ALTER	COBOL	DAY-OF-WEEK
ALTERNATE	CODE	DE
AND	CODE-SET	DEBUG-CONTENTS
ANY	COLLATING	DEBUG-ITEM
ARE	COLUMN	DEBUG-LINE
AREA	COMMA	DEBUG-NAME
AREAS	COMMON	DEBUG-SUB-1
ASCENDING	COMMUNICATION	DEBUG-SUB-2
ASSIGN	COMP	DEBUG-SUB-3
AT	COMPUTATIONAL	DEBUGGING
AUTHOR	COMPUTE	DECIMAL-POINT
	CONFIGURATION	DECLARATIVES
BEFORE	CONTAINS	DELETE

DELIMITED   EVERY   JUST
DELIMITER   EXCEPTION   JUSTIFIED
DEPENDING   EXIT
DESCENDING   EXTEND   KEY
DESTINATION   EXTERNAL
DETAIL   LABEL
DISABLE   FALSE   LAST
DISPLAY   FD   LEADING
DIVIDE   FILE   LEFT
DIVISION   FILE-CONTROL   LENGTH
DOWN   FILLER   LESS
DUPLICATES   FINAL   LIMIT
DYNAMIC   FIRST   LIMITS
                     FOOTING   LINAGE
EGI   FOR   LINAGE-COUNTER
ELSE   FROM   LINE
EMI   LINE-COUNTER
ENABLE   GENERATE   LINES
END   GIVING   LINKAGE
END-ADD   GLOBAL   LOCK
END-CALL   GO   LOW-VALUE
END-COMPUTE   GREATER   LOW-VALUES
END-DELETE   GROUP
END-DIVIDE   MEMORY
END-EVALUATE   HEADING   MERGE
END-IF   HIGH-VALUE   MESSAGE
END-MULTIPLY   HIGH-VALUES   MODE
END-OF-PAGE   MODULES
END-PERFORM   I-O   MOVE
END-READ   I-O-CONTROL   MULTIPLE
END-RECEIVE   IDENTIFICATION   MULTIPLY
END-RETURN   IF
END-REWRITE   IN   NATIVE
END-SEARCH   INDEX   NEGATIVE
END-START   INDEXED   NEXT
END-STRING   INDICATE   NO
END-SUBTRACT   INITIAL   NOT
END-UNSTRING   INITIALIZE   NUMBER
END-WRITE   INITIATE   NUMERIC
ENTER   INPUT   NUMERIC-EDITED
ENVIRONMENT   INPUT-OUTPUT
EOP   INSPECT   OBJECT-
EQUAL   INSTALLATION   COMPUTER
ERROR   INTO   OCCURS
ESI   INVALID   OF
EVALUATE   IS   OFF

OMITTED
OPEN
OPTIONAL
ORDER
ORGANIZATION
OTHER
OVERFLOW

PACKED-DECIMAL
PADDING
PAGE
PAGE-COUNTER
PERFORM
PIC
PICTURE
PLUS
POINTER
POSITION
POSITIVE
PRINTING
PROCEDURE
PROCEDURES
PROCEED
PROGRAM
PROGRAM-ID
PURGE

QUEUE
QUOTE
QUOTES

RANDOM
READ
RECEIVE
RECORD
RECORDS
REDEFINES
REEL
REFERENCE
REFERENCES

RELATIVE
RELEASE
REMAINDER
REMOVAL
RENAMES
REPLACE
REPLACING
REPORT
REPORTING
REPORTS
RERUN
RESERVE
RESET
RETURN
REVERSED
REWIND
REWRITE
RIGHT
ROUNDED
RUN

SAME
SEARCH
SECTION
SECURITY
SELECT
SEND
SENTENCE
SEPARATE
SEQUENCE
SEQUENTIAL
SET
SIGN
SIZE
SORT
SORT-MERGE
SOURCE
SOURCE-
    COMPUTER
SPACE
SPACES

SPECIAL-NAMES
STANDARD
STANDARD-1
STANDARD-2
START
STATUS
STRING
SUB-QUEUE-1
SUB-QUEUE-2
SUB-QUEUE-3
SUBTRACT
SUM
SUPPRESS
SYMBOLIC
SYNC
SYNCHRONIZED

TABLE
TALLYING
TAPE
TERMINAL
TERMINATE
TEST
TEXT
THAN
THEN
THROUGH
THRU
TIME
TIMES
TO
TOP
TRAILING
TRUE
TYPE

UNIT
UNSTRING
UNTIL
UP
UPON
USAGE
USE
USING

VALUE	ZERO	+
VALUES	ZEROES	−
VARYING	ZEROS	*
		/
WHEN		**
WITH		>
WORDS		<
WORKING-		=
STORAGE		>=
WRITE		<=

Appendix D
ANS COBOL 85 Language Formats

These formats represent the full ANS COBOL 85 language excluding the following which are not discussed in this book:

(i) the Communications facilities,
(ii) features marked as obsolete and destined for deletion in the next standard.

For certain Input/Output Procedure Division statements, an italic letter to the left indicates that their use is restricted to a particular feature as follows:

S Sequential files
R Relative files
I Indexed files
W Report Writer module

GENERAL FORMAT FOR NESTED SOURCE PROGRAMS

IDENTIFICATION DIVISION.

PROGRAM-ID. program-name-1 [IS INITIAL PROGRAM].

[ENVIRONMENT DIVISION. environment-division-content]

[DATA DIVISION. data-division-content]

[PROCEDURE DIVISION. procedure-division-content]

[[nested-source-program] ...

END PROGRAM program-name-1.]

GENERAL FORMAT FOR NESTED-SOURCE-PROGRAM

IDENTIFICATION DIVISION.

PROGRAM-ID.   program-name-2 $\left[\text{IS} \left\{ \left| \begin{array}{c} \underline{\text{COMMON}} \\ \underline{\text{INITIAL}} \end{array} \right| \right\} \text{PROGRAM} \right]$.

[ENVIRONMENT DIVISION. environment-division-content]

[DATA DIVISION. data-division-content]

[PROCEDURE DIVISION. procedure-division-content]

[nested-source-program] ...

END PROGRAM program-name-2.

GENERAL FORMAT FOR A SEQUENCE OF SOURCE PROGRAMS

{IDENTIFICATION DIVISION.

 PROGRAM-ID. program-name-3 [IS INITIAL PROGRAM].

[ENVIRONMENT DIVISION. environment-division-content]

[DATA DIVISION. data-division-content]

[PROCEDURE DIVISION. procedure-division-content]

{nested-source-program] ...

 END PROGRAM program-name-3.} ...

 IDENTIFICATION DIVISION.

 PROGRAM-ID. program-name-4 [IS INITIAL PROGRAM].

[ENVIRONMENT DIVISION. environment-division-content]

[DATA DIVISION. data-division-content]

[PROCEDURE DIVISION. procedure-division-content]

[[nested-source-program] ...

 END PROGRAM program-name-4.]

GENERAL FORMAT FOR ENVIRONMENT DIVISION

[ENVIRONMENT DIVISION.

[CONFIGURATION SECTION.

```
[SOURCE-COMPUTER.  [computer-name [WITH DEBUGGING MODE].]]

[OBJECT-COMPUTER.  [computer-name
```

$$
\left[\text{MEMORY SIZE integer-1} \left\{ \begin{array}{l} \text{WORDS} \\ \text{CHARACTERS} \\ \text{MODULES} \end{array} \right\} \right]
$$

```
    [PROGRAM COLLATING SEQUENCE IS alphabet-name-1]

    [SEGMENT-LIMIT IS segment-number].]]


[SPECIAL-NAMES.  [[ implementor-name-1
```

$$
\left\{ \begin{array}{l} \text{IS mnemonic-name-1 [ON STATUS IS condition-name-1 [OFF STATUS IS condition-name-2]]} \\ \text{IS mnemonic-name-2 [OFF STATUS IS condition-name-2 [ON STATUS IS condition-name-1]]} \\ \text{ON STATUS IS condition-name-1 [OFF STATUS IS condition-name-2]} \\ \text{OFF STATUS IS condition-name-2 [ON STATUS IS condition-name-1]} \end{array} \right\} \dots
$$

```
    [ALPHABET alphabet-name-1 IS
```

$$
\left\{ \begin{array}{l} \text{STANDARD-1} \\ \text{STANDARD-2} \\ \text{NATIVE} \\ \text{implementor-name-2} \\ \left\{ \text{literal-1} \left[\left\{ \begin{array}{l} \text{THROUGH} \\ \text{THRU} \end{array} \right\} \text{literal-2} \atop \{\text{ALSO literal-3}\} \dots \right] \right\} \dots \end{array} \right\} \dots
$$

$$
\left[\text{SYMBOLIC CHARACTERS} \left\{ \left\{ \{\text{symbolic-character-1}\} \dots \left\{ \begin{array}{l} \text{IS} \\ \text{ARE} \end{array} \right\} \{\text{integer-1}\} \dots \right\} \dots \right. \right.
$$

$$
\left. \left. [\text{IN alphabet-name-2}] \right\} \right] \dots
$$

$$
\left[\text{CLASS class-name-1 IS} \left\{ \text{literal-4} \left[\left\{ \begin{array}{l} \text{THROUGH} \\ \text{THRU} \end{array} \right\} \text{literal-5} \right] \right\} \dots \right] \dots
$$

```
    [CURRENCY SIGN IS literal-6]

    [DECIMAL-POINT IS COMMA].]]]
```

GENERAL FORMAT FOR IDENTIFICATION DIVISION

```
IDENTIFICATION DIVISION.
```

$$
\text{PROGRAM-ID. program-name} \left[\text{IS} \left\{ \left| \begin{array}{l} \text{COMMON} \\ \text{INITIAL} \end{array} \right| \right\} \text{PROGRAM} \right] .
$$

```
[AUTHOR.  [comment-entry] ... ]

[INSTALLATION.  [comment-entry] ... ]

[DATE-WRITTEN.  [comment-entry] ... ]

[DATE-COMPILED.  [comment-entry] ... ]

[SECURITY.  [comment-entry] ... ]
```

GENERAL FORMAT FOR ENVIRONMENT DIVISION

[INPUT-OUTPUT SECTION.

FILE-CONTROL.

    {file-control-entry} ...

[I-O-CONTROL.

$$\left[\left[\left[\text{RERUN} \left[\text{ON} \begin{Bmatrix} \text{file-name-1} \\ \text{implementor-name-1} \end{Bmatrix}\right]\right] \text{EVERY} \begin{Bmatrix} \begin{Bmatrix} [\text{END OF}] \begin{Bmatrix} \text{REEL} \\ \text{UNIT} \end{Bmatrix} \\ \text{integer-1 RECORDS} \end{Bmatrix} \text{OF file-name-2} \\ \text{integer-2 CLOCK-UNITS} \\ \text{condition-name-1} \end{Bmatrix}\right] \cdots\right.$$

$$\left[\text{SAME} \begin{bmatrix} \text{RECORD} \\ \text{SORT} \\ \text{SORT-MERGE} \end{bmatrix} \text{AREA FOR file-name-3 } \{\text{file-name-4}\} \cdots \right] \cdots$$

    [MULTIPLE FILE TAPE CONTAINS {file-name-5 [POSITION integer-3]} ...] ... .]]]]

GENERAL FORMAT FOR FILE CONTROL ENTRY

SEQUENTIAL FILE:

SELECT [OPTIONAL] file-name-1

    ASSIGN TO $\begin{Bmatrix} \text{implementor-name-1} \\ \text{literal-1} \end{Bmatrix}$ ...

    $\left[\text{RESERVE integer-1} \begin{bmatrix} \text{AREA} \\ \text{AREAS} \end{bmatrix}\right]$

    [[ORGANIZATION IS] SEQUENTIAL]

    $\left[\text{PADDING CHARACTER IS} \begin{Bmatrix} \text{data-name-1} \\ \text{literal-2} \end{Bmatrix}\right]$

    $\left[\text{RECORD DELIMITER IS} \begin{Bmatrix} \text{STANDARD-1} \\ \text{implementor-name-2} \end{Bmatrix}\right]$

    [ACCESS MODE IS SEQUENTIAL]

    [FILE STATUS IS data-name-2].

RELATIVE FILE:

SELECT [OPTIONAL] file-name-1

    ASSIGN TO $\begin{Bmatrix} \text{implementor-name-1} \\ \text{literal-1} \end{Bmatrix}$ ...

    $\left[\text{RESERVE integer-1} \begin{bmatrix} \text{AREA} \\ \text{AREAS} \end{bmatrix}\right]$

[ORGANIZATION IS] RELATIVE

$$\left[\text{ACCESS MODE IS} \left\{ \begin{array}{l} \text{SEQUENTIAL} \quad [\text{RELATIVE KEY IS data-name-1}] \\ \left\{ \begin{array}{l} \text{RANDOM} \\ \text{DYNAMIC} \end{array} \right\} \text{RELATIVE KEY IS data-name-1} \end{array} \right\} \right]$$

[FILE STATUS IS data-name-2].

GENERAL FORMAT FOR FILE CONTROL ENTRY

INDEXED FILE:

SELECT [OPTIONAL] file-name-1

    ASSIGN TO $\left\{ \begin{array}{l} \text{implementor-name-1} \\ \text{literal-1} \end{array} \right\}$ ...

$$\left[\text{RESERVE integer-1} \left[\begin{array}{l} \text{AREA} \\ \text{AREAS} \end{array} \right] \right]$$

[ORGANIZATION IS] INDEXED

$$\left[\text{ACCESS MODE IS} \left\{ \begin{array}{l} \text{SEQUENTIAL} \\ \text{RANDOM} \\ \text{DYNAMIC} \end{array} \right\} \right]$$

RECORD KEY IS data-name-1

[ALTERNATE RECORD KEY IS data-name-2   [WITH DUPLICATES]] ...

[FILE STATUS IS data-name-3].

SORT OR MERGE FILE:

SELECT file-name-1 ASSIGN TO $\left\{ \begin{array}{l} \text{implementor-name-1} \\ \text{literal-1} \end{array} \right\}$ ...

GENERAL FORMAT FOR FILE CONTROL ENTRY

REPORT FILE:

SELECT [OPTIONAL] file-name-1

    ASSIGN TO $\left\{ \begin{array}{l} \text{implementor-name-1} \\ \text{literal-1} \end{array} \right\}$ ...

$$\left[\text{RESERVE integer-1} \left[\begin{array}{l} \text{AREA} \\ \text{AREAS} \end{array} \right] \right]$$

[[ORGANIZATION IS] SEQUENTIAL]]

$$\left[\underline{\text{PADDING}} \text{ CHARACTER IS } \left\{ \begin{matrix} \text{data-name-1} \\ \text{literal-2} \end{matrix} \right\} \right]$$

$$\left[\underline{\text{RECORD}} \text{ } \underline{\text{DELIMITER}} \text{ IS } \left\{ \begin{matrix} \underline{\text{STANDARD-1}} \\ \text{implementor-name-2} \end{matrix} \right\} \right]$$

[<u>ACCESS</u> MODE IS <u>SEQUENTIAL</u>]

[FILE <u>STATUS</u> IS data-name-2].

<u>GENERAL FORMAT FOR DATA DIVISION</u>

[<u>DATA</u> <u>DIVISION</u>.

[<u>FILE</u> <u>SECTION</u>.

$$\left[\begin{matrix} \text{file-description-entry \{record-description-entry\} ...} \\ \text{sort-merge-file-description-entry \{record-description-entry\} ...} \\ \text{report-file-description-entry} \end{matrix} \right] \text{ ...} \right]$$

[<u>WORKING-STORAGE</u> <u>SECTION</u>.

$$\left[\begin{matrix} \text{77-level-description-entry} \\ \text{record-description-entry} \end{matrix} \right] \text{ ...} \right]$$

[<u>LINKAGE</u> <u>SECTION</u>.

$$\left[\begin{matrix} \text{77-level-description-entry} \\ \text{record-description-entry} \end{matrix} \right] \text{ ...} \right]$$

[<u>REPORT</u> <u>SECTION</u>.

[report-description-entry {report-group-description-entry} ...] ...]]

<u>GENERAL FORMAT FOR FILE DESCRIPTION ENTRY</u>

<u>SEQUENTIAL FILE</u>:

<u>FD</u> file-name-1

    [IS <u>EXTERNAL</u>]

    [IS <u>GLOBAL</u>]

$$\left[\underline{\text{BLOCK}} \text{ CONTAINS } [\text{integer-1} \underline{\text{TO}}] \text{ integer-2} \left\{ \begin{matrix} \underline{\text{RECORDS}} \\ \text{CHARACTERS} \end{matrix} \right\} \right]$$

$$\left[\underline{\text{RECORD}} \quad \left\{ \begin{array}{l} \text{CONTAINS integer-3 CHARACTERS} \\ \text{IS } \underline{\text{VARYING}} \text{ IN SIZE [[FROM integer-4] [\underline{TO} integer-5] CHARACTERS]} \\ \qquad \text{[\underline{DEPENDING} ON data-name-1]} \\ \text{CONTAINS integer-6 \underline{TO} integer-7 CHARACTERS} \end{array} \right\} \right]$$

$$\left[\underline{\text{LABEL}} \quad \left\{ \begin{array}{l} \underline{\text{RECORD}} \text{ IS} \\ \underline{\text{RECORDS}} \text{ ARE} \end{array} \right\} \quad \left\{ \begin{array}{l} \underline{\text{STANDARD}} \\ \underline{\text{OMITTED}} \end{array} \right\} \right]$$

$$\left[\underline{\text{VALUE}} \ \underline{\text{OF}} \quad \left\{ \text{implementor-name-1 IS} \quad \left\{ \begin{array}{l} \text{data-name-2} \\ \text{literal-1} \end{array} \right\} \right\} \ \ldots \right]$$

$$\left[\underline{\text{DATA}} \quad \left\{ \begin{array}{l} \underline{\text{RECORD}} \text{ IS} \\ \underline{\text{RECORDS}} \text{ ARE} \end{array} \right\} \quad \{\text{data-name-3}\} \ \ldots \right]$$

$$\left[\underline{\text{LINAGE}} \text{ IS} \quad \left\{ \begin{array}{l} \text{data-name-4} \\ \text{integer-8} \end{array} \right\} \text{ LINES} \quad \left[\text{WITH } \underline{\text{FOOTING}} \text{ AT} \quad \left\{ \begin{array}{l} \text{data-name-5} \\ \text{integer-9} \end{array} \right\} \right] \right.$$

$$\left. \left[\text{LINES AT } \underline{\text{TOP}} \quad \left\{ \begin{array}{l} \text{data-name-6} \\ \text{integer-10} \end{array} \right\} \right] \left[\text{LINES AT } \underline{\text{BOTTOM}} \quad \left\{ \begin{array}{l} \text{data-name-7} \\ \text{integer-11} \end{array} \right\} \right] \right]$$

[\underline{CODE-SET} IS alphabet-name-1].

GENERAL FORMAT FOR FILE DESCRIPTION ENTRY

RELATIVE FILE:

<u>FD</u> file-name-1

   [IS <u>EXTERNAL</u>]

   [IS <u>GLOBAL</u>]

$$\left[\underline{\text{BLOCK}} \text{ CONTAINS} \quad [\text{integer-1 } \underline{\text{TO}}] \quad \text{integer-2} \quad \left\{ \begin{array}{l} \underline{\text{RECORDS}} \\ \underline{\text{CHARACTERS}} \end{array} \right\} \right]$$

$$\left[\underline{\text{RECORD}} \quad \left\{ \begin{array}{l} \text{CONTAINS integer-3 CHARACTERS} \\ \text{IS } \underline{\text{VARYING}} \text{ IN SIZE [[FROM integer-4] [\underline{TO} integer-5] CHARACTERS]} \\ \qquad \text{[\underline{DEPENDING} ON data-name-1]} \\ \text{CONTAINS integer-6 \underline{TO} integer-7 CHARACTERS} \end{array} \right\} \right]$$

$$\left[\underline{\text{LABEL}} \quad \left\{ \begin{array}{l} \underline{\text{RECORD}} \text{ IS} \\ \underline{\text{RECORDS}} \text{ ARE} \end{array} \right\} \quad \left\{ \begin{array}{l} \underline{\text{STANDARD}} \\ \underline{\text{OMITTED}} \end{array} \right\} \right]$$

$$\left[\underline{\text{VALUE}} \ \underline{\text{OF}} \quad \left\{ \text{implementor-name-1 IS} \quad \left\{ \begin{array}{l} \text{data-name-2} \\ \text{literal-1} \end{array} \right\} \right\} \ \ldots \right]$$

$$\left[\underline{\text{DATA}} \quad \left\{ \begin{array}{l} \underline{\text{RECORD}} \text{ IS} \\ \underline{\text{RECORDS}} \text{ ARE} \end{array} \right\} \quad \{\text{data-name-3}\} \ \ldots \right].$$

GENERAL FORMAT FOR FILE DESCRIPTION ENTRY

INDEXED FILE:

FD file-name-1

   [IS EXTERNAL]

   [IS GLOBAL]

$$
\left[\underline{\text{BLOCK}} \text{ CONTAINS } [\text{integer-1 } \underline{\text{TO}}] \text{ integer-2 } \left\{ \begin{array}{l} \text{RECORDS} \\ \text{CHARACTERS} \end{array} \right\} \right]
$$

$$
\left[\underline{\text{RECORD}} \left\{ \begin{array}{l} \text{CONTAINS integer-3 CHARACTERS} \\ \text{IS } \underline{\text{VARYING}} \text{ IN SIZE } [[\text{FROM integer-4}] \ [\underline{\text{TO}} \text{ integer-5}] \text{ CHARACTERS}] \\ \qquad [\underline{\text{DEPENDING}} \text{ ON data-name-1}] \\ \text{CONTAINS integer-6 } \underline{\text{TO}} \text{ integer-7 CHARACTERS} \end{array} \right\} \right]
$$

$$
\left[\underline{\text{LABEL}} \left\{ \begin{array}{l} \underline{\text{RECORD}} \text{ IS} \\ \underline{\text{RECORDS}} \text{ ARE} \end{array} \right\} \left\{ \begin{array}{l} \underline{\text{STANDARD}} \\ \underline{\text{OMITTED}} \end{array} \right\} \right]
$$

$$
\left[\underline{\text{VALUE}} \ \underline{\text{OF}} \ \left\{ \text{implementor-name-1 IS } \left\{ \begin{array}{l} \text{data-name-2} \\ \text{literal-1} \end{array} \right\} \right\} \ ... \right]
$$

$$
\left[\underline{\text{DATA}} \left\{ \begin{array}{l} \underline{\text{RECORD}} \text{ IS} \\ \underline{\text{RECORDS}} \text{ ARE} \end{array} \right\} \{\text{data-name-3}\} \ ... \right] \ .
$$

GENERAL FORMAT FOR FILE DESCRIPTION ENTRY

SORT-MERGE FILE:

SD file-name-1

$$
\left[\underline{\text{RECORD}} \left\{ \begin{array}{l} \text{CONTAINS integer-1 CHARACTERS} \\ \text{IS } \underline{\text{VARYING}} \text{ IN SIZE } [[\text{FROM integer-2}] \ [\underline{\text{TO}} \text{ integer-3}] \text{ CHARACTERS}] \\ \qquad [\underline{\text{DEPENDING}} \text{ ON data-name-1}] \\ \text{CONTAINS integer-4 } \underline{\text{TO}} \text{ integer-5 CHARACTERS} \end{array} \right\} \right.
$$

$$
\left. \left[\underline{\text{DATA}} \left\{ \begin{array}{l} \underline{\text{RECORD}} \text{ IS} \\ \underline{\text{RECORDS}} \text{ ARE} \end{array} \right\} \{\text{data-name-2}\} \ ... \right] \right] \ .
$$

REPORT FILE:

FD file-name-1

   [IS EXTERNAL]

   [IS GLOBAL]

$$
\left[\underline{\text{BLOCK}} \text{ CONTAINS } [\text{integer-1 } \underline{\text{TO}}] \text{ integer-2 } \left\{ \begin{array}{l} \text{RECORDS} \\ \text{CHARACTERS} \end{array} \right\} \right]
$$

$$\left[\underline{\text{RECORD}} \quad \begin{Bmatrix} \text{CONTAINS integer-3 CHARACTERS} \\ \text{CONTAINS integer-4 } \underline{\text{TO}} \text{ integer-5 CHARACTERS} \end{Bmatrix}\right]$$

$$\left[\underline{\text{LABEL}} \quad \begin{Bmatrix} \underline{\text{RECORD}} \text{ IS} \\ \underline{\text{RECORDS}} \text{ ARE} \end{Bmatrix} \begin{Bmatrix} \underline{\text{STANDARD}} \\ \underline{\text{OMITTED}} \end{Bmatrix}\right]$$

$$\left[\underline{\text{VALUE}} \ \underline{\text{OF}} \ \left\{\text{implementor-name-1 IS} \ \begin{Bmatrix} \text{data-name-1} \\ \text{literal-1} \end{Bmatrix}\right\} \ldots\right]$$

[<u>CODE-SET</u> IS alphabet-name-1]

$$\begin{Bmatrix} \underline{\text{REPORT}} \text{ IS} \\ \underline{\text{REPORTS}} \text{ ARE} \end{Bmatrix} \ \{\text{report-name-1}\} \ldots \quad .$$

<u>GENERAL FORMAT FOR DATA DESCRIPTION ENTRY</u>

<u>FORMAT 1</u>:

$$\text{level-number} \quad \begin{bmatrix} \text{data-name-1} \\ \text{FILLER} \end{bmatrix}$$

[<u>REDEFINES</u> data-name-2]

[IS <u>EXTERNAL</u>]

[IS <u>GLOBAL</u>]

$$\left[\begin{Bmatrix} \underline{\text{PICTURE}} \\ \underline{\text{PIC}} \end{Bmatrix} \text{ IS character-string}\right]$$

$$\left[[\underline{\text{USAGE}} \text{ IS}] \begin{Bmatrix} \underline{\text{BINARY}} \\ \underline{\text{COMPUTATIONAL}} \\ \underline{\text{COMP}} \\ \underline{\text{DISPLAY}} \\ \underline{\text{INDEX}} \\ \underline{\text{PACKED-DECIMAL}} \end{Bmatrix}\right]$$

$$\left[[\underline{\text{SIGN}} \text{ IS}] \begin{Bmatrix} \underline{\text{LEADING}} \\ \underline{\text{TRAILING}} \end{Bmatrix} [\underline{\text{SEPARATE}} \text{ CHARACTER}]\right]$$

$$\left[\begin{array}{l} \underline{\text{OCCURS}} \text{ integer-2 TIMES} \\[4pt] \quad \left[\begin{Bmatrix} \underline{\text{ASCENDING}} \\ \underline{\text{DESCENDING}} \end{Bmatrix} \text{ KEY IS } \{\text{data-name-3}\} \ldots\right] \ldots \\[8pt] \quad [\underline{\text{INDEXED}} \text{ BY } \{\text{index-name-1}\} \ldots] \\[6pt] \underline{\text{OCCURS}} \text{ integer-1 } \underline{\text{TO}} \text{ integer-2 TIMES } \underline{\text{DEPENDING}} \text{ ON data-name-4} \\[4pt] \quad \left[\begin{Bmatrix} \underline{\text{ASCENDING}} \\ \underline{\text{DESCENDING}} \end{Bmatrix} \text{ KEY IS } \{\text{data-name-3}\} \ldots\right] \ldots \\[8pt] \quad [\underline{\text{INDEXED}} \text{ BY } \{\text{index-name-1}\} \ldots] \end{array}\right]$$

$$\left[\begin{Bmatrix} \underline{\text{SYNCHRONIZED}} \\ \underline{\text{SYNC}} \end{Bmatrix} \begin{bmatrix} \underline{\text{LEFT}} \\ \underline{\text{RIGHT}} \end{bmatrix}\right]$$

$$\left[\begin{Bmatrix} \underline{JUSTIFIED} \\ \underline{JUST} \end{Bmatrix} \text{ RIGHT}\right]$$

[BLANK WHEN ZERO]

[VALUE IS literal-1].

GENERAL FORMAT FOR DATA DESCRIPTION ENTRY

FORMAT 2:

66 data-name-1 RENAMES data-name-2 $\left[\begin{Bmatrix} \underline{THROUGH} \\ \underline{THRU} \end{Bmatrix} \text{ data-name-3}\right]$.

FORMAT 3:

88 condition-name-1 $\begin{Bmatrix} \underline{VALUE} \text{ IS} \\ \underline{VALUES} \text{ ARE} \end{Bmatrix}$ $\left\{ \text{literal-1} \left[\begin{Bmatrix} \underline{THROUGH} \\ \underline{THRU} \end{Bmatrix} \text{ literal-2}\right]\right\}$ ... .

GENERAL FORMAT FOR REPORT DESCRIPTION ENTRY

RD   report-name-1

[IS GLOBAL]

[CODE literal-1]

$$\left[\begin{Bmatrix} \underline{CONTROL} \text{ IS} \\ \underline{CONTROLS} \text{ ARE} \end{Bmatrix} \begin{Bmatrix} \{\text{data-name-1}\} \ ... \\ \underline{FINAL} \text{ [data-name-1] } ... \end{Bmatrix}\right]$$

$$\left[\underline{PAGE} \begin{bmatrix} \text{LIMIT IS} \\ \text{LIMITS ARE} \end{bmatrix} \text{ integer-1} \begin{bmatrix} \text{LINE} \\ \text{LINES} \end{bmatrix} \text{ [}\underline{HEADING}\text{ integer-2]}\right.$$

[FIRST DETAIL integer-3]   [LAST DETAIL integer-4]

$$\left. \text{[}\underline{FOOTING}\text{ integer-5]}\right].$$

GENERAL FORMAT FOR REPORT GROUP DESCRIPTION ENTRY

FORMAT 1:

01 [data-name-1]

$$\left[\text{LINE NUMBER IS } \begin{Bmatrix} \text{integer-1 \quad [ON \underline{NEXT} PAGE]} \\ \underline{PLUS} \text{ integer-2} \end{Bmatrix}\right]$$

$$\left[\underline{NEXT} \ \underline{GROUP} \text{ IS } \begin{Bmatrix} \text{integer-3} \\ \underline{PLUS} \text{ integer-4} \\ \underline{NEXT} \ \underline{PAGE} \end{Bmatrix}\right]$$

$$\underline{TYPE} \text{ IS } \begin{Bmatrix} \begin{Bmatrix} \underline{REPORT} \ \underline{HEADING} \\ \underline{RH} \end{Bmatrix} \\ \begin{Bmatrix} \underline{PAGE} \ \underline{HEADING} \\ \underline{PH} \end{Bmatrix} \\ \begin{Bmatrix} \underline{CONTROL} \ \underline{HEADING} \\ \underline{CH} \end{Bmatrix} \begin{Bmatrix} \text{data-name-2} \\ \underline{FINAL} \end{Bmatrix} \\ \begin{Bmatrix} \underline{DETAIL} \\ \underline{DE} \end{Bmatrix} \\ \begin{Bmatrix} \underline{CONTROL} \ \underline{FOOTING} \\ \underline{CF} \end{Bmatrix} \begin{Bmatrix} \text{data-name-3} \\ \underline{FINAL} \end{Bmatrix} \\ \begin{Bmatrix} \underline{PAGE} \ \underline{FOOTING} \\ \underline{PF} \end{Bmatrix} \\ \begin{Bmatrix} \underline{REPORT} \ \underline{FOOTING} \\ \underline{RF} \end{Bmatrix} \end{Bmatrix}$$

[[USAGE IS] DISPLAY].

GENERAL FORMAT FOR REPORT GROUP DESCRIPTION ENTRY

FORMAT 2:

level-number [data-name-1]

$$\left[\underline{LINE} \text{ NUMBER IS } \begin{Bmatrix} \text{integer-1 \quad [ON \underline{NEXT} PAGE]} \\ \underline{PLUS} \text{ Integer-2} \end{Bmatrix}\right]$$

[[USAGE IS] DISPLAY].

FORMAT 3:

level-number [data-name-1]

$$\begin{Bmatrix} \underline{PICTURE} \\ \underline{PIC} \end{Bmatrix} \text{ IS character-string}$$

[[USAGE IS] DISPLAY]

$$\left[[\underline{SIGN} \text{ IS}] \begin{Bmatrix} \underline{LEADING} \\ \underline{TRAILING} \end{Bmatrix} \underline{SEPARATE} \text{ CHARACTER} \right]$$

$$\left[\begin{Bmatrix} \underline{JUSTIFIED} \\ \underline{JUST} \end{Bmatrix} \text{ RIGHT} \right]$$

[BLANK WHEN ZERO]

$$\left[\underline{LINE} \text{ NUMBER IS } \begin{Bmatrix} \text{integer-1 } [\text{ON } \underline{NEXT} \ \underline{PAGE}] \\ \underline{PLUS} \text{ integer-2} \end{Bmatrix} \right]$$

[COLUMN NUMBER IS integer-3]

$$\left\{ \begin{array}{l} \underline{SOURCE} \text{ IS identifier-1} \\[4pt] \underline{VALUE} \text{ IS literal-1} \\[4pt] \{\underline{SUM} \ \{\text{identifier-2}\} \ \dots \ [\underline{UPON} \ \{\text{data-name-2}\} \ \dots \ ]\} \ \dots \\[4pt] \qquad \left[\underline{RESET} \text{ ON } \begin{Bmatrix} \text{data-name-3} \\ \underline{FINAL} \end{Bmatrix} \right] \end{array} \right\}$$

[GROUP INDICATE].

GENERAL FORMAT FOR PROCEDURE DIVISION

FORMAT 1:

[PROCEDURE DIVISION [USING {data-name-1} ...].

[DECLARATIVES.

{section-name SECTION [segment-number].

    USE statement.

[paragraph-name.

    [sentence] ...] ... } ...

  END DECLARATIVES.]

{section-name SECTION [segment-number].

[paragraph-name.

    [sentence] ...] ... } ...]

FORMAT 2:

[PROCEDURE DIVISION [USING {data-name-1} ...].

{paragraph-name.

    [sentence] ... } ...]

GENERAL FORMAT FOR COBOL VERBS

ACCEPT identifier-1 [FROM mnemonic-name-1]

ACCEPT identifier-2 FROM $\begin{Bmatrix} \text{DATE} \\ \text{DAY} \\ \text{DAY-OF-WEEK} \\ \text{TIME} \end{Bmatrix}$

ADD $\begin{Bmatrix} \text{identifier-1} \\ \text{literal-1} \end{Bmatrix}$ ... TO {identifier-2 [ROUNDED]} ...

   [ON SIZE ERROR imperative-statement-1]

   [NOT ON SIZE ERROR imperative-statement-2]

   [END-ADD]

ADD $\begin{Bmatrix} \text{identifier-1} \\ \text{literal-1} \end{Bmatrix}$ ... TO $\begin{Bmatrix} \text{identifier-2} \\ \text{literal-2} \end{Bmatrix}$

   GIVING {identifier-3 [ROUNDED]} ...

   [ON SIZE ERROR imperative-statement-1]

   [NOT ON SIZE ERROR imperative-statement-2]

   [END-ADD]

ADD $\begin{Bmatrix} \text{CORRESPONDING} \\ \text{CORR} \end{Bmatrix}$ identifier-1 TO identifier-2 [ROUNDED]

   [ON SIZE ERROR imperative-statement-1]

   [NOT ON SIZE ERROR imperative-statement-2]

   [END-ADD]

ALTER {procedure-name-1 TO [PROCEED TO] procedure-name-2} ...

CALL $\begin{Bmatrix} \text{identifier-1} \\ \text{literal-1} \end{Bmatrix}$ $\left[\text{USING} \begin{Bmatrix} \text{[BY REFERENCE]} & \text{\{identifier-2\} ...} \\ \text{BY CONTENT} & \text{\{identifier-2\} ...} \end{Bmatrix} \cdots \right]$

   [ON OVERFLOW imperative-statement-1]

   [END-CALL]

GENERAL FORMAT FOR COBOL VERBS

CALL $\begin{Bmatrix} \text{identifier-1} \\ \text{literal-1} \end{Bmatrix}$ $\left[\underline{\text{USING}} \begin{Bmatrix} [\text{BY } \underline{\text{REFERENCE}}] & \{\text{identifier-2}\} \dots \\ \text{BY } \underline{\text{CONTENT}} & \{\text{identifier-2}\} \dots \end{Bmatrix} \dots \right]$

    [ON <u>EXCEPTION</u> imperative-statement-1]

    [<u>NOT</u> ON <u>EXCEPTION</u> imperative-statement-2]

    [<u>END-CALL</u>]

<u>CANCEL</u> $\begin{Bmatrix} \text{identifier-1} \\ \text{literal-1} \end{Bmatrix} \dots$

SW <u>CLOSE</u> $\left\{ \text{file-name-1} \left[\begin{Bmatrix} \underline{\text{REEL}} \\ \underline{\text{UNIT}} \end{Bmatrix} [\text{FOR } \underline{\text{REMOVAL}}] \\ \text{WITH } \begin{Bmatrix} \text{NO } \underline{\text{REWIND}} \\ \underline{\text{LOCK}} \end{Bmatrix} \right] \right\} \dots$

RI <u>CLOSE</u> {file-name-1 [WITH <u>LOCK</u>]} ...

    <u>COMPUTE</u> {identifier-1 [<u>ROUNDED</u>]} ... = arithmetic-expression-1

        [ON <u>SIZE</u> <u>ERROR</u> imperative-statement-1]

        [<u>NOT</u> ON <u>SIZE</u> <u>ERROR</u> imperative-statement-2]

        [<u>END-COMPUTE</u>]

    <u>CONTINUE</u>

    <u>DELETE</u> file-name-1 RECORD

        [<u>INVALID</u> KEY imperative-statement-1]

        [<u>NOT</u> <u>INVALID</u> KEY imperative-statement-2]

        [<u>END-DELETE</u>]

GENERAL FORMAT FOR COBOL VERBS

<u>DISPLAY</u> $\begin{Bmatrix} \text{identifier-1} \\ \text{literal-1} \end{Bmatrix}$ ...   [<u>UPON</u> mnemonic-name-1]   [WITH <u>NO</u> <u>ADVANCING</u>]

<u>DIVIDE</u> $\begin{Bmatrix} \text{identifier-1} \\ \text{literal-1} \end{Bmatrix}$ <u>INTO</u> {identifier-2 [<u>ROUNDED</u>]} ...

   [ON <u>SIZE</u> <u>ERROR</u> imperative-statement-1]

   [<u>NOT</u> ON <u>SIZE</u> <u>ERROR</u> imperative-statement-2]

   [<u>END-DIVIDE</u>]

<u>DIVIDE</u> $\begin{Bmatrix} \text{identifier-1} \\ \text{literal-1} \end{Bmatrix}$ <u>INTO</u> $\begin{Bmatrix} \text{identifier-2} \\ \text{literal-2} \end{Bmatrix}$

   <u>GIVING</u> {identifier-3 [<u>ROUNDED</u>]} ...

   [ON <u>SIZE</u> <u>ERROR</u> imperative-statement-1]

   [<u>NOT</u> ON <u>SIZE</u> <u>ERROR</u> imperative-statement-2]

   [<u>END-DIVIDE</u>]

<u>DIVIDE</u> $\begin{Bmatrix} \text{identifier-1} \\ \text{literal-1} \end{Bmatrix}$ <u>BY</u> $\begin{Bmatrix} \text{identifier-2} \\ \text{literal-2} \end{Bmatrix}$

   <u>GIVING</u> {identifier-3 [<u>ROUNDED</u>]} ...

   [ON <u>SIZE</u> <u>ERROR</u> imperative-statement-1]

   [<u>NOT</u> ON <u>SIZE</u> <u>ERROR</u> imperative-statement-2]

   [<u>END-DIVIDE</u>]

<u>DIVIDE</u> $\begin{Bmatrix} \text{identifier-1} \\ \text{literal-1} \end{Bmatrix}$ <u>INTO</u> $\begin{Bmatrix} \text{identifier-2} \\ \text{literal-2} \end{Bmatrix}$ <u>GIVING</u> identifier-3 [<u>ROUNDED</u>]

   <u>REMAINDER</u> identifier-4

   [ON <u>SIZE</u> <u>ERROR</u> imperative-statement-1]

   [<u>NOT</u> ON <u>SIZE</u> <u>ERROR</u> imperative-statement-2]

   [<u>END-DIVIDE</u>]

GENERAL FORMAT FOR COBOL VERBS

<u>DIVIDE</u> $\left\{\begin{array}{l}\text{identifier-1}\\ \text{literal-1}\end{array}\right\}$ <u>BY</u> $\left\{\begin{array}{l}\text{identifier-2}\\ \text{literal-2}\end{array}\right\}$ <u>GIVING</u> identifier-3 [<u>ROUNDED</u>]

   <u>REMAINDER</u> identifier-4

   [ON <u>SIZE</u> <u>ERROR</u> imperative-statement-1]

   [<u>NOT</u> ON <u>SIZE</u> <u>ERROR</u> imperative-statement-2]

   [<u>END-DIVIDE</u>]

<u>EVALUATE</u> $\left\{\begin{array}{l}\text{identifier-1}\\ \text{literal-1}\\ \text{expression-1}\\ \underline{\text{TRUE}}\\ \underline{\text{FALSE}}\end{array}\right\}$ $\left[\underline{\text{ALSO}} \left\{\begin{array}{l}\text{identifier-2}\\ \text{literal-2}\\ \text{expression-2}\\ \underline{\text{TRUE}}\\ \underline{\text{FALSE}}\end{array}\right\}\right]$ ...

  {{<u>WHEN</u>

$\left\{\begin{array}{l}\underline{\text{ANY}}\\ \text{condition-1}\\ \underline{\text{TRUE}}\\ \underline{\text{FALSE}}\\ [\underline{\text{NOT}}] \left\{\begin{array}{l}\text{identifier-3}\\ \text{literal-3}\\ \text{arithmetic-expression-1}\end{array}\right\} \left[\left\{\begin{array}{l}\underline{\text{THROUGH}}\\ \underline{\text{THRU}}\end{array}\right\} \left\{\begin{array}{l}\text{identifier-4}\\ \text{literal-4}\\ \text{arithmetic-expression-2}\end{array}\right\}\right]\end{array}\right\}$

  [<u>ALSO</u>

$\left\{\begin{array}{l}\underline{\text{ANY}}\\ \text{condition-2}\\ \underline{\text{TRUE}}\\ \underline{\text{FALSE}}\\ [\underline{\text{NOT}}] \left\{\begin{array}{l}\text{identifier-5}\\ \text{literal-5}\\ \text{arithmetic-expression-3}\end{array}\right\} \left[\left\{\begin{array}{l}\underline{\text{THROUGH}}\\ \underline{\text{THRU}}\end{array}\right\} \left\{\begin{array}{l}\text{identifier-6}\\ \text{literal-6}\\ \text{arithmetic-expression-4}\end{array}\right\}\right]\end{array}\right\}$ ... } ...

  imperative-statement-1} ...

[<u>WHEN</u> <u>OTHER</u> imperative-statement-2]

[<u>END-EVALUATE</u>]

<u>GENERAL FORMAT FOR COBOL VERBS</u>

<u>EXIT</u>

<u>EXIT</u> <u>PROGRAM</u>

<u>GENERATE</u> $\begin{Bmatrix} \text{data-name-1} \\ \text{report-name-1} \end{Bmatrix}$

<u>GO</u> TO [procedure-name-1]

<u>GO</u> TO {procedure-name-1} ...   <u>DEPENDING</u> ON identifier-1

<u>IF</u> condition-1 THEN $\begin{Bmatrix} \text{\{statement-1\} ...} \\ \underline{\text{NEXT}} \ \underline{\text{SENTENCE}} \end{Bmatrix}$ $\begin{Bmatrix} \underline{\text{ELSE}} \ \text{\{statement-2\} ... } [\underline{\text{END-IF}}] \\ \underline{\text{ELSE}} \ \underline{\text{NEXT}} \ \underline{\text{SENTENCE}} \\ \underline{\text{END-IF}} \end{Bmatrix}$

<u>INITIALIZE</u> {identifier-1} ...

$$\left[\underline{\text{REPLACING}} \ \left\{ \begin{Bmatrix} \underline{\text{ALPHABETIC}} \\ \underline{\text{ALPHANUMERIC}} \\ \underline{\text{NUMERIC}} \\ \underline{\text{ALPHANUMERIC-EDITED}} \\ \underline{\text{NUMERIC-EDITED}} \end{Bmatrix} \ \text{DATA} \ \underline{\text{BY}} \ \begin{Bmatrix} \text{identifier-2} \\ \text{literal-1} \end{Bmatrix} \right\} \ ... \right]$$

<u>INITIATE</u> {report-name-1} ...

<u>INSPECT</u> identifier-1 <u>TALLYING</u>
$$\left\{ \text{identifier-2} \ \underline{\text{FOR}} \ \left\{ \begin{matrix} \text{CHARACTERS} \left[\begin{Bmatrix} \underline{\text{BEFORE}} \\ \underline{\text{AFTER}} \end{Bmatrix} \text{INITIAL} \begin{Bmatrix} \text{identifier-4} \\ \text{literal-2} \end{Bmatrix} \right] ... \\ \begin{Bmatrix} \underline{\text{ALL}} \\ \underline{\text{LEADING}} \end{Bmatrix} \begin{Bmatrix} \text{identifier-3} \\ \text{literal-1} \end{Bmatrix} \left[\begin{Bmatrix} \underline{\text{BEFORE}} \\ \underline{\text{AFTER}} \end{Bmatrix} \text{INITIAL} \begin{Bmatrix} \text{identifier-4} \\ \text{literal-2} \end{Bmatrix} \right] ... \end{matrix} \right\} ... \right\} ...$$

<u>INSPECT</u> identifier-1 <u>REPLACING</u>
$$\left\{ \begin{matrix} \text{CHARACTERS} \ \underline{\text{BY}} \ \begin{Bmatrix} \text{identifier-5} \\ \text{literal-3} \end{Bmatrix} \left[\begin{Bmatrix} \underline{\text{BEFORE}} \\ \underline{\text{AFTER}} \end{Bmatrix} \text{INITIAL} \begin{Bmatrix} \text{identifier-4} \\ \text{literal-2} \end{Bmatrix} \right] ... \\ \begin{Bmatrix} \underline{\text{ALL}} \\ \underline{\text{LEADING}} \\ \underline{\text{FIRST}} \end{Bmatrix} \begin{Bmatrix} \text{identifier-3} \\ \text{literal-1} \end{Bmatrix} \ \underline{\text{BY}} \ \begin{Bmatrix} \text{identifier-5} \\ \text{literal-3} \end{Bmatrix} \left[\begin{Bmatrix} \underline{\text{BEFORE}} \\ \underline{\text{AFTER}} \end{Bmatrix} \text{INITIAL} \begin{Bmatrix} \text{identifier-4} \\ \text{literal-2} \end{Bmatrix} \right] ... \end{matrix} \right\} ...$$

GENERAL FORMAT FOR COBOL VERBS

<u>INSPECT</u> identifier-1 <u>TALLYING</u>

$$\left\{ identifier\text{-}2 \ \underline{FOR} \left\{ \begin{array}{l} \underline{CHARACTERS} \left[\left\{ \begin{array}{l} \underline{BEFORE} \\ \underline{AFTER} \end{array} \right\} INITIAL \ \left\{ \begin{array}{l} identifier\text{-}4 \\ literal\text{-}2 \end{array} \right\} \right] \ \ldots \\ \left\{ \begin{array}{l} \underline{ALL} \\ \underline{LEADING} \end{array} \right\} \ \left\{ \begin{array}{l} identifier\text{-}3 \\ literal\text{-}1 \end{array} \right\} \left[\left\{ \begin{array}{l} \underline{BEFORE} \\ \underline{AFTER} \end{array} \right\} INITIAL \ \left\{ \begin{array}{l} identifier\text{-}4 \\ literal\text{-}2 \end{array} \right\} \right] \ \ldots \right\} \ \ldots \right\} \ \ldots$$

<u>REPLACING</u>

$$\left\{ \begin{array}{l} \underline{CHARACTERS} \ \underline{BY} \ \left\{ \begin{array}{l} identifier\text{-}5 \\ literal\text{-}3 \end{array} \right\} \left[\left\{ \begin{array}{l} \underline{BEFORE} \\ \underline{AFTER} \end{array} \right\} INITIAL \ \left\{ \begin{array}{l} identifier\text{-}4 \\ literal\text{-}2 \end{array} \right\} \right] \ \ldots \\ \left\{ \begin{array}{l} \underline{ALL} \\ \underline{LEADING} \\ \underline{FIRST} \end{array} \right\} \ \left\{ \begin{array}{l} identifier\text{-}3 \\ literal\text{-}1 \end{array} \right\} \ \underline{BY} \ \left\{ \begin{array}{l} identifier\text{-}5 \\ literal\text{-}3 \end{array} \right\} \left[\left\{ \begin{array}{l} \underline{BEFORE} \\ \underline{AFTER} \end{array} \right\} INITIAL \ \left\{ \begin{array}{l} identifier\text{-}4 \\ literal\text{-}2 \end{array} \right\} \right] \ \ldots \right\} \ \ldots$$

<u>INSPECT</u> identifier-1 <u>CONVERTING</u> $\left\{ \begin{array}{l} identifier\text{-}6 \\ literal\text{-}4 \end{array} \right\}$ <u>TO</u> $\left\{ \begin{array}{l} identifier\text{-}7 \\ literal\text{-}5 \end{array} \right\}$

$$\left[\left\{ \begin{array}{l} \underline{BEFORE} \\ \underline{AFTER} \end{array} \right\} INITIAL \ \left\{ \begin{array}{l} identifier\text{-}4 \\ literal\text{-}2 \end{array} \right\} \right] \ \ldots$$

<u>MERGE</u> file-name-1 $\left\{ ON \ \left\{ \begin{array}{l} \underline{ASCENDING} \\ \underline{DESCENDING} \end{array} \right\} KEY \ \{data\text{-}name\text{-}1\} \ \ldots \right\} \ \ldots$

[COLLATING <u>SEQUENCE</u> IS alphabet-name-1]

<u>USING</u> file-name-2 {file-name-3} ...

$$\left\{ \begin{array}{l} \underline{OUTPUT} \ \underline{PROCEDURE} \ IS \ procedure\text{-}name\text{-}1 \left[\left\{ \begin{array}{l} \underline{THROUGH} \\ \underline{THRU} \end{array} \right\} procedure\text{-}name\text{-}2 \right] \\ \underline{GIVING} \ \{file\text{-}name\text{-}4\} \ \ldots \end{array} \right\}$$

<u>MOVE</u> $\left\{ \begin{array}{l} identifier\text{-}1 \\ literal\text{-}1 \end{array} \right\}$ <u>TO</u> {identifier-2} ...

<u>MOVE</u> $\left\{ \begin{array}{l} \underline{CORRESPONDING} \\ \underline{CORR} \end{array} \right\}$ identifier-1 <u>TO</u> identifier-2

<u>MULTIPLY</u> $\left\{ \begin{array}{l} identifier\text{-}1 \\ literal\text{-}1 \end{array} \right\}$ <u>BY</u> {identifier-2 [<u>ROUNDED</u>]} ...

[ON <u>SIZE</u> <u>ERROR</u> imperative-statement-1]

[<u>NOT</u> ON <u>SIZE</u> <u>ERROR</u> imperative-statement-2]

[<u>END-MULTIPLY</u>]

GENERAL FORMAT FOR COBOL VERBS

MULTIPLY $\begin{Bmatrix} \text{identifier-1} \\ \text{literal-1} \end{Bmatrix}$ BY $\begin{Bmatrix} \text{identifier-2} \\ \text{literal-2} \end{Bmatrix}$

    GIVING {identifier-3 [ROUNDED]} ...

    [ON SIZE ERROR imperative-statement-1]

    [NOT ON SIZE ERROR imperative-statement-2]

    [END-MULTIPLY]

S OPEN $\begin{Bmatrix} \text{INPUT} \left\{ \text{file-name-1} \begin{bmatrix} \underline{\text{REVERSED}} \\ \text{WITH } \underline{\text{NO}} \text{ REWIND} \end{bmatrix} \right\} \cdots \\ \text{OUTPUT } \{\text{file-name-2 [WITH } \underline{\text{NO}} \text{ REWIND]}\} \cdots \\ \text{I-O } \{\text{file-name-3}\} \cdots \\ \text{EXTEND } \{\text{file-name-4}\} \cdots \end{Bmatrix}$ ...

RI OPEN $\begin{Bmatrix} \text{INPUT } \{\text{file-name-1}\} \cdots \\ \text{OUTPUT } \{\text{file-name-2}\} \cdots \\ \text{I-O } \{\text{file-name-3}\} \cdots \\ \text{EXTEND } \{\text{file-name-4}\} \cdots \end{Bmatrix}$ ...

W OPEN $\begin{Bmatrix} \text{OUTPUT } \{\text{file-name-1 [WITH } \underline{\text{NO}} \text{ REWIND]}\} \cdots \\ \text{EXTEND } \{\text{file-name-2}\} \cdots \end{Bmatrix}$ ...

    PERFORM $\left[\text{procedure-name-1} \left[\begin{Bmatrix} \underline{\text{THROUGH}} \\ \underline{\text{THRU}} \end{Bmatrix} \text{procedure-name-2} \right] \right]$

        [imperative-statement-1 END-PERFORM]

    PERFORM $\left[\text{procedure-name-1} \left[\begin{Bmatrix} \underline{\text{THROUGH}} \\ \underline{\text{THRU}} \end{Bmatrix} \text{procedure-name-2} \right] \right]$

        $\begin{Bmatrix} \text{identifier-1} \\ \text{integer-1} \end{Bmatrix}$ TIMES [imperative-statement-1 END-PERFORM]

    PERFORM $\left[\text{procedure-name-1} \left[\begin{Bmatrix} \underline{\text{THROUGH}} \\ \underline{\text{THRU}} \end{Bmatrix} \text{procedure-name-2} \right] \right]$

    $\left[\text{WITH } \underline{\text{TEST}} \begin{Bmatrix} \underline{\text{BEFORE}} \\ \underline{\text{AFTER}} \end{Bmatrix} \right]$ UNTIL condition-1

    [imperative-statement-1 END-PERFORM]

GENERAL FORMAT FOR COBOL VERBS

PERFORM $\left[\text{procedure-name-1}\ \left[\left\{\begin{matrix}\underline{\text{THROUGH}}\\ \underline{\text{THRU}}\end{matrix}\right\}\ \text{procedure-name-2}\right]\right]$

$\left[\text{WITH}\ \underline{\text{TEST}}\ \left\{\begin{matrix}\underline{\text{BEFORE}}\\ \underline{\text{AFTER}}\end{matrix}\right\}\right]$

$\underline{\text{VARYING}}\ \left\{\begin{matrix}\text{identifier-2}\\ \text{index-name-1}\end{matrix}\right\}\ \underline{\text{FROM}}\ \left\{\begin{matrix}\text{identifier-3}\\ \text{index-name-2}\\ \text{literal-1}\end{matrix}\right\}$

$\underline{\text{BY}}\ \left\{\begin{matrix}\text{identifier-4}\\ \text{literal-2}\end{matrix}\right\}\ \underline{\text{UNTIL}}\ \text{condition-1}$

$\left[\underline{\text{AFTER}}\ \left\{\begin{matrix}\text{identifier-5}\\ \text{literal-3}\end{matrix}\right\}\ \underline{\text{FROM}}\ \left\{\begin{matrix}\text{identifier-6}\\ \text{index-name-4}\\ \text{literal-3}\end{matrix}\right\}\right.$

$\left.\underline{\text{BY}}\ \left\{\begin{matrix}\text{identifier-7}\\ \text{literal-4}\end{matrix}\right\}\ \underline{\text{UNTIL}}\ \text{condition-2}\right]$ ...

[imperative-statement-1 END-PERFORM]

SRI READ file-name-1 [NEXT] RECORD [INTO identifier-1]

[AT END imperative-statement-1]

[NOT AT END imperative-statement-2]

[END-READ]

R READ file-name-1 RECORD [INTO identifier-1]

[INVALID KEY imperative-statement-3]

[NOT INVALID KEY imperative-statement-4]

[END-READ]

GENERAL FORMAT FOR COBOL VERBS

I READ file-name-1 RECORD [INTO identifier-1]

    [KEY IS data-name-1]

    [INVALID KEY imperative-statement-3]

    [NOT INVALID KEY imperative-statement-4]

    [END-READ]

  RELEASE record-name-1 [FROM identifier-1]

  RETURN file-name-1 RECORD [INTO identifier-1]

    AT END imperative-statement-1

    [NOT AT END imperative-statement-2]

    [END-RETURN]

S REWRITE record-name-1 [FROM identifier-1]

RI REWRITE record-name-1 [FROM identifier-1]

    [INVALID KEY imperative-statement-1]

    [NOT INVALID KEY imperative-statement-2]

    [END-REWRITE]

GENERAL FORMAT FOR COBOL VERBS

<u>SEARCH</u> identifier-1 $\left[\underline{VARYING}\ \begin{Bmatrix} \text{identifier-2} \\ \text{index-name-1} \end{Bmatrix}\right]$

  [AT <u>END</u> imperative-statement-1]

$\begin{Bmatrix}\underline{WHEN}\ \text{condition-1}\ \begin{Bmatrix}\text{imperative-statement-2} \\ \underline{NEXT}\ \underline{SENTENCE}\end{Bmatrix}\end{Bmatrix} \ldots$

  [<u>END-SEARCH</u>]

<u>SEARCH</u> <u>ALL</u> identifier-1   [AT <u>END</u> imperative-statement-1]

    $\underline{WHEN}\quad \begin{Bmatrix}\text{data-name-1}\ \begin{Bmatrix}\text{IS}\ \underline{EQUAL}\ \text{TO} \\ \text{IS}\ = \end{Bmatrix}\ \begin{Bmatrix}\text{identifier-3} \\ \text{literal-1} \\ \text{arithmetic-expression-1}\end{Bmatrix} \\ \text{condition-name-1}\end{Bmatrix}$

    $\left[\underline{AND}\ \begin{Bmatrix}\text{data-name-2}\ \begin{Bmatrix}\text{IS}\ \underline{EQUAL}\ \text{TO} \\ \text{IS}\ = \end{Bmatrix}\ \begin{Bmatrix}\text{identifier-4} \\ \text{literal-2} \\ \text{arithmetic-expression-2}\end{Bmatrix} \\ \text{condition-name-2}\end{Bmatrix}\right] \ldots$

    $\begin{Bmatrix}\text{imperative-statement-2} \\ \underline{NEXT}\ \underline{SENTENCE}\end{Bmatrix}$

  [<u>END-SEARCH</u>]

<u>SET</u> $\begin{Bmatrix}\text{index-name-1} \\ \text{identifier-1}\end{Bmatrix} \ldots \quad \underline{TO}\ \begin{Bmatrix}\text{index-name-2} \\ \text{identifier-2} \\ \text{integer-1}\end{Bmatrix}$

<u>SET</u> {index-name-3} $\ldots \begin{Bmatrix}\underline{UP}\ \underline{BY} \\ \underline{DOWN}\ \underline{BY}\end{Bmatrix}\ \begin{Bmatrix}\text{identifier-3} \\ \text{integer-2}\end{Bmatrix}$

<u>SET</u> $\begin{Bmatrix}\text{\{mnemonic-name-1\}} \ldots \quad \underline{TO}\ \begin{Bmatrix}\underline{ON} \\ \underline{OFF}\end{Bmatrix}\end{Bmatrix} \ldots$

<u>SET</u> {condition-name-1} $\ldots \quad \underline{TO}\ \underline{TRUE}$

GENERAL FORMAT FOR COBOL VERBS

$$\underline{\text{SORT}} \text{ file-name-1} \left\{ \text{ON} \left\{ \begin{array}{l} \underline{\text{ASCENDING}} \\ \underline{\text{DESCENDING}} \end{array} \right\} \text{KEY } \{\text{data-name-1}\} \dots \right\} \dots$$

[WITH <u>DUPLICATES</u> IN ORDER]

[COLLATING <u>SEQUENCE</u> IS alphabet-name-1]

$$\left\{ \begin{array}{l} \underline{\text{INPUT}} \ \underline{\text{PROCEDURE}} \text{ IS procedure-name-1} \ \left[\left\{ \begin{array}{l} \underline{\text{THROUGH}} \\ \underline{\text{THRU}} \end{array} \right\} \text{procedure-name-2}\right] \\ \underline{\text{USING}} \ \{\text{file-name-2}\} \ \dots \end{array} \right\}$$

$$\left\{ \begin{array}{l} \underline{\text{OUTPUT}} \ \underline{\text{PROCEDURE}} \text{ IS procedure-name-3} \ \left[\left\{ \begin{array}{l} \underline{\text{THROUGH}} \\ \underline{\text{THRU}} \end{array} \right\} \text{procedure-name-4}\right] \\ \underline{\text{GIVING}} \ \{\text{file-name-3}\} \ \dots \end{array} \right\}$$

$$\underline{\text{START}} \text{ file-name-1} \left[\underline{\text{KEY}} \left\{ \begin{array}{l} \text{IS } \underline{\text{EQUAL}} \text{ TO} \\ \text{IS } = \\ \text{IS } \underline{\text{GREATER}} \text{ THAN} \\ \text{IS } > \\ \text{IS } \underline{\text{NOT}} \ \underline{\text{LESS}} \text{ THAN} \\ \text{IS } \underline{\text{NOT}} < \\ \text{IS } \underline{\text{GREATER}} \text{ THAN } \underline{\text{OR}} \ \underline{\text{EQUAL}} \text{ TO} \\ \text{IS } >= \end{array} \right\} \text{data-name-1} \right]$$

[<u>INVALID</u> KEY imperative-statement-1]

[<u>NOT</u> <u>INVALID</u> KEY imperative-statement-2]

[<u>END–START</u>]

$$\underline{\text{STOP}} \left\{ \begin{array}{l} \underline{\text{RUN}} \\ \text{literal-1} \end{array} \right\}$$

GENERAL FORMAT FOR COBOL VERBS

STRING $\begin{Bmatrix} \text{identifier-1} \\ \text{literal-1} \end{Bmatrix}$ ... DELIMITED BY $\begin{Bmatrix} \text{identifier-2} \\ \text{literal-2} \\ \underline{\text{SIZE}} \end{Bmatrix}$ ...

    INTO identifier-3

    [WITH POINTER identifier-4]

    [ON OVERFLOW imperative-statement-1]

    [NOT ON OVERFLOW imperative-statement-2]

    [END-STRING]

SUBTRACT $\begin{Bmatrix} \text{identifier-1} \\ \text{literal-1} \end{Bmatrix}$ ... FROM {identifier-3 [ROUNDED]} ...

    [ON SIZE ERROR imperative-statement-1]

    [NOT ON SIZE ERROR imperative-statement-2]

    [END-SUBTRACT]

SUBTRACT $\begin{Bmatrix} \text{identifier-1} \\ \text{literal-1} \end{Bmatrix}$ ... FROM $\begin{Bmatrix} \text{identifier-2} \\ \text{literal-2} \end{Bmatrix}$

    GIVING {identifier-3 [ROUNDED]} ...

    [ON SIZE ERROR imperative-statement-1]

    [NOT ON SIZE ERROR imperative-statement-2]

    [END-SUBTRACT]

SUBTRACT $\begin{Bmatrix} \underline{\text{CORRESPONDING}} \\ \underline{\text{CORR}} \end{Bmatrix}$ identifier-1 FROM identifier-2 [ROUNDED]

    [ON SIZE ERROR imperative-statement-1]

    [NOT ON SIZE ERROR imperative-statement-2]

    [END-SUBTRACT]

SUPPRESS PRINTING

TERMINATE {report-name-1} ...

GENERAL FORMAT FOR COBOL VERBS

UNSTRING identifier-1

$$\left[\underline{\text{DELIMITED}} \text{ BY } [\underline{\text{ALL}}] \begin{Bmatrix} \text{identifier-2} \\ \text{literal-1} \end{Bmatrix} \left[\underline{\text{OR}} [\underline{\text{ALL}}] \begin{Bmatrix} \text{identifier-3} \\ \text{literal-2} \end{Bmatrix}\right] \dots\right]$$

INTO {identifier-4 [DELIMITER IN identifier-5] [COUNT IN identifier-6]} ...

[WITH POINTER identifier-7]

[TALLYING IN identifier-8]

[ON OVERFLOW imperative-statement-1]

[NOT ON OVERFLOW imperative-statement-2]

[END-UNSTRING]

SRI USE [GLOBAL] AFTER STANDARD $\begin{Bmatrix} \text{EXCEPTION} \\ \text{ERROR} \end{Bmatrix}$ PROCEDURE ON $\begin{Bmatrix} \{\text{file-name-1}\} \dots \\ \text{INPUT} \\ \text{OUTPUT} \\ \text{I-O} \\ \text{EXTEND} \end{Bmatrix}$

W USE AFTER STANDARD $\begin{Bmatrix} \text{EXCEPTION} \\ \text{ERROR} \end{Bmatrix}$ PROCEDURE ON $\begin{Bmatrix} \{\text{file-name-1}\} \dots \\ \text{OUTPUT} \\ \text{EXTEND} \end{Bmatrix}$

USE [GLOBAL] BEFORE REPORTING identifier-1

GENERAL FORMAT FOR COBOL VERBS

S WRITE record-name-1 [FROM identifier-1]

$$
\left[\begin{Bmatrix} \underline{BEFORE} \\ \underline{AFTER} \end{Bmatrix} \text{ADVANCING} \begin{Bmatrix} \begin{Bmatrix} \text{identifier-2} \\ \text{integer-1} \end{Bmatrix} \begin{bmatrix} \text{LINE} \\ \text{LINES} \end{bmatrix} \\ \begin{Bmatrix} \text{mnemonic-name-1} \\ \underline{PAGE} \end{Bmatrix} \end{Bmatrix} \right]
$$

$$
\left[\text{AT} \begin{Bmatrix} \underline{END-OF-PAGE} \\ \underline{EOP} \end{Bmatrix} \text{imperative-statement-1} \right]
$$

$$
\left[\underline{NOT} \text{ AT} \begin{Bmatrix} \underline{END-OF-PAGE} \\ \underline{EOP} \end{Bmatrix} \text{imperative-statement-2} \right]
$$

[END-WRITE]

RI WRITE record-name-1 [FROM identifier-1]

[INVALID KEY imperative-statement-1]

[NOT INVALID KEY imperative-statement-2]

[END-WRITE]

GENERAL FORMAT FOR COPY AND REPLACE STATEMENTS

$$
\underline{COPY} \text{ text-name-1} \left[\begin{Bmatrix} \underline{OF} \\ \underline{IN} \end{Bmatrix} \text{library-name-1} \right]
$$

$$
\left[\underline{REPLACING} \begin{Bmatrix} \begin{Bmatrix} ==\text{pseudo-text-1}== \\ \text{identifier-1} \\ \text{literal-1} \\ \text{word-1} \end{Bmatrix} \underline{BY} \begin{Bmatrix} ==\text{pseudo-text-2}== \\ \text{identifier-2} \\ \text{literal-2} \\ \text{word-2} \end{Bmatrix} \end{Bmatrix} \dots \right]
$$

$\underline{REPLACE}$ {==pseudo-text-1== $\underline{BY}$ ==pseudo-text-2==} ...

$\underline{REPLACE}$ $\underline{OFF}$

GENERAL FORMAT FOR CONDITIONS

RELATION CONDITION:

$$
\left\{\begin{array}{l}\text{identifier-1}\\\text{literal-1}\\\text{arithmetic-expression-1}\\\text{index-name-1}\end{array}\right\}
\left\{\begin{array}{l}\text{IS [NOT] GREATER THAN}\\\text{IS [NOT] >}\\\text{IS [NOT] LESS THAN}\\\text{IS [NOT] <}\\\text{IS [NOT] EQUAL TO}\\\text{IS [NOT] =}\\\text{IS GREATER THAN OR EQUAL TO}\\\text{IS >=}\\\text{IS LESS THAN OR EQUAL TO}\\\text{IS <=}\end{array}\right\}
\left\{\begin{array}{l}\text{identifier-2}\\\text{literal-2}\\\text{arithmetic-expression-2}\\\text{index-name-2}\end{array}\right\}
$$

CLASS CONDITION:

$$
\text{identifier-1 IS [NOT] }\left\{\begin{array}{l}\text{NUMERIC}\\\text{ALPHABETIC}\\\text{ALPHABETIC-LOWER}\\\text{ALPHABETIC-UPPER}\\\text{class-name-1}\end{array}\right\}
$$

CONDITION-NAME CONDITION:

condition-name-1

SWITCH-STATUS CONDITION:

condition-name-1

SIGN CONDITION:

$$
\text{arithmetic-expression-1 IS [NOT] }\left\{\begin{array}{l}\text{POSITIVE}\\\text{NEGATIVE}\\\text{ZERO}\end{array}\right\}
$$

NEGATED CONDITION:

NOT condition-1

COMBINED CONDITION:

$$
\text{condition-1 }\left\{\left\{\begin{array}{l}\text{AND}\\\text{OR}\end{array}\right\}\text{ condition-2}\right\}\ \ldots
$$

ABBREVIATED COMBINED RELATION CONDITION:

$$
\text{relation-condition }\left\{\left\{\begin{array}{l}\text{AND}\\\text{OR}\end{array}\right\}\text{ [NOT] [relational-operator] object}\right\}\ \ldots
$$

Index